Expert Systems in Law

Expert Systems in Law

A Jurisprudential Inquiry

RICHARD E. SUSSKIND

CLARENDON PRESS · OXFORD
1987

Oxford University Press, Walton Street, Oxford OX2 6DP

Oxford New York Toronto
Delhi Bombay Calcutta Madras Karachi
Pataling Jaya Singapore Hong Kong Tokyo
Nairobi Dar es Salaam Cape Town
Melbourne Auckland
and associated companies in
Beirut Berlin Ibadan Nicosia

Oxford is a trade mark of Oxford University Press

Published in the United States
by Oxford University Press, New York

British Library Cataloguing in Publication Data
Susskind, Richard E.
Expert Systems in law.
1. Law—Data processing   2. Expert
systems (Computer science)
I. Title
340'.028'5633   K87
ISBN 0–19–825582–9

Library of Congress Cataloging in Publication Data
Susskind, Richard E.
Expert systems in law
Bibliography: p.
Includes index.
1. Information storage and retrieval systems—Law.
2. Legal research—Data processing.   I. Title.
K87.S87 1987   343'.0999   87–12254
ISBN 0–19–825582–9   342.3999

Eta Services, Beccles, Suffolk

Printed in Great Britain by
Thomson Litho Ltd, East Kilbride, Scotland

I dedicate this book to the four people who encourage me the most,

my wife, Michelle,
my brother, Alan,
and my parents.

Preface

This book is a general inquiry into expert systems in law. It is a revised and updated version of a doctoral thesis submitted in the University of Oxford in May 1986. The conclusions, arguments, and recommendations are based largely on the legally orientated findings of a collaborative research project in expert systems in law that involved the Law Faculty and the Programming Research Group of the University of Oxford. The project ran from 1983 until 1986 and is referred to throughout the book as the 'Oxford project'.

Although the book is intimately concerned with one branch of computer science, it was, nevertheless, not written from a computational perspective. Nor was it conceived as a rigorous, formal, and directly implementable specification of an expert system in law. Rather, it was composed from the point of view of jurisprudence (legal theory).

My central argument is that there are no theoretical obstacles, from the point of view of jurisprudence, to the development of rule-based expert systems in law of limited scope. I support this claim throughout the text not only by jurisprudential argumentation, but also by reference to the prototype system in Scottish divorce law that was developed in the course of the Oxford project. I articulate the underlying computational theories of law and legal reasoning upon which the system was designed and in so doing state the jurisprudential and practical limitations of expert systems in law. The theories themselves are shown to be derived from consensus located in many contemporary, yet often thought to be radically incompatible, works of analytical jurisprudence.

The book is divided into three parts. Part One is devoted to various preliminary matters concerning expert systems in law. Its purpose is to offer a comprehensive introduction to the field of artificial intelligence and legal reasoning: current projects in the field are assessed, central concepts are analysed and clarified, and basic features of systems are considered. Drawing extensively from modern analytical jurisprudence, Part Two identifies the types of legal knowledge that will need to be stored in an expert system in law, and recommends a particular way of organising and representing that knowledge. Finally, in Part Three, through examination and evaluation of many classical jurisprudential arguments in opposition to deductive legal reasoning, an account of logical legal inference is developed, and the limitations of the kind of expert system being recommended are identified.

I hope the book will be of interest to four classes of person. First, it is intended as a text of fresh perspective for workers in the field of artificial intelligence and legal reasoning. Secondly, the book is for all those professional advisers—particularly lawyers—who administer and reason with the law and are eager to know of technological developments within their professions. Thirdly, this inquiry is for jurisprudents (legal theorists and philosophers), who will find in it both an intensely practical application for their subject and a new range of problems over which I would very much like debate to ensue. Finally, the book is directed at computer and artificial intelligence scientists who find in law a suitable domain of application for expert systems work: I have sought to provide coherent but nevertheless informal models of law and legal reasoning, together with an accompanying commentary, which will be of guidance to those wishing to build expert systems in law.

The terminology of the book is firmly rooted in the tradition of analytical jurisprudence. Accordingly, it will be relatively foreign to more than half of my projected readership. However, I urge those averse to the language of legal theory to persevere: new terms and concepts are introduced and explained during the course of the book. With any luck, computer persons will find use for the novel vocabulary while practising lawyers will be encouraged to re-examine—or commence study of—the world of legal philosophy.

I am extremely grateful to many individuals and institutions for encouraging me, and allowing me the opportunity, to pursue the research that led to this book.

I am indebted particularly to Colin Tapper, who with enormous patience, exceedingly good humour, and unparalleled knowledge of computers and law, supervised my doctoral research and advised on its revision for publication. His guidance and support were invaluable.

The examiners of my thesis, Neil MacCormick and Jon Bing, also made many useful suggestions and I am very grateful to them for their advice and encouragement.

My interest in the field of artificial intelligence and legal reasoning dates to 1981 when I worked in the field as a student of jurisprudence in the University of Glasgow. I would like to express my thanks to the Department of Jurisprudence there for introducing me to the subject.

I have benefited greatly from the advice of my oldest friend, David Gold, who, as the other major part of the Oxford project, implemented many of the ideas of this book in a computer program. His detailed comments on succeeding drafts of the computationally orientated parts of my thesis continually kept me aware of the rigorous demands of the programmer.

Having read drafts of my work, many other individuals offered me invaluable advice, criticism, and encouragment during the course of my research and my preparation of this book: most notably, Robin Downie, Donald Harris, Anthony Kenny, Alan Paterson, and Joseph Raz. I am very grateful to all of them.

With his characteristic fly's eye for detail, my good friend Howard Beach purged an earlier draft of this book of more errors, slips, and impurities than I would care to discuss. Thank you, H. And in correction of the final proofs, my wife Michelle patiently read the book in a last elimination of all manner of mistakes: the book is as much hers as mine.

Thanks are also due to those of the Oxford University Computing Laboratory who for three years allowed me the use of the facilities of the Programming Research Group. It was a pleasure to work in such a congenial atmosphere. Within the Laboratory, Jeremy Jacob deserves particular mention for tirelessly teaching me about the intricacies and idiosyncrasies of the text editor, QED, and for introducing me to the ZIP family, which processed my manuscript.

The bulk of the funding for my project was provided by the Scottish Education Department and the Snell Trust.

An earlier version of part of Chapter 1 of this book appeared in *The Modern Law Review* in March 1986.

My editor at OUP, Richard Hart, directed the book through the publishing process with great efficiency: his advice and effort are very much appreciated.

Penultimately, at Ernst & Whinney, I would like to thank John

Barney, Nick Land, Andrew Pawlowicz, and James Tucker for encouraging me to bring expert systems in law out of the research laboratory and into the marketplace.

Finally, and most importantly, my family and friends deserve endless thanks for their endless support. My parents, in the past few years, as they always have done, have lovingly encouraged and helped me in my activities: their contribution to my work cannot be overestimated. And Michelle, as devoted girlfriend, fiancée, and now wife, more than anyone has both tolerantly endured my fascination with my work and has, with love, offered unflagging support in the writing of this book.

14 June 1987
Bushey Heath   R.E.S.

Contents

Contents

Abbreviations

NA   von Wright, *Norm and Action* (1963)

NLNR Finnis, *Natural Law and Natural Rights* (1980)

NS   Alchourron and Bulygin, *Normative Systems* (1971)

OLG   Bentham, *Of Laws in General* (1970)

PAI   Nilsson, *Principles of Artificial Intelligence* (1982)

PL   Haack, *Philosophy of Logics* (1978)

PLP   Castberg, *Problems of Legal Philosophy* (1957)

'PPL'   Hart, 'Problems of the Philosophy of Law' (1967)

'PSLM' Hart, 'Positivism and the Separation of Law and Morals' (1958)

PTL   Kelsen, *The Pure Theory of Law* (1967)

PRBES Buchanan and Duda, *Principles of Rule-Based Expert Systems* (1982)

SLS   Walker, *The Scottish Legal System* (1981)

TRS   Dworkin, *Taking Rights Seriously* (1977)

PART ONE

PRELIMINARY CONSIDERATIONS CONCERNING EXPERT SYSTEMS IN LAW

1

Computer Applications to the Law

It is now widely accepted that much of the data with which lawyers must deal can be processed by computers more efficiently than by human beings. This is true not just of all the administrative data which confronts lawyers as it must any office executive, but also of the specifically legal data—the primary sources of law—that can now be stored in vast quantity and retrieved with little difficulty by current computer systems. This legal data is regarded here as the raw material of the legal reasoning and legal problem-solving processes. Though computers are used extensively by lawyers for legal data storage and retrieval purposes, they have not yet been satisfactorily programmed to interpret this raw material or to provide assistance in reasoning with, drawing inferences from, and offering advice on the basis of, the formal sources of the law. This requires the design of computer systems that are capable of knowledge processing, that is, of applying their knowledge of the law to the problem data presented to them. Such systems can be called knowledge-based, as opposed to database, systems in law.

Expert systems in law are a type of knowledge-based system in law, and I introduce them in this chapter in more detail by relating them, in the first instance, in Section 1.1, to those existing and commonly used computer applications to the law that belong to the field of traditional data processing. In Section 1.2, the terms artificial intelligence and expert systems are discussed, resulting, in Section 1.3, in a characterization of knowledge-based and expert systems in law. In Section 1.4, I offer a brief summary of some of the significant projects in the field of artificial intelligence and legal reasoning. The idea of injecting jurisprudential rigour into the process of building expert systems in law is first advanced in Section 1.5, and is developed in Section 1.6, which pertains to consensus and disagreement within legal theory. Finally, in Section 1.7, in my concluding remarks, I identify the many problems that research workers in the field of expert systems in law must confront, and then point to those that are the specific concern of this book.

1.1 DATABASE SYSTEMS IN LAW

As in most office environments, many tedious and repetitive administrative duties in the law office can now be discharged with the assistance of computers. Most legal practitioners are now aware of the potential not only of the general filing and storage facilities of computers, but also of word processors, which compose letters, documents, and deeds, and so forth in a fraction of the time of, and at considerably less expense than, conventional (electronic or manual) typewriters. Moreover, the computerization of legal and trust accounting procedures, of time-costing and time-recording systems, of the practice of conveyancing, of inter-office communications, and of court administration, together with the development of computer-assisted decision support systems, are all contributing to a more cost-effective and efficient provision of legal services than was possible in the past.[1] In a sense, all these computer applications are instances of database systems in law. In this book, however, it is database systems in law that store and retrieve the substantive law that I take to be paradigmatic of this category. The first twenty-five years of research into the application of computer technology to the law were devoted largely to the development of these latter systems and they are generally—but, I shall argue, misleadingly—termed legal information retrieval systems.

Many legal practitioners and academics are now familiar with the operation and capabilities of these systems, the best known of which in the United Kingdom is LEXIS. Though the precise sequence of operations to be followed in their actual use varies from system to system, ordinarily the user operates through a terminal and, having initially executed various preliminary instructions in order to gain access to the system, then enters one or more keywords, that is, words he considers to be important for, relevant to, and characteristic of, his inquiry. The computer then compares these keywords with

---

[1] On computer use in the law office generally, see National Law Library, *The Slot Report* (1983), Bellord, *Computers for Lawyers* (1983), Ruoff, *The Solicitor and the Automated Office* (1984), and *Computers and Law*—The Journal of the Society for Computers and Law.

the concordance of the full-text (or perhaps only head-notes) of that section of the database in which the user has chosen to search. (The concordance is an alphabetical index of almost all the database's words and their addresses.) Seconds later, the number of occurrences of the selected keywords in the material searched appears on the screen. If that number is too great to be managed easily or too small to be of assistance, then the search can be modified by entering additional or alternative keywords or by the addition of further conditions. When the number is deemed convenient, the computer can be instructed to display them on the screen in one of a variety of ways: first, perhaps, by presenting those parts of the text that contain the keywords and then, if the user so chooses, by exhibiting the full-text itself. After browsing the user may then instruct the computer to print out any desired portions of text.[2]

In order to appreciate their various shortcomings, it is necessary to have a rudimentary understanding of certain key aspects of these systems' operation. One of the first steps in their construction is the creation of a database which involves the loading of selected materials (for example, statutes and case-reports) into the computer's memory, using it as a sort of library. This source material may be stored on a full-text, abbreviated-text, or head-notes basis. At this stage, when the legal material is input, the system assembles its concordance. While in operation, the system identifies and then matches the string of characters (that constitutes the keyword) with this concordance. In more complex search requests, involving several keywords and connectors (for instance, the disjunctive connector 'or', and the conjunctive connector 'and'), the system compares the addresses of these words in a fashion stipulated by the relationships established through the use of the connectors. The occurrence of the keyword(s) in the full-text (or head-notes) of documents, therefore, is the determinative factor with regard to the *relevance*, or otherwise, of the data retrieved.

Although it is now generally accepted that computers can be used in the way just outlined as highly efficient tools for the recovery of the substantive law, many believe, nevertheless, that this criterion of relevance implicit in the systems is unsatisfactory. As a result, it is argued, many searches deliver an excess of irrelevant documents, or

---

[2] For relevant historical and explanatory accounts of database systems for the retrieval of substantive law, see Tapper, 'Lawyers and Machines' (1963), pp. 121–37, *CATL*, chs. 4–7, and Bing (ed.), *Handbook of Legal Information Retrieval* (1984).

they often fail to produce the bulk of those relevant texts that are in fact stored within the database. Illustrations of these alleged shortcomings can be found in the *LEXIS Handbook*,[3] where it is pointed out that if a hypothetical researcher, who intends to retrieve data containing the words 'executor' and 'executrix', enters the search request 'execut!', he will be confronted not only by texts carrying those terms he is looking for, but also those holding 'execute', 'execution', and 'executive'. (The use, in this example, of the exclamation mark, known as the super-universal character, results in the computer searching its concordance for all strings of characters with the prefix 'execut'.) Another interesting example given indicates how relevant texts may be missed: the user who enters the keywords 'warehouseman's lien' will miss some of those texts where that concept is referred to as 'warehouseman's possessory lien', 'lien of a warehouseman', 'warehousekeeper's lien', or 'warehouse keeper's lien'.

It can be forcefully argued, of course, that many of the putative deficiencies of systems such as LEXIS in fact amount to no more than the inability of users to formulate suitable search requests. Yet, most researchers do recognize that there are serious problems. Some have endeavoured to develop other methods of searching stored documents (for example by 'citation vectors'[4]) remaining, none the less, within the paradigm of what I term legal database systems. Others, however, with a similar goal in mind—that of improving the performance of computer systems used to recover legal data—have sought to examine the possibility of knowledge-based systems in law.

Still others, for an entirely different reason, have also been motivated to the investigation of knowledge-based systems. This last group subscribe to the view that the so-called legal information retrieval systems are of minimal utility to the majority of practising lawyers, whereas systems that could hold the kind of know-how laid out in such materials as practitioners' texts and handbooks might, in contrast, prove to be of inestimable practical value.[5]

There has, then, been a gradual appreciation by many workers in the field that it is now necessary to attempt to develop computer sys-

---

[3] Butterworth Telepublishing (1981), pp. 24 and 12.

[4] e.g. Tapper, *An Experiment in the Use of Citation Vectors in the Area of Legal Data* (1982).

[5] For evidence of the contention that many lawyers have less need for access to primary legal sources than to lawyers' 'know-how', see National Law Library, *The Slot Report* (1983), pp. 33–4. Also see pp. 36–40, and p. 124.

tems in law that can be said to embody knowledge, and even exhibit intelligence. Achievements over the last twenty years, in the branch of computer science referred to as Artificial Intelligence (AI), have perhaps now provided the appropriate technological framework within which the construction of such knowledge-based systems in law might now be undertaken. Indeed, although similar such systems were anticipated by Loevinger in 1949[6] and by Mehl in 1958,[7] it is unlikely that their aspirations would now be receiving such serious consideration but for the apparently stunning advances that have been made recently by computer scientists involved with AI.

1.2 ARTIFICIAL INTELLIGENCE AND EXPERT SYSTEMS

The idea of artificial intelligence is perhaps the most intellectually stimulating issue to have arisen from the advent of computer technology.[8] This topic has attracted comment from exponents of many diverse disciplines. Many problems of philosophy of mind and of cognitive psychology, for instance, are now being contemplated in a fresh context, relating them to this novel possibility of imbuing a machine—a computer—with artificial intelligence. As a result, much debate on AI, pertaining as it does to the metaphorical relationship between man and machine, can hardly be regarded as an unfamiliar province of academic inquiry; Western philosophers have puzzled over the nature of intelligence and related concepts for countless centuries and, more recently, even prior to serious AI work of any kind, intelligence was under thorough experimental and theoretical scrutiny by cognitive psychologists. Though many of the issues that are discussed under the rubric of AI are of intense interest to representatives of certain academic disciplines, it is sufficient for those concerned with AI and legal reasoning to characterize AI in a fashion that avoids, in particular, the many conceivable philosophical, psychological, and linguistic technicalities.

In the present context, the term 'artificial intelligence' can perhaps best be regarded not as derived, by analogy, from the rigorous con-

---

[6] 'Jurimetrics: The Next Step Forward' (1949).

[7] 'Automation in the Legal World: From the Machine Processing of Legal Information to the "Law Machine"' (1958).

[8] On the origin of the much-criticized term of 'Artificial Intelligence' see McCorduck, *Machines Who Think* (1979), p. 96.

ceptions of philosophers, psychologists, and linguistic scientists, but as a label used to refer to what it seems that certain computer systems possess to some degree. Such systems—having been so designed and constructed to perform those tasks and solve those problems that together if performed by human beings are taken by us to be indicative of intelligence—can be said to exhibit artificial intelligence. On this account, then, the term artificial intelligence connotes a prima facie intelligence and this designation, while perhaps lacking in philosophical rigour, serves simply as an explanatory and metaphorically framed classification. This book, therefore, is not directly concerned with the core AI question of whether machines can meaningfully be said to *think*. The expert systems in law discussed here are no more capable of thinking, in the sense of having cognitive states, than legal textbooks.[9]

There are many tasks that computer scientists are currently endeavouring to program computers to perform which are deemed to result in artificially intelligent computer behaviour: the understanding and translation of natural language (Natural Language Processing); the understanding of the spoken word (Speech Understanding); the recognition of images and objects of the physical world (Vision and Perception); the playing of complex games such as chess (Game Playing); learning from examples and precedents (Machine Learning); the writing of programs, that is, computer programs that can themselves generate programs (Automatic Programming); the sophisticated education of human users (Intelligent Computer-aided Instruction or Tutors); intelligent problem-solving and reasoning (Intelligent Knowledge-based Systems (IKBS) or Expert Systems). Moreover, attempts to build intelligent robot systems (Robotics), and the study of the human mind using the computer as a means of testing hypotheses and modelling human behaviour, that is, using what is commonly referred to as the Computational Metaphor, are also considered to be contributions to the study of AI.[10]

The particular aspect of AI from which the legal profession may well benefit is sometimes regarded as the applied branch of the field and is usually known as Intelligent Knowledge-Based Systems

⁹ On machine thought, see Turing, 'Computing Machinery and Intelligence' (1950), Searle, *Minds, Brains and Science* (1984), and Hofstadter and Dennett, *The Mind's I* (1982).

¹⁰ On artificial intelligence, generally, see particularly *AI, AINM, CC, FG, IS, PAI*. Also see Section 3 of the Bibliography of this book.

(IKBS). These are systems that contain representations of knowledge which can be deployed in the solving of given problems. Expert Systems (despite the fact that this term is often considered to be synonymous with IKBS), are, more precisely, a type of IKBS. Expert systems are computer programs that have been constructed (with the assistance of human experts) in such a way that they are capable of functioning at the standard of (and sometimes even at a higher standard than) human experts in given fields. They are used as high-level intellectual aids to their users, which explains one of their alternative epithets: intelligent assistants. They differ from IKBS in that the latter may recognize speech, perceive images, or indeed solve problems in a fashion that undoubtedly is dependent on knowledge yet that requires no particular human expertise. Only those IKBS that embody a depth and richness of knowledge that permit them to perform at the level of an expert in a particular (and normally highly specialized) domain, therefore, ought then to be designated expert systems.

The above characterization of expert systems, however, can be refined considerably by reference to various attributes that are generally expected of them (although there is some confusion even amongst computer scientists over what programs can correctly be termed expert systems[11]). Expert systems are usually: (1) transparent, which means that they can generate explanations of the lines of reasoning that lead them to their conclusions; (2) heuristic, by which is meant they reason with the informal, judgmental, experiential, and often procedural knowledge that underlies expertise in a given field (as well as with the more formal knowledge of the domain in question); and (3) flexible, a term that refers to the ability of these systems to allow, without any great difficulty, modifications to their *knowledge bases*, that is, to their stores of knowledge.[12]

Further insight into expert systems can be gained through appreciation of the three major research issues in this wing of computer science.[13] First, there is the matter of knowledge acquisition. Work on this topic addresses the manner in which the requisite knowledge,

---

[11] On this confusion, see *PRBES*, p. 1. On expert systems generally, see *AGES*, *BES*, Michie (ed.), *Introductory Readings in Expert Systems* (1982) and *Expert Systems in the Micro-electronic Age* (1979), and Goodall, *The Guide to Expert Systems* (1985). Also see Department of Industry, *The Alvey Report* (1982), pp. 32–5, and Section 3 of the Bibliography of this book.

[12] See *PRBES*, p. 1.

[13] See Feigenbaum, 'Knowledge Engineering: The Applied Side' (1983), pp. 37–55.

particularly the heuristic knowledge, can be extracted from human experts, and then articulated with a view to representing it in the system. Second is the issue of knowledge representation, which concerns the techniques to be adopted in the process of restructuring the body of knowledge of a particular domain so that it can be represented as data structures within the computer's memory. This has to be done in a fashion that not only facilitates subsequent alterations to the knowledge base, but also makes for easy access during the problem-solving routines. Further, this representation is required to be a configuration faithful in meaning to the original corpus of knowledge. Third is the question of knowledge utilization, which pertains to the inference procedures, that is, to the methods of reasoning, to be used by the system in the process of problem-solving. So that conclusions may be drawn, all expert systems require an inference engine—the mechanism by which the knowledge base interacts and reasons with the data relating to any problem at hand. The inference engine, then, can be said to contain general problem-solving (but *not* domain) knowledge. The person whose role it is to build expert systems, and, therefore, to consider appropriate methods of knowledge acquisition, representation, and utilization in respect of any project with which he may be concerned, is known as the knowledge engineer.

Applications of expert systems have been many and various.[14] Arguably the first sustained, and ultimately successful, work in this field, was initiated in 1965. This was the DENDRAL project, carried out at Stanford University and inspired by Feigenbaum, one of the fathers of AI. By harnessing the formal and heuristic knowledge both of Lederberg (a professor of genetics and Nobel laureate), and of Djerassi (a physical chemist renowned for having invented the birth-control pill), Feigenbaum wrote a program that can infer the molecular structure of an unknown molecule given the mass spectroscopic data that would normally be available to a physical chemist engaged in such a task. The system's capabilities in this sphere are now said to exceed those of any single human being (including its designers), and it is used in university and industrial environments throughout the world. Another expert system, PROSPECTOR, functions as an intelligent assistant for geologists by offering advice on the location of ore deposits based on geological data. As a direct re-

14 For details, see *AGES*, chs. 24–6.

sult of its advice (its knowledge base contains the heuristic and formal knowledge of scientists of the US Geological Survey), it is claimed that a molybdenum find, valued at 100 million dollars, was made in 1982.

Perhaps the most widely known expert systems are those that perform medical diagnoses. MYCIN, for instance, a system developed by Shortliffe, a doctor-cum-computer scientist, provides consultative advice on diagnosis and antibiotic therapy for infectious diseases such as blood infections and meningitis. CADUCEUS (formerly INTERNIST) performs diagnoses (at a level of expertise that permits it to cope with the case studies of the Clinical Pathological Conferences), in the field of internal medicine, 80–85 per cent of which domain is represented in its knowledge base. Finally, CASNET diagnoses and advocates therapeutic measures for the disease process of glaucoma, doing so in a fashion, it is averred, that ophthalmologists have acclaimed to be akin to that of an expert in the field.

Inspired by such successes, some lawyers have suggested the possibility of 'legal diagnostics'[15] and expert systems for lawyers,[16] while various computer scientists, flush with their colleagues' achievements, have turned to the domain of law in order that they might widen their range of conquests.

1.3 KNOWLEDGE-BASED AND EXPERT SYSTEMS IN LAW

There is, no doubt, a wide range of potential applications for expert systems in the legal domain.[17] Indeed whenever human expertise is required for some legally orientated assignment—for instance, drafting documents, interviewing clients, or scheduling court appearances—it is conceivable that an expert system could be of help. However, this book is concerned with only one use of expert systems in the legal context: expert systems that reason with, solve problems on the basis of, and offer advice on the strength of, the substantive law.

[15] Chalton, 'Legal Diagnostics' (1980).
[16] Niblett, 'Expert Systems for Lawyers' (1981).
[17] For an extended listing of such applications, see Gray, 'Law & Technology Conference: Expert System Workshop Report' (1985). In a sense, the forerunners of knowledge-based systems in law are the computer-aided instruction in law systems (CAI systems), see Park and Burris, 'Computer-Aided Instruction in Law: Theories, Techniques and Trepidations' (1978), p. 42. On expert systems as teaching aids, see Susskind, 'Artificial Intelligence, Expert Systems, and the Teaching of Law' (1986).

Following from the discussion of the previous section, expert systems in substantive law, meaningfully so-called, might be expected to correspond to the following tentative characterization. They are computer programs that have been written with the aid of legal experts in particular, and usually highly specialized, areas of law. (Systems lacking the specialization requirement, yet possessing those other expert systems' attributes mentioned in the previous section, might more correctly be termed IKBS in law.) These expert systems are designed to function as intelligent assistants in the process of legal problem-solving (and can also be used as teaching aids). The users of such systems are intended to be general legal practitioners, who, when faced with legal problems beyond their range of knowledge and experience, rather than always having to turn to appropriately qualified legal specialists or to unwieldy legal textbooks, may instead consult their expert systems in law. Such systems ask questions of their users and guide them through the problem-solving process, utilizing the embodied heuristic and formal knowledge of the experts who assisted in their design. Moreover, these systems offer explanations for their lines of reasoning and may be required to provide citations of the authoritative sources of all assertions made and conclusions drawn.

It will become increasingly apparent during the course of this book why I suggest that the users of expert systems in law should be lawyers, or at least those with considerable familiarity with the workings of the legal and court systems. Suffice it to say, at this stage for a system to be used responsibly, the user must be aware of the possible role in legal reasoning of 'principles' (Sections 5.2, 5.7, and 6.6) and of 'purpose' (Sections 5.7 and 6.6). Moreover, he must be sensitive to the drawbacks and implications of 'compartmentalizing' the law (Section 2.4), and capable too of recognizing those occasions when some legal aid cannot help him with any problem at hand (Section 6.7).

Although in the literature there are several claims of existing expert systems in law, as is apparent from the analysis given in Appendix 1, close examination of the documentation of the systems invariably reveals these pronouncements to be exaggerated. It is clear, however, when fully operational expert systems in law of the type envisaged above are developed (as seems likely), that the output of these systems will be of a very different nature to that of the legal database systems in law such as LEXIS that are currently assisting legal practitioners and academics in their research into the substantive law. Expert systems will not be designed to provide the legal profession with the raw *data* (the formal sources of law) of the legal reasoning and legal problem-solving processes, based upon search requests formulated in terms of keywords in combination, as existing database systems in law do; but, rather, they will serve as the embodiment of a corpus of *knowledge*—the result of interpretation of the raw data—to which users may gain access. Both database systems in law and expert systems in law have been said to offer their users *information* about the law, but because of the ambiguity of that word this description of the function of these computer facilities obscures the nature of the material with which the lawyer will be furnished. The former systems process and provide uninterpreted legal data for manipulation by the human user in his own subsequent interpretative reasoning procedures. The latter systems process and provide knowledge of the law which itself is, in part, the consequence of previous intellectual operations by human beings upon legal data: in that way, much of the knowledge processing and reasoning is carried out by the expert system rather than by the user and thereby the new technology is harnessed in a legal context to relieve further intellectual toil.

In truth, then, we might question whether database systems in law do indeed offer us 'information' about the law. Much confusion in this field, as indeed in many others, has been occasioned by the ambiguity of the term 'information', a concept in relation to which two radically diverging analyses are often offered by information theorists.[18] On one account, information can (logically) come about only subsequent to the operation of the interpretative processes of some cognitive agent on some more basic raw material. In law, Niblett seems to defend this thesis.[19] He contends that computer systems such as LEXIS are not, strictly, *information* retrieval systems at all. Rather, Niblett argues, these are 'document' retrieval systems, because in any search session a user is provided with texts of possibly relevant documents and not with solutions to the problem that he is investigating.

Proponents of the other school of thought in information theory maintain that advocates of the first confuse the notions of *informa-*

---

[18] See generally Dretske, *Knowledge and the Flow of Information* (1981).
[19] 'Expert Systems for Lawyers' (1981), p. 2.

tion and *meaning*. If this conceptual error is corrected, they argue, then information can be regarded, in the words of Dretske, 'as an objective commodity, something whose generation, transmission, and reception do not require or in any way presuppose interpretive processes'. He concludes, then, that the 'raw material *is* information'[20]. This conception of information is favoured implicitly, in law, by all, like Mehl,[21] who consider there to be no attendant linguistic infelicity in the usage of the expression 'legal information' in respect of the produce of LEXIS and other similar systems. In law, however, there is also a third camp, occupants of which seem content to wield the term information wildly and with little discretion.[22] These commentators deploy the title 'legal informatics' on all occasions, exercising it as a generic term for many activities involving the application of computer technology to the law. Thus, they seem to find no problems in the practice of referring both to systems such as LEXIS, as well as to systems that might actually solve legal problems, as 'legal information systems'. Yet, as I have said, this practice tends to obscure our vision of what systems have actually been designed to do—how it is conceived that they should function as aids to the legal profession.

It would be advantageous for practitioners and theorists alike, because of the uncertainty of its range of reference, if the word 'information' were to be banished from the vocabulary of all those who profess an interest in computer applications to the law. In its stead, it is submitted that a more appropriate distinction of law machines, based on a systems design approach, is between database systems in law and knowledge-based systems in law.[23] Because the term 'information' is so firmly entrenched in the minds of so many, however, as a compromise, where it would be unavoidable to phrase it otherwise, we might distinguish also between legal database information systems and legal knowledge-based information systems. The former systems are designed to function as non-intelligent supportive

---

[20] *Knowledge and the Flow of Information* (1981), p. vii, (emphasis added) and *passim*.
[21] 'Automation in the Legal World: From the Machine Processing of Legal Information to the "Law Machine"' (1958).
[22] e.g. see the collection of articles in *AILIS*. Note, however, that the Italian term *informatica* means 'computer science' or 'information science', which perhaps explains the Italian commentators' wide usage of the word information.
[23] This distinction accords with the common usage of computer scientists—see Wiederhold, 'Knowledge and Database Management' (1984).

components in the general legal problem-solving process, while the latter (which may embody or interface with the former), assist in the more specific interpretative processes requiring a level of knowledge normally associated only with intelligent human beings. (It is likely, in the future, that further problems, akin to those arising because of the vagueness of the term 'information', will emerge as a result of the imprecise notion of 'knowledge'.)

While it would be a premature and indeed a misconceived exercise to detail all the conceivable advantages of expert systems in law, one striking and direct consequence of their widespread use bears mention: these systems would provide the legal profession with the possibility of overcoming difficulties resulting from intense specialization in the law. This phenomenon has itself been occasioned, amongst other factors, by the continual expansion of the statute books as well as by the growth in number of reported cases, as a result of which lawyers are now incapable of keeping apace with many legal developments. Despite the availability and considerable use of database systems in law, it is undeniable that many lawyers are still heavily reliant on the resources of the legal expert and his ability, culled from years of experience in the field, to direct his specialist knowledge to given legal problems.

The general practitioner is less likely now than in the past to be able himself to offer counsel to his client and is becoming increasingly dependent on expert advice for problems beyond his range of legal knowledge. The capability of the legal expert to identify, classify, and analyse the problem domain, then to adopt an appropriate mode of systematic inquiry, to follow this up by skilful and relevant consultation, and finally to formulate his opinion, having evaluated various alternatives, is indeed a valuable legal resource. This resource, often transitory, even volatile in nature, surely is worthy of nurture and preservation. Untimely departures of senior partners from law firms, of scholars from the groves of academe, or indeed of members of the judiciary from the Bench can, without adequate educational preparation, wreak havoc in given specialized fields of law. It may now be possible, however, by use of expert systems in law, to preserve indefinitely and to put at the disposal of others the wealth of legal knowledge and expertise of various experts hitherto bestowed upon the legal world in transient and indiscriminate doses. More than this, a computer may now be able to offer assistance of a quality possibly greater than that of any one individual human legal expert. In the next section, I introduce the various projects that have contributed to the possibility of the development of such machines.

1.4 SIGNIFICANT PROJECTS IN ARTIFICIAL INTELLIGENCE AND LEGAL REASONING

The first serious recommendation that research into the application of AI techniques to legal reasoning should be undertaken was made in 1970 in a joint paper by Buchanan, an eminent computer scientist who was closely involved with the DENDRAL project, and Headrick, of Stanford Law School.[24] They argued then that it was time for interdisciplinary work in this field and foresaw benefits both for jurisprudence and artificial intelligence. Since 1970, no more than twenty-five sustained research projects have been launched in this field, most of which are introduced in this section, summarized in Appendix I, and discussed in the remainder of the chapter.[25]

The most thorough and sophisticated contribution so far has been made by McCarty, whose TAXMAN project, initiated in 1972 and now involving both TAXMAN I and II, concerns the development of a program, using classical AI tools, that can perform 'a very rudimentary form of "legal reasoning"' in corporate taxation law.[26] Meldman also commenced his MIT Project in the early 1970s, the prototype of which engages in 'legal analysis' in relation to the torts of assault and battery. Meldman's system was partially implemented by King in 1976. Two other significant efforts originating in that period were Popp and Schlink's JUDITH, which operates on the German Civil Code, and Sprowl's ABF, a computer system that uses legal regulations to draft legal documents.

Substantial advances in AI led to the launching of many later projects: Hafner's LIRS, which adopts a knowledge-based approach to the retrieval of documents pertaining to the law of negotiable instruments; Waterman and Peterson's Rand Project whose goal is to develop—using expert systems techniques—rule-based computer models of the decision-making processes of experts involved with

---

[24] 'Some Speculation about Artificial Intelligence and Legal Reasoning' (1970).

[25] References to the projects mentioned in this section can be found in Section I of the Bibliography of this book.

[26] 'Reflections on TAXMAN: An Experiment in Artificial Intelligence and Legal Reasoning' (1977), p. 838.

settlement and evaluation of claims in civil litigation; The Prolog Projects, the best known of which were developed at Imperial College, London, which seek both to represent various legal domains using the much favoured Fifth Generation logic programming tool, Prolog, and often also to run translations of legislation in a general expert system shell;[27] Michaelsen's TAXADVISOR program, which advises on federal tax planning, and runs on the expert system shell, EMYCIN; deBessonet's CCLIPS (Civil Code Legal Information Processing System), one of whose chief goals is 'scientifically' to codify parts of the Louisiana Civil Code using AI techniques; Leith's ELI (Expert Legislative Information) program which operates on welfare law; and Gardner's Stanford Project relating to offer and acceptance law.

Other related projects are LEGOL/NORMA, carried on at the London School of Economics, SARA, developed at the Norwegian Research Center for Computers and Law, and POLYTEXT/ARBIT, conducted under the auspices of the Swedish National Defence Research Institute. Moreover, two lawyers, Bellord of the UK, and Hellawell of the USA, have also written programs that are relevant in this context—ATAXIS and CORPTAX respectively.

Finally, worthy of note are the many quasi-legal applications currently being developed on the general expert system shells that are available today on a commercial basis. The Data Protection Adviser (DPA)—built on the Crystal shell—is a suitable example of such a system.[28]

For further details on each of the above projects and programs, reference may be made to the systematic and comparative assessment presented in tabulated form in Appendix I. Many of the projects have made considerable impact on our general understanding of the AI/legal reasoning field, but, as I shall now argue, there has been insufficient attention paid so far to the jurisprudential pre-

---

[25] 'Shells', as shall be seen in Section 4.7, are ready-made inference mechanisms upon which expert systems may be built.

[28] The Data Protection Adviser is reviewed in Susskind, 'Expert Systems in Law and the Data Protection Adviser' (1987). ESP/Advisor is also a relevant shell: its designers claim that its ability to 'animate' text renders it suitable for the handling of complex rules, and indeed some of its sample knowledge bases have law as their domain of application: see Goodall, *The Guide to Expert Systems* (1985), pp. 68–9, 83–4, 113–14, and 141. A final shell to note is xi, on which a system that clarifies employment law was written: see Keen and McBride, 'Expert Systems in Clarifying Employment Law' (1986).

suppositions of building expert systems in law. And I turn to that matter in the next section.

1.5 A NEW JOB FOR JURISPRUDENCE

Many conclusions can be drawn from the tabulated survey of the AI/legal reasoning field given in Appendix I, but none surely more remarkable than the fact that despite the fairly extensive, and undoubtedly growing, interest in the field, and notwithstanding the widespread use of many of the classical tools of AI, there has not yet been developed on a commercial basis a fully operational expert system in substantive law, of the sort sketched in Section 1.3, to serve today as a useful tool for the legal profession. The collective achievements of all the projects do, however, suggest that, in terms of the necessary computational tools, the construction of expert systems in law (at least of limited scope), as I have envisaged them, is now technically feasible. That is to say there do not seem, on the face of it, to be any insurmountable *computational* barriers preventing the development of such systems. Most of the features expected of any expert system have been incorporated in one or other of the prototypes mentioned. The important attribute of flexibility, for instance, has been achieved in the design of most of the major systems. (It is in relation to this that we can see the limitations of CORPTAX, the tax systems on sale in most leading department stores and, as McCarty has noted,[29] the computer-assisted instruction systems in law, all of which are inflexible.) Moreover, more than half of the systems exhibit transparency, although it must be stressed that most of those that do offer explanations of their lines of reasoning do so simply by regurgitating the rules that are used by the programs in coming to their conclusions. While it should be conceded that if a system is to replicate a human legal expert it ought to provide more penetrating explanations (by clarifying the rules and, as Bellord realizes, also by stating the authoritative legal sources of all material propositions advanced), these modifications do not present profound computational problems.

Notwithstanding this apparently optimistic analysis of the computational feasibility of building expert systems in law, it is funda-

---

[29] 'Intelligent Legal Information Systems: Problems and Prospects' (1984), p. 145.

mental that workers in this field be urged to consider why it is that inquiries over the last fifteen years into the possibility of knowledge-based computer-assisted legal reasoning have yielded far fewer positive results than comparable efforts in other disciplines. It might seem intuitively obvious that this lack of success stems from the differences between the nature of legal reasoning and the nature of other enterprises such as diagnosing illnesses, mineral prospecting, and inferring chemical structures. The latter, we generally agree, are rooted, ultimately, in the empirically based, causal, descriptive laws of the natural sciences, whereas legal reasoning involves the manipulation of the prescriptive laws of the legal order, discoverable, in the main, not from uniformities or patterns in the external world but through scrutiny of the formal sources of the law. No attempts have been made, however, to examine in detail this intuitive reaction to what is regarded by some as an epistemological issue.[30] This lack of interest in such theoretical matters is typified by the paucity of attention exhibited, in the writings pertaining to the projects I have mentioned, towards the relationship between jurisprudence and AI/legal reasoning.

In the explanatory papers pertaining to KRL, the Rand Project, ABF, LIRS, POLYTEXT/ARBIT, and TAXADVISOR, as in the writings of Bellord and Hellawell, for instance, there are no references or allusions to jurisprudence. In the commentaries on the MIT Project, JUDITH, the Prolog Projects, LEGOL/NORMA, and CCLIPS, legal theory is mentioned but is not considered to be of fundamental significance as a source of guidance. In short, with the exceptions of SARA,[31] the Stanford Project, and ELI, the relationship manifested in the literature between jurisprudence and the application of AI to legal reasoning has been unidirectional; that is, the projects constitute marginal contributions to, rather than exploitations of, the wealth of jurisprudential resources that I shall argue are available and indeed

---

[30] See Sloman, 'Epistemology and Artificial Intelligence' (1979), pp. 235–41.

[31] SARA was developed by the Norwegian Research Center for Computers and the Law (NRCCL), a body which carries out exemplary interdisciplinary inquiries into the computer/law interface. NRCCL's research is exceptional amongst the projects discussed in this book, because its works are permeated with an acute awareness of the complexities of jurisprudence and its intimate involvement with the task of designing systems to assist in legal reasoning. Much of their work on legal reasoning and computers is based on the writings of the Norwegian legal theorists Eckhoff and Sundby. For a very recent example of this, see Hansen, *Simulation and Automation of Legal Decisions* (1986).

invaluable for the would-be scholar or builder of expert systems in law.

In this connection, Niblett has claimed that 'a successful expert system is likely to contribute more to jurisprudence than the other way round'.[32] This book casts grave doubt on that suggestion. In any event, if the majority of the projects mentioned in the previous section are indicative of quality, then it is unlikely that many commentaries on expert systems will exhibit the analytical rigour and sophistication of argument that characterize today's major contributions to legal theory. More importantly, it is submitted that in the first instance jurisprudence can and ought to supply the models of law and legal reasoning that are required for computerized implementation in the process of building all expert systems in law. If this be the case, it is difficult to imagine that any subsequent contribution of expert systems to jurisprudence could be of such import as to overshadow the latter's initial endowment.

No doubt it may well transpire that, in Niblett's words, 'the value of an expert system will reside not in its conformity to some jurisprudential theory',[33] if by this he means in conformity with a pre-existing theory, such as that of Hart, Dworkin, Finnis, or Raz. It is beyond argument, however, that all expert systems must conform to some jurisprudential theory because *all expert systems in law necessarily make assumptions about the nature of law and legal reasoning.* To be more specific, all expert systems must embody theories of legal knowledge, legal science, the structure of rules, the individuation of laws, legal systems and sub-systems, legal reasoning, and of logic and the law (as well perhaps as elements of a semantic theory, a sociology, and a psychology of law), theories that must all themselves rest on more basic philosophical foundations. If this is so, it would seem prudent that the general theory of law implicit in expert systems should be explicitly articulated using (where appropriate) the relevant works of seasoned theoreticians of law. Perhaps the reason that there is, as yet, no overwhelmingly successful system is that the vast corpus of apposite jurisprudential material has not yet been tapped in the construction process.

It has been naïve to suppose, as shall emerge in this book, that computer scientists could talk unobjectionably and unassailably of issues such as representing legal knowledge and legal inference pro-

---

[32] 'Expert Systems for Lawyers' (1981), p. 3.
[33] Ibid.

cedures. These are highly complex matters of jurisprudence that require the attention of workers of that field. It is submitted that we now have sufficient experience of the general field of AI and legal reasoning for the immediate commencement of a systematic jurisprudential inquiry into the various stages of legal knowledge engineering and expert systems in law together with the development of a compatible theory of law, to the extent that such a theory is required in this context. The principal goal of this study is to make such an inquiry and to present the foundations of such a general theory, and in so doing I shall thereby remedy a defect identified in the following terms by Fiedler in 1979: 'On the side of legal theory up till now there has been but very little interest in the computerized implementation of law... For legal theory, this lack of interest is a deplorable deficiency.'[34]

The need for jurisprudential involvement in this field can be appreciated more fully on consideration of the various approaches that have thus far been adopted in the design of AI systems in law, in relation to the three major research issues in expert systems that I identified in Section 1.2—knowledge acquisition, knowledge representation, and knowledge utilization.

Most AI theorists are agreed that knowledge acquisition—the process by which, as it is said, domain-specific expertise is extracted from the domain specialist(s)—is the major remaining obstacle to be tackled by expert systems research workers.[35] However, few of the projects that I have mentioned even approach the hurdle of *legal* knowledge acquisition, still less attempt to negotiate it. In general, the systems that have been developed to date have minimal heuristic content and no methods have yet been suggested that might eliminate this deficit. The knowledge represented in the systems usually consists of restructured statutory source material (case law has received far less treatment) and even in the statutory domain the researchers remain unsettled over whether superficial coverage of an extensive legal domain should be attempted, as in LEGOL/NORMA, or whether intensive coverage of a far more restricted area is more effective as in, say, the MIT Project. Insight into these problems can be found in works of jurisprudence. For it is in writings of legal theory that we find observations about the nature of the knowledge thought to be necessary and sufficient for legal problem-solving, and

[34] 'Functional Relations between Legal Regulations and Software' (1980), p. 143.
[35] See e.g. *FG*, p. 75.

arguments for the necessity, in common law jurisdictions, of taking cognizance not just of statutory material but also of case law, these being found together with guidelines outlining how judicial precedents might most effectively be tackled.

Most of the projects mentioned in the last section are chiefly concerned with *legal* knowledge representation. In this book, this is shown to be the central issue of the study of *legal* knowledge engineering, a conclusion that is supported by reflection on the differences between database and knowledge-based systems. In the full-text species of the former, the formal legal sources are stored in the computer memory in computer-readable format and are retrieved by the user as documents identical in content to the printed statute books and law reports of conventional law libraries. The legal data is not *interpreted* for this purpose, but is simply fed into the computer as the raw material of the process of legal reasoning. In knowledge-based systems in law, in contrast, these sources must be *represented*, that is, restructured so that they can be stored in the memory and utilized in the reasoning process. The activity of legal knowledge representation, therefore, involves the operation of interpretative processes whereby the legal data of part of a legal system, valid at one particular point in time (that is, the legal data of a momentary legal system[36]) is scrutinized, analysed, and eventually reformulated in a fashion that is both faithful in meaning to the original source materials and that allows for the requisite transparency and flexibility of expert systems in law.

As Appendix I indicates, many different computational methods have been used to represent legal knowledge. The importance of adopting a suitable method of knowledge representation cannot be overstated: the efficiency of the system depends largely on this matter. In this connection McCarty has argued that 'the most critical task in the development of an intelligent legal information system, either for document retrieval or for expert advice, is the construction of a *conceptual model* of the relevant legal domain'.[37] He calls for the development in law of 'deep' systems akin to that of the glaucoma diagnosis expert system, CASNET, in which the disease is represented as a dynamic process structured as a network of causally connected pathophysiological states, in contrast to the 'shallow rule-based'

---

[36] See *CLS*, pp. 34–5, *NS*, pp. 88–9, and *LLS*, pp. 42–3 and 49–50.
[37] 'Intelligent Legal Information Systems: Problems and Prospects' (1984), p. 126. (Original emphasis.)

MYCIN which contains no internal representation of the disease process. Whereas TAXMAN aspires to the CASNET mode of representation, McCarty claims that Sprowl's ABF and Hellawell's CORPTAX can be likened in this respect to MYCIN.

However, no thorough examination of the relative merits of all the various approaches to the representation of legal knowledge has yet been attempted. It might be thought that this is simply a matter for computer scientists to work out. Yet that view reflects a misunderstanding of the enterprise of representing knowledge of the law, as it is quite clear that the fundamental issues involved here are jurisprudential. The object of the exercise is to describe the law in a fashion that can suitably be embodied, together with the experts' heuristics, in the knowledge base. The activity of describing the law while remaining faithful to its meaning has received considerable attention from eminent legal theorists. We need, as Dworkin has admitted, 'a strategy of exposition',[38] and where better to initiate our search for that strategy than, say, the writings of Kelsen and Harris on legal science, Bentham's and Raz's theories of the individuation of laws, and the studies of Ross, von Wright, Alchourron, and Bulygin on normative discourse?[39]

It would be bold to question the relevance of the works of Kelsen who, in the preface to his *General Theory of Law and State*, states that he intends to provide the legal scientist with the 'fundamental concepts by which the positive law of a definite legal community can be described'. Kelsen's general theory of law must be pertinent for theorists of legal knowledge engineering, for its aim is said to be 'to enable the jurist concerned with a particular legal order, the lawyer, the judge, the legislator, or the law-teacher' and, it may not unreasonably be inferred, the legal knowledge engineer, 'to understand and to describe as exactly as possible his own positive law'.[40] When we 'describe' the law in a computer program, we will be engaging, as Alchourron and Bulygin put it, in a 'reformulation',[41] or, as Golding suggests, in a 'rational reconstruction',[42] of an area of the law, and the comments of these theorists on these matters cannot sensibly be ignored. Likewise, with regard to the principles in accordance

---

[38] *TRS*, p. 75.
[39] See e.g. Kelsen, *GTLS* and *PTL*, Harris, *LLS*, Bentham, *OLG*, Raz, *CLS*, Ross, *DN*, von Wright, *NA*, and Alchourron and Bulygin, *NS*.
[40] See p. xiii. See also Harris, *LLS*, *passim*.
[41] *NS*, p. 71.
[42] Golding, 'Kelsen and the Concept of "Legal System"' (1961), *passim*.

with which we may divide up our formal legal sources, surely we must pay heed to the limiting and guiding requirements with which Raz furnishes us for this purpose.[43] Moreover, once we have individuated our legal rules, we must then decide upon their precise structure for representational purposes. This is no easy task, for as Harris has said, 'The law does not announce, on its face, into what units it can be most usefully split up.'[44] It can be seen from Appendix I that many researchers in AI/legal reasoning (for example, Waterman and Peterson, Popp and Schlink, and deBessonet), have represented the law as a system of rules. Laying aside the obvious jurisprudential difficulties involved in this process,[45] it is striking that the internal structures of the rules represented in the respective systems are crude in comparison to, say, the components of laws that Ross and von Wright identify.[46] Again, to disregard these theorists would be folly indeed.

Although, of course, not all legal theorists agree over the manner in which we ought to describe, individuate, and structure the law, having surveyed the relevant jurisprudential literature and having noted both the concordance and dissent, we shall surely then be better equipped to discuss with computer scientists how legal knowledge bases might be built. In that way too, it will be possible to remove the law from the Procrustean bed into which many computer scientists have remorselessly thrust it in order that they might demonstrate the versatility of their favoured computer programming languages.[47] Furthermore, with models of law drawn from legal theory, we shall then also be in a position to consider the possibility, desirability, and indeed the necessity of following McCarty's claim regarding 'deep conceptual models' and expert systems in law.

With regard to the challenge of designing the inference procedures of an expert system in law—the problem of *legal* knowledge utilization—this too raises interesting jurisprudential questions for the legal knowledge engineer. The commentators Solomon, Grossman,

---

[43] *CLS*, pp. 140–7.

[44] *LLS*, p. 92.

[45] The question of whether or not the law is exclusively a system of rules is central to the Hart/Dworkin debate. See e.g. *TRS*, chs. 2–3.

[46] See *DN*, ch. 5 and *NA*, ch. 5.

[47] Some of the workers on the Prolog Projects, for instance, were, in a sense, committed to the use of Prolog prior to the selection of the law as an apposite domain of application. And the goal of some of their projects, then, was to represent chosen pieces of legislation in Prolog come what may!

and Morrise[48] all place great emphasis on the distinction between *deductive* and *analogical* approaches adopted in the projects—a confusion that obscures the actual jurisprudential orientations and functions of the systems. For it is misleading to categorize, as these writers have done, TAXMAN I and II and the MIT Project as analogical systems. McCarty does not stress in any of the papers cited in this book that either TAXMAN I or II are to be regarded as systems that reason by analogy. Moreover, Meldman's definition of 'legal analysis', together with his emphasis that his model simplifies the notion of analogy,[49] imply that he, too, would be reluctant to characterize his system as predominantly an analogical one. (King's implementation of the MIT Project, on the other hand, is principally concerned with analogy.) Despite any allegations to the contrary, it seems undeniable that the distinguishing characteristic of the overwhelming majority of the systems is their dependence on deductive inference procedures. (This will become clearer when, in Chapter 6, I clarify various inference mechanisms currently used.) In consequence, all those objections to deductive legal reasoning that pervade the jurisprudential literature seem to be germane to legal knowledge utilization, and indeed Part Three of this book is devoted largely to an examination of the implications of these arguments for designers and users of expert systems in law.

Given, as I have claimed, that all expert systems in law necessarily make assumptions about the nature of law and legal reasoning, in what ways can jurisprudence be of relevance to the study of these systems? In this book, I show that jurisprudence is of importance to expert systems in law in two significant respects. First, I demonstrate—through reference to the design and implementation of the Oxford prototype expert system in Scottish Divorce Law—how jurisprudence can be an invaluable source of guidance for legal knowledge engineers, and is not simply a field of discourse to be mentioned in passing. (Guidance, it should be noted, is sorely needed in this area, as none of the workers in the field has offered useful practical advice on the strength of which other projects might be launched.) Second, I shall articulate the latent jurisprudential presuppositions, assumptions, and implications of the Oxford system, and, it transpires, of most other expert systems in law, so that

---

[48] In 'Computers and Legal Reasoning' (1982) and (1983), and 'Emerging Computer-Assisted Legal Analysis Systems' (1980), respectively.
[49] 'A Structural Model for Computer-Aided Legal Analysis' (1977), p. 67.

evaluation of this field might now become the province of representatives of the legal profession as well as of computer scientists.

In a sense, I can be said to have found for jurisprudence 'a new
job',[50] and one of intense practical significance if indeed on its
strength a powerful tool for the lawyer emerges. It should perhaps
be emphasized that while it is submitted that it is both possible and
desirable to assign this new role to jurisprudence, it is not suggested
that it is *necessary* for all legal knowledge engineers to use jurisprudence as their guide. Just as it is not necessary for a legal textbook writer explicitly to use jurisprudence during his process of
composition and indeed many writers (for better or for worse) have
apparently paid no heed to legal theory,[51] similarly, expert systems
may in the future be built without jurisprudential insight. It is likely,
however, that such systems will be of poor quality. Because successful legal knowledge engineering presupposes so profound a familiarity with the nature of law and legal reasoning, it is scarcely
imaginable that such a mastery could be gained other than through
immersion in jurisprudence. Moreover, at their current stage of research and development, it is conceivable that some jurisprudential
(as opposed to computational) input may accelerate the possibility
of their widespread use by the legal profession. It is to the substan-
tiation of these last rather bald assertions that much of this book is
directed.

1.6 CONSENSUS AND DISAGREEMENT IN LEGAL THEORY

In response to the previous arguments regarding the use of jurisprudence for legal knowledge engineering purposes, the cynical critic
of jurisprudence would probably retort that there is a degree of disagreement and dissent so great between legal theorists themselves
that no points of contact between their competing theories could

---

[50] Despite the historical, educational, and intrinsic value of jurisprudence, its utility and importance have often been called into question in the past, as a consequence
of which its proponents have felt urged to allocate the discipline specific 'jobs'. See
Harvey, 'A Job for Jurisprudence' (1944), Kennedy, 'Another Job for Jurisprudence'
(1945), and Twining, 'Some Jobs for Jurisprudence' (1974). Also see Harris, *LLS*, pp.
14–23, where he assigns 'tasks' for jurisprudence. Of relevance too is MacCormick,
'The Democratic Intellect and the Law' (1985).

[51] On jurisprudence and legal textbooks, see Simmonds, *The Decline of Juridical
Reason: Doctrine and Theory in the Legal Order* (1984), ch. 1.

possibly be located, as a result of which, therefore, legal theory has little to offer for the purposes suggested. However, I believe that the divergence of views within jurisprudence has been unrealistically accentuated by the typical foci of inquiry, in that legal theorists tend to concentrate on the inherently contentious issues while ignoring 'straightforward' matters (which themselves may indeed raise insurmountable difficulties for the less capable). There may very well be *consensus* over many jurisprudential questions that has remained unarticulated on grounds of it being simplistic or mundane. Indeed, it may be in virtue of this presupposed, unifying substratum of concordance that dialogue between the various schools has been possible. For instance, as I show in Part Three, theorists do seem to agree on the forms of legal argument that are both possible and desirable in the clearest of cases, although this unanimity may not be apparent from the literature because 'hard cases' and not 'crystal clear cases' have invariably been jurists' object of study.

If there is such a concurrence of approach in relation to legal reasoning as well as to legal theory in general, then it is a model culled from that harmony that should be implemented in expert systems in law. If there is not, and if these conflicts affect the expert system enterprise, then a model that clashes as little as possible with the widely accepted theories should be developed. In this study, I endeavour to determine the extent to which such consensus within jurisprudence (albeit of mundane and limited application) can be located. A practical consequence of this exercise, if completed satisfactorily, is that it would render unnecessary the repetition of such exegeses in respect of all expert systems in the future if these were built in accordance with the principles offered in this initial theoretical exposition.

Given that one of the goals of the Oxford project was to divine consensus in legal theory, methodological considerations now fall to be examined. More specifically, it is necessary to clarify (as no others who have seen the relevance of jurisprudence have done), on what basis, and deploying what criteria, certain jurisprudential writings were chosen to serve as points of departure. Although analytical jurisprudence was identified as being of chief concern, because the literature even on this one branch of jurisprudence is voluminous, we were committed to being selective; which inevitably raised those perennial problems concerning bias and subjectivity that smite investigators in all fields of discourse. It is as well at the outset, then, to state the nature of the sources that were consulted (for their value-relevance, of course). With the notable exceptions of the works of Bentham and Kelsen, the vast majority of the materials surveyed were British writings of analytical jurisprudence (and philosophy) written since the mid-fifties and early sixties. In the period since then, there have been unparalleled instances of punctilious legal analyses, particularly in relation to the nature of reasoning and rules, the impetus for which was derived very largely from the publications of H. L. A. Hart. It was considered that the most rigorous of these writings constituted the source materials with greatest potential given our overall purpose. Accordingly, the conclusions reached in this book are undoubtedly open to falsification in light of further jurisprudential work that accounts for a still broader range of legal theories.

It is also desirable at this stage, in light of my method of approaching jurisprudence, to offer an explanation of why theorists accounting for the nature of law and legal reasoning have failed to agree; for clarification of this matter will permit a less hindered search for consensus (not only in this context, but for others with broadly similar aims). It is submitted that disagreements in legal theory can be understood in terms of one or more of the following five reasons. (No doubt there are others.) First, they do not concur over more basic philosophical issues, which disparity manifests itself in their theories of law. Second, their purposes in theorizing about the law are often vastly different as they are engaging in jurisprudence (in a broad sense) from the perspectives of their own respective disciplines. Third, even those whose academic orientations are at one will disagree over what is 'important' and 'significant' within their enterprise, and, therefore, will propound quite distinct theses. Fourth, theoretical accounts differ because of terminological divergences. Fifth, some theories are simply unacceptable (for many reasons), and members of this last group clearly are often found to be at odds with others. I shall look at each of these in turn.[52]

Any comprehensive historical account of Western thought will attest to the fact that there are many fundamental questions over which human beings have failed to agree since the dawn of philosophical speculation in the sixth century BC. In turn, the problems

---

[52] Cf. Friedmann, *Legal Theory* (1967), ch. 6: most of the antinomies in legal theory identified there are subsumable under my various explanations of disagreements. Also relevant is Summers, 'Notes on Criticism in Legal Philosophy' (1971).

raised by these controversies permeate the disputes that have arisen over explanation in the natural, social, behavioural, and historical sciences, debates which necessarily intrude on the pursuit of legal theory. Indeed, many jurisprudential controversies, modern and ancient—all those embodied in the literature produced in the era (of over two millenia) between, say Plato's *The Laws* and an important modern contribution such as Finnis's *Natural Law and Natural Rights*—are explicable in terms of more fundamental philosophical issues. The competent legal theorist does not generate his arguments in a philosophical vacuum, but rather tends to propound his theses on the philosophical foundations laid by others. Thus, for instance, we know Kelsen's intellectual roots to have been planted by Kant and the Neo-Kantians, Cohen and Cassirer; while much of Hart's philosophical inspiration was provided by the school of linguistic philosophy, and, in particular, the teachings of J. L. Austin.

Many perennial philosophical problems thus impregnate works of jurisprudence, as a result of which many issues of legal theory cannot be settled by any rational process currently available for the resolution of philosophical disputes. It is therefore not presently possible to establish consensus over these issues, and I shall refer to such apparently impenetrable jurisprudential problems as ones that are *currently philosophically insoluble*. This is not to suggest, of course, that these problems will never be solved, but simply that we do not seem to have, at present, the necessary apparatus required to resolve the difficulties. The existence of these currently philosophically insoluble problems is not necessarily fatal for present purposes, as I show in the course of this study.[53]

The second proposed reason for differing accounts of the nature of law relates to the fact that many workers from many disciplines are interested in the nature of law. This reason 'entails the denial of any univocal theory of "law"', according to Harris.[54] The study of the nature and operation of law is not the exclusive province of lawyers and legal theorists—anthropologists, criminologists, economists, historians, philosophers, political scientists, and theologians (amongst others) also have a justifiable claim to that pursuit. As a consequence of this widespread concern with the law, it is misconceived to seek interdisciplinary unanimity in response to the well-

---

[53] Cf. MacIntyre, *After Virtue* (1981), pp. 6 ff.
[54] *LLS*, p. 20. Also see p. 35.

worn query 'What is law?' For, as Harris has pointed out,
the law is not something one can lay hold of independently of a focus of
interest. Is one engaged in descriptive or critical legal science, or in political
philosophy, social psychology, sociology, or anthropology? Answer that,
and then one can say which conception of 'rule' or 'system' will be the primary point of reference, the 'law', so far as that discipline is concerned. An
over-all view of the law must be a phenomenological one which takes
account of shifting focuses of interest.[55]

A further illustration of what might be referred to as *disciplinary
divergences* as being the source of differing legal theories is offered by
Finnis. He emphasizes, at the start of his *Natural Law and Natural
Rights*, that while his study was written in the tradition of analytical
jurisprudence, 'someone who shared my theory of natural law, but
whose focus of interest and competence was, say, sociological jurisprudence or political theory or moral theology, would have written a
different book'.[56] It might be thought, then, that those who seek to
elucidate the nature of law from the same disciplinary orientation
will offer substantially similar accounts. In virtue of the next argument, however, this is not so.

This third reason is also convincingly explained by Finnis, who
seeks to explain why the descriptions of *descriptive* legal theorists
such as Austin, Bentham, Fuller, Hart, Kelsen, and Raz are at vari-
ance with one another, and concludes, 'It is obvious, then, that the
differences in description derive from differences in opinion,
amongst the descriptive theorists, about what is *important* and *significant* in the field of data and experience with which they are all
equally and thoroughly familiar'.[57]

Notwithstanding common 'focuses of interest', it is submitted,
following Finnis, that theorists' expositions tend to deviate because
they fail to subscribe to the same judgments as to what is 'important'
and 'significant' in their sphere. I shall refer to this species of disagreement in legal theory as a *disagreement over relevance*.

Much confusion and apparent disagreement in jurisprudence
arises from what shall be called *terminological discrepancies*. This
has two aspects: on the one hand, theorists often use the same term

---

[55] Ibid. p. 166.

[56] *NLNR*, p. vi. Also see Summers, 'Notes on Criticism in Legal Philosophy'
(1971), pp. 14–15.

[57] *NLNR*, p. 9. Original emphasis.

to denote entirely different notions (for example, 'legal science'—see Section 3.1), and on the other hand, writers deal with identical subject matters under seemingly unrelated headings.

For our purposes, consensus in jurisprudence is reached in respect of those matters that are accepted by analytical jurisprudents (and not necessarily by any of the many other interested parties), once any terminological confusions are eliminated and certain judgments are accepted as to what is important and significant in the discipline of legal knowledge engineering. As can be seen from this book, however, such consensus barely extends beyond explanations of 'clear cases' (see Section 6.6).

In searching for consensus in jurisprudence with a view to building expert systems in law, it is necessary, however, also to bear in mind that some disagreements are not rooted in any of the above four reasons, but are due to actual theories of law themselves being *theoretically untenable*. A theory of law (like any theory) can be defective in many respects: it may lack clarity; it might suffer from internal inconsistency (logical, empirical, or normative); it may be empirically inadequate; it may fail to explain all the phenomena within the relevant field of discourse; it may not be preferred to a competing theory whose greater simplicity is considered to contribute to its more immediate acceptance. For our purposes, we can safely disregard those theories (or aspects of those theories) which are demonstrably false or patently defective for the above or other appropriate reasons. False conclusions that have been invalidly drawn (even from acceptable premises) must also be rejected.

It is helpful to bear these five sources of disagreement in mind when surveying the jurisprudential literature for any reason. Indeed, most theorists usually do just that when propounding a new thesis, for they feel it incumbent upon them to explain in what ways theirs differs from, in what way theirs accords with, and why theirs is to be preferred to, the traditional competing theories, and in so explaining, they invariably adduce one or more of the above five reasons.

1.7 CONCLUSION

In this chapter, I have summarized both the extent to which the data-processing functions of the lawyer have actually been successfully computerized, and, moreover, the progress that has been made thus far in developing knowledge-based systems in law. It has emerged there are many problems that research workers in the field of expert systems in law must recognize and confront:

1. There are no commercially available, satisfactorily operating expert systems in both statute and case law, that have a high heuristic content and that are, moreover, at once transparent and flexible.

2. No guidelines have been offered by the cognoscenti in the field for those others who are interested in attempting to build such systems but who rightly have little desire to try to overcome problems that have already been successfully tackled.

3. There has been minimal jurisprudential input to the field, much of the work having been produced from a computational perspective.

4. The prototypes that are currently in operation cannot be instructed in natural language—the facts of a case cannot simply be described to a computer in, say, English—but require computer language or very restricted natural language input and/or responses to questions asked of the user.

5. There is little agreement over suitable terminology in the field, to the extent that researchers disagree over what constitutes an expert system in law properly so-called.

6. The possibility of expert systems interfacing with existing database computerized legal information retrieval systems has not been sufficiently examined (a matter discussed in Section 2.6).

The above problems will require many years of attention from the most skilful exponents in the field. It is the object of this book to examine and provide the basis for tentative solutions to all of them (excluding problem 4, which is clearly beyond the scope of the study as it constitutes a major AI research topic in itself—natural language processing). My point of departure shall be legal theory, and systematic inquiries into legal knowledge representation and utilization shall be made with a view to identifying jurisprudential consensus upon which the future development of expert systems in law may be premissed. With regard to representing legal knowledge, having surveyed the relevant literature, I shall endeavour to develop methods of describing, individuating, and structuring any legal subsystem (not confining attention just to statutory material). I discuss legal knowledge utilization through examination of many commentaries on the notion of deductive legal reasoning. In that way, I determine the utility and limitations of deductive legal inference engines.

My revelation of the underlying jurisprudential theorems implicit in expert systems work cannot, of course, in the present study, be dissociated from the deployment of jurisprudence in the design of the program for the Oxford project, for these two activities, at the research stage, progressed concurrently and had mutual impact. At the outset, the project commenced on the basis of a very rudimentary and tentative hypothesis based on a familiarity with both the content of much analytical jurisprudence and the requirements of artificial intelligence. The results of further immersion in relevant works of legal theory whose aim was to pinpoint consensus within jurisprudence were refined to accommodate the specific requirements of designing and implementing our working system.[58] (It should be noted that it is beyond the scope of this general jurisprudential inquiry into expert systems in law to describe our computer program in detail: that has been done in a computational work.[59])

Finally, it should be said that I do not consider it necessary in this context to enter that arid debate in legal theory over what jurisprudence is.[60] It seems to be widely agreed that jurisprudence strives for a general and systematic understanding of law, and of its administration in society. Beyond this brief remark, however, it is intended, from the nature and content of the arguments presented here in the name of jurisprudence, and, more specifically, analytical jurisprudence, that it will be sufficiently clear what is meant by these notions. Definitional matters, then, need not detain us. Clarification of central concepts, in contrast, is of central concern, and it is to that activity that much of the next chapter is devoted.

[58] The methodology adopted could be considered to be Popperian in nature, essentially a feedback process, theory being propounded in conjunction with practice, tentative solutions and procedures being refined through elimination of errors and shortcomings. See Popper, *Objective Knowledge: An Evolutionary Approach* (1972).

[59] For a detailed account of the system that was developed on the basis of the findings of this book, see Gold, 'Specification and Implementation of an Expert System in Law' (1987).

[60] On the nature of jurisprudence, see Tur, 'What is Jurisprudence?' (1978), and *IJ*, pp. 1–7.

2

Prolegomenon to Building Expert Systems in Law

THE person who designs and constructs expert systems, and, therefore, has to consider appropriate methods of knowledge acquisition, representation, and utilization in respect of each project with which he is concerned, is known as the knowledge engineer. For most domains of application of expert systems, it has sufficed that computer programmers fulfil the demands of knowledge engineering. Yet many computer scientists who have embarked on the task of *legal* knowledge engineering have promptly realized that issues such as the representation of formal sources of law and legal inference procedures are more complex than the corresponding processes in other fields. Moreover, a few have recognized that in that corpus of writings invariably referred to as jurisprudence (and, in particular, analytical jurisprudence) there seems to be much pertinent material for those who are seeking to build expert systems in law.

To gain a satisfactory understanding of the intricacies of analytical jurisprudence, familiarity both with the workings of legal systems and with the methods of philosophical inquiry is required. The assimilation of that knowledge is indeed a daunting assignment for any computer scientist and one for which his educational background has rarely equipped him. Research into the topic of legal knowledge engineering may fruitfully proceed, however, as an interdisciplinary activity—the jurisprudential models of law and legal reasoning can be provided by the legal theorist for implementation by the computer scientist in expert systems in law. In collaboration, these exponents from diverse disciplines can provide the basis for the design and construction of computer programs that can reason as experts do in particular and specialized fields of law.

The success of this proposed plan of action, however, is clearly contingent on the development by the jurisprudents of suitable models which the programmer will subsequently manipulate and

34

embody in his systems. It is the task of legal theory to provide these models. It would indeed be embarrassing for all concerned with jurisprudence if it transpired that we had to admit to computer scientists that, though we have been speculating about the nature of law and legal reasoning for well in excess of two thousand years, no matters of controversy have been settled, no agreement attained, in consequence of which legal theory has little to offer to the development of techniques of legal knowledge engineering. Such an admission is, of course, not necessary if legal theorists confine the bulk of their attention, as I do in this book, to identifying consensus within jurisprudence. It is my purpose, then, in so far as is feasible, to lay bare and articulate those relevant matters over which legal theorists have no quarrel.

However, prior to embarking on this task in detail, it will prove helpful in this chapter to discuss several preliminary matters pertaining to expert systems in law. In Section 2.1, I introduce a jurisprudential taxonomy which will provide a useful vocabulary for use throughout the book. Thereafter, in Section 2.2, I briefly reflect on the nature of legal reasoning. Section 2.3 concerns the nature of legal knowledge and its suitability for inclusion within expert systems. The more specific question of the suitability of particular branches of law is addressed in Section 2.4. The terms 'legal expertise' and 'legal expert' are examined in Section 2.5, and Section 2.6 shows how expert systems could usefully operate in conjunction with database systems in law. In Section 2.7, I advocate a suitable way in which users may interact with their expert systems in law, and in Section 2.8 I make concluding observations.

2.1 LAW-FORMULATIONS, LAW-STATEMENTS, LAW, AND VALID FORMAL SOURCES

It might be thought that a sensible initial step in a detailed inquiry into expert systems in law would be a detailed conceptual analysis of the concept of law itself. Yet a satisfactory and succinct elucidation of the idea of law will no doubt elude legal knowledge engineers in the future as it has legal theorists in the past. Some jurisprudents have argued that the law is a body of commands issued by a sovereign and supported by the threatened imposition of sanctions; others have said it to be a mass of cognitive states continually induced through the repeated proclamation of categorical imperatives; still others have maintained that it is no more than a set of forecasts of official or judicial behaviour; while yet another group claim it to be a field of meaning of predominantly normative content; and one final school of thought asserts the law to exist only in social situations in which regularity of behaviour coincides with certain intentional phenomena directed at such conduct, the criteria of validity on this account being an exclusively empirical matter. It is clear (probably for all five reasons for disagreement identified in Section 1.6) that these theories of the nature of law (being but a small selection) diverge to an extent that renders the quest for consensus in this respect futile. (I shall identify shortly just why some of these theories diverge.)

It is, of course, not the purpose of this book to address in detail fundamental problems of legal theory such as the question of the ontological status of law, but, where possible, to engage in jurisprudential inquiry at another level—where the basic premises perhaps diverge but the conclusions concur. With this in mind, I can usefully begin our discussion by looking at those widely accepted sources of legal systems that themselves, in a sense, belong to the external physical world, namely, the paper and print known as legislation and case reports.[1] These I shall refer to as *law-formulations*, thereby emphasizing that they are linguistic entities, verbally formulated as written sentences that are themselves composed of written words.[2] Acts of Parliament, as published by HMSO, and the *Law Reports*, are good examples of law-formulations. Law-formulations are also held in full-text format in database systems such as LEXIS. Although, as emerges from Section 3.4, both legal practitioners and legal theorists alike have questioned whether knowledge of law-formulations is sufficient for thorough practice and understanding of the law, no one can sensibly deny the necessity for lawyers of knowing their contents.

In legal discourse, however, not only do we refer to law-

---

[1] I take the term 'legislation' to include all written bodies of laws, rules, and regulations, and 'case reports' to encompass written reports of all court and tribunal hearings.

[2] The jurisprudential taxonomy in this section was influenced by many writings, but most notably: von Wright, *NA*, ch. 6; Raz, *CLS*, pp. 45–50, 234–8, *Practical Reason and Norms* (1975), pp. 170–7, *AL*, pp. 62–5; Kelsen, *GTLS*, p. 45, *PTL*, p. 6; Alchourron and Bulygin, 'The Expressive Conception of Norms' (1981).

formulations, but we also deploy *law-statements*—statements about what the content of the law is. These can be understood as being existential statements about law-formulations. They are second-order statements that describe the linguistic symbols that are law-formulations. Law-statements, therefore, have truth-value,[3] the existence of the law-formulation being described being the truth-ground of any law-statement. Characteristically, as Raz has shown,[4] law-statements are expressed through the use of sentence-forming operators such as 'It is the law that...', or 'Legally...', or 'There is a law that...', although, as he also says, 'often no linguistic indication is given to show that a sentence is used to make a legal statement [*a law-statement, in my terminology*]'.[5] When an operator is not used, therefore, a law-statement may well be expressed in identical terms to the law-formulation that it describes.

The above distinction between law-statements and law-formulations, to which I shall refer regularly in this book, is surely consistent with all theoretically tenable legal theories, for this approach is not incompatible with either one of the two philosophically irreconcilable jurisprudential ontologies that underpin the diverging accounts of the nature of law stated at the start of this section. On the one hand, there is a legal ontology in accordance with which the law can best be regarded as existing in some non-linguistic and non-physical form as some kind of abstract system of concepts and entities distinct from the marks on paper that are the material symbols of it. On this view, law-formulations are expressive of the law: the law is to the law-formulation what the *proposition* is to the *sentence*.[6] The law, then, is the *semantic content* of law-formulations. On the other hand, the second ontology, espoused by more empiricist theorists, eschews accounts such as the first by denying that they can be accommodated in any acceptable calculus of meaningful discourse. On this latter view, talk of abstract entities is to be avoided, and the articulation or promulgation of law-formulations in accordance with some pre-existing standards is of

---

[3] But, as Lloyd and Freeman seem to be saying in this context, their truth or falsity 'will depend not on factual verification but on whatever tests are accorded by that [the legal] system' (*IJ*, p. 13 n. 81).

[4] See *AL*, p. 63, and 'The Problem About the Nature of Law' (1982), in *IJ*, pp. 474–6.

[5] *AL*, p. 63.

[6] On the sentence/proposition distinction, see Hospers, *An Introduction to Philosophical Analysis* (1967), p. 78.

itself considered to be *creative* of the law. In other words, the law comes about *as a result of* the use of (usually prescriptive) language, and the law cannot be said to exist prior to some linguistic formulation. According to this second view, and in contrast to the first, the law is dependent on language; indeed it is constituted by our use of language. These two conceptions of law are, as Alchourron and Bulygin say of a similar distinction, 'radically different and incompatible; there is no room for any eclecticism'. But, as they also point out, 'many authors do not clearly adhere to either of the two conceptions, or rather seem to adhere to both of them'.[7]

It is not crucial for the current enterprise, however, that consensus on the question of the ontology of law is unattainable because it is not necessary here to favour one side or the other in that debate (although it is useful to know of the controversy). For it is law-statements, as I shall argue, that are at the core of any legal knowledge base, and we derive these statements from law-formulations. And my account of law-formulations neither prejudices nor presupposes either theory of the nature of law just outlined. All that I assume is that the law can be expressed in natural language, and that this is possible, as Alchourron and Bulygin also say (this time in their *Normative Systems*) is 'incontrovertible'.[8]

Yet law-formulations are not without their own jurisprudential problems, and there is one issue in particular that must be addressed. It results from the fact that legal knowledge engineers are surely required to represent as law-statements only those law-formulations that are deemed 'valid'. Any jurisprudentially sound account of expert systems in law must articulate the criteria of legal validity presupposed by the designers of acceptable expert systems in law. However, this is a very complex matter: the questions of the ascription of validity, the alleged authority and bindingness and the methods of recognition and identification of valid law, and many other related issues, have received extensive consideration by analytical jurists, and the promise of locating consensus once more seems remote.[9]

Some would deny the import of such allegedly relevant philosophical conundrums, and may suggest that citizens, lawyers, legisla-

---

[7] 'The Expressive Conception of Norms', (1981) pp. 97–8. Their distinction is between 'hyletic' and 'expressive' conceptions of norms—see pp. 95–100.

[8] (1971), p. 60.

[9] Two writings that reveal the complexity of the question of validity are Raz, *AL*, ch. 8, and Harris, *LLS*, ch. 4.

tors, legal officials, judges, and so forth all seem to interact with the legal system in a manner consistent enough to suggest that for those concerned with actually obeying, utilizing, and administering the law, the questions of the validity and authority of legal systems and laws is usually of little moment: for the most part, legal systems function effectively despite the many conceivable but latent problems of legal theory. The jurisprudential sceptic may then be surprised to be told, therefore, that many leading theorists, of diverse inclinations, do not disagree that problems of legal validity for the most part do not, and should not, interfere with the daily administration of the law. But the fact that the problems are not articulated is, for them, significant. For example, in respect of lawyers: for Hart, it is symptomatic of their critical reflective attitude towards some rule of recognition;[10] for Kelsen, it is evidence of their unconscious and implicit assumption of some basic norm;[11] and, for Finnis, it reveals the necessary practical device used so that legal solutions can in practice be found.[12] What emerges from all these (and other) theorists' explanations of validity is not consensus over the nature of that concept (probably because, as Harris has shown, it is not 'univocal'[13]), but acceptance that it is possible to articulate and render explicit a reasoning agent's (and, therefore, an expert system's) implicit presuppositions about some of those materials that count for him (or it) as the sources of valid law. This articulation can be grounded in terms of such philosophically diverse concepts as Hart's rule of recognition or Kelsen's basic norm: yet the functional similarity of these two notions suggests it is not necessary here to be committed on the more fundamental question of the nature of validity, but can simply state for our purposes what law-formulations legal knowledge engineers should treat as being valid sources of law.[14] In the remainder of this section, I briefly outline our criteria of validity, and in Chapter 3 go beyond these in some detail by suggesting all those entities that ought to be represented within a legal knowledge base. (It would no doubt be possible to reduce the

---

[10] *CL*, p. 105.

[11] *GTLS*, pp. 116–17.

[12] *NLNR*, pp. 279–80.

[13] *LLS*, ch. 4.

[14] On the similarity between Hart's rule of recognition and Kelsen's basic norm, see Hart, *CL*. pp. 245–6, and MacCormick, 'Contemporary Legal Philosophy: The Rediscovery of Practical Reason' (1983), in *IJ*, p. 461.

suggestions of this section and of Chapter 3 to some metaphysically unpresumptuous rule not unlike Harris's basic legal science fiat.[15]) The most basic principle, consonant with the ethos of expert systems, is:

1. Those materials that are regarded by legal experts as being formal sources of the law ought to be accepted as such by legal knowledge engineers without further jurisprudential question. Such sources, it will invariably transpire, will be valid also in most, if not all, of the first four senses of 'valid' that Harris identifies,[16] in that they will usually conform to higher rules, will be consistent parts of legal normative fields of meaning, will correspond with social reality, and *may* have inherent claims to fulfilment (although clearly the requirements of this last conception of validity may not always be satisfied). In accordance with the consensus approach adopted in this book, therefore, the law to be embodied in expert systems will be valid in most of the senses in which that term is used by different legal theorists. The formal sources of any developed legal system are those sources that establish or confirm the validity and authority of rules or principles derived from them. The formal sources of the Scottish Legal System, for instance, are legislation (comprising that of the European Communities, of the Parliaments of Scotland, Great Britain, and the United Kingdom, as well as subordinate or delegated legislation), judicial precedents, Institutional Writings and certain other treatises, custom, equity, and other accepted 'extraneous sources'.[17] However, disputes have often arisen over what actual legal regime or system is in force or valid at any one time to the extent that legal experts themselves disagree. The above approach is of little use in respect of such legal systems, so the first guideline must be supplemented with a second:

2. Where there is doubt amongst experts as to the legal system which is in force—that is, over what sources are valid—then that system or those sources are not suitable for being represented in expert systems in law. (See also Principle 4 in Section 2.4.)

---

[15] *LLS*, p. 70.
[16] Ibid, ch. 4.
[17] See Walker, *SLS*, p. 343. In this book, attention is confned to the representation of legislation, judicial precedents, and related entities, but the methods advocated could also be used with but little adaptation in respect of all other formal sources (e.g. Institutional Writings).

2.2 A PRELIMINARY ANALYSIS OF THE NATURE OF LEGAL
REASONING

Because legal knowledge engineers strive to construct programs that
can assist in the solving of legal problems, they are in some way concerned with legal reasoning. Correspondingly, this book too is about
legal reasoning, and it is useful at the outset to consider rudiment-
arily the nature both of the activity of legal reasoning and of theories
pertaining to it. More specifically, in this section I shall discuss the
function of legal reasoning, the human agents that may be involved
in the process, the distinction between descriptive and prescriptive
theories of legal reasoning, and, finally, the relationship of theories
of legal reasoning to legal theory in general.

Legal reasoning has always been one of the central concerns of the
study of jurisprudence, but while few eminent theorists have neglected the topic, not all discussions that claim to pertain to it focus
on the same issues. There is, on the face of it, fundamental disagreement even over the *function* of legal reasoning, that is, over the purpose of engaging in the process.[18] Three functions in particular have
received attention. First, it has been said, in respect of judicial legal
reasoning, that justification is its prime function, in that judges are
generally expected to offer at least ostensible reasons for their decisions by way of what seems indeed to be a form of justificatory
argument.[19] Second, it has been suggested, especially by the so-
called American Legal Realists, that the function of legal reasoning
is prediction: lawyers' reasoning is about predicting judicial and
official behaviour, while judges' reasoning is of an instrumentally
predictive nature pertaining to whether or not laws will work for
society.[20] A third function that has been identified is that of persuasion, whereby the lawyer's task is conceived as that of convincing the
court of the argument he is presenting; or the law reformer's charge
is that of inclining the legislature in favour of his recommendations.[21]

These three functions, however, are not fundamentally incompatible with one another, for the divergence of views is often explicable

---

[18] I shall not analyse the complex concept of function, for it does not seem that
jurisprudential controversy has arisen because of the term itself.

[19] See e.g. MacCormick, *LRLT*; Wasserstrom, *JD*; and Harris, *LLS* and *LP*.

[20] On the American Legal Realists, see Twining, *Karl Llewellyn and the Realist
Movement* (1973), and *IJ*, ch. 8.

[21] See e.g. Perelman, *Justice, Law and Argument* (1980).

in terms of the legal reasoning agent being discussed. That agent might, for instance, be a judge, jurist, advocate, legal adviser, legal academic, law reformer, civil servant, or indeed a citizen. And the accuracy of characterizing the reasoning processes of each of these persons in terms of any one or more of the adduced functions will no doubt vary greatly. (The nature of the jurisdiction involved— common law system, civil law system, or, like that in Scotland, a hybrid system—will often also be a significant factor.)

Given that there are several functions of legal reasoning, does this mean the legal knowledge engineer, before designing any system, has to decide if his program is to assist in justification, prediction, or persuasion? At this stage in the research and development of expert systems in law, I suggest the answer to that question should be 'no'. For there is an underlying, more restricted, and yet fundamental, model of legal reasoning, common to all three accounts of function just noted, that should be at the core of all current systems. Those who claim that the function of legal reasoning is one of justification, prediction, or persuasion share several assumptions about the nature of legal reasoning. First, they acknowledge the possibility of legal reasoning, that is, of an activity whereby legal consequences *can* be attached to acts, events, and states of affairs of our world (although some may be cynical about how the facts and the law can be manipulated). Second, in deploying the term 'reasoning' and ascribing it a function, they thereby recognize legal reasoning to be an activity guided in some sense if not by logical principles then at least by principles of rationality. Third, and this factor is not unrelated to the previous two, they all presuppose a more fundamental function, namely, that of stating what is true or false within the universe of legal discourse (a domain whose existence is assumed), together with that of deriving the implications of such truth or falsity in respect of particular facts of particular cases. In short, before any justifying, predicting, or persuading goes on, it seems to be assumed that there is a rational process by which a body of legal knowledge can usually be applied to the facts of a case in order to yield a legal conclusion (although that is not to say that a legal conclusion can always be yielded with ease or that the conclusion will correspond to a final judicial determination). Once the conclusion is derived, some will set about justifying it (perhaps in terms of the rational process); others will use it as one (not necessarily overriding) element in their predictive calculus; and still others will bring it to bear (perhaps again in terms of the rational process, and again not necessarily as an overriding element) in their rhetorical deliverances.

It is suggested that expert systems in law be designed today to perform this most fundamental operation of drawing legal conclusions based on the universe of legal discourse (as represented in the legal knowledge base), through the deployment of some rational reasoning mechanism (embodied in the legal inference engine, whose rationality, I shall argue, may well be that of deductive logic). From this book, it will be seen that such a system could indeed be augmented to perform a justificatory function through the implementation of a purely backward-chaining search strategy (Section 6.2) or a predictive function through the addition to the knowledge base of predictive heuristic knowledge (Chapter 3). And with regard to persuasion, what more convincing argument could there be than one based on deductive logic, particularly when reinforced (through the system's transparency) both with legal authority for each proposition asserted, and with fully articulated lines of reasoning supporting each conclusion inferred?

Turning now to theories of legal reasoning, note that this book is concerned with them in two ways. On the one hand, in works of jurisprudence, I shall find in pre-existing theories of legal reasoning many valuable insights that illuminate problems that beset legal knowledge engineers. On the other hand, in recommending a method of legal knowledge utilization, I shall myself be explicitly propounding a theory of legal reasoning (as others do implicitly when they build or seek to build expert systems in law). In consequence of my concern with theories of legal reasoning, there are two meta-theoretical issues that should be borne in mind.

First, it should be remembered that many theories of legal reasoning do not simply offer a reportive account of what the process involves but also recommend how the process ought to be carried out. The former can be called the descriptive (explanatory or factual) component of a theory, and the latter the prescriptive (normative or evaluative) aspect. Despite the problems of practical philosophy over whether there can be a truly dichotomous division between description and prescription and whether pure description is possible, it remains the case that some theories of legal reasoning are heavily biased towards description, while others seem to be quite unambiguously prescribing particular methods of reasoning in law. It should be noted too that many theorists, such as Dworkin and Mac-

Cormick, write about legal reasoning in a manner that is at once explicitly descriptive and prescriptive, on the sound basis, as Mac-Cormick says, that 'one can be censor as well as expositor without necessarily confusing the two roles'.[22] Jurisprudential writings and commentaries on AI and legal reasoning should always be examined with this description/prescription distinction in mind. For the purposes of the Oxford project, it was necessary to decide whether the goal was to design a program to emulate faithfully the process that we thought was human expert legal reasoning, or to recommend a mode of reasoning that we intended would produce the same legal conclusions as human legal expert reasoning (but through different means). As can be seen from Chapters 5 and 6, our proposed method of legal knowledge utilization constitutes an account of legal reasoning that has significant descriptive and prescriptive elements (like the theories of legal reasoning of Dworkin and MacCormick).

The second meta-theoretical issue that is worthy of note concerns the connection between a theory of legal reasoning and a theory of law. MacCormick is surely correct when he suggests that 'a theory of legal reasoning requires and is required by a theory of law',[23] for any account of legal reasoning necessarily makes assumptions about, and has manifest implications in relation to, the nature of law. As Wasserstrom agrees, 'It is impossible to discuss legal decision procedures without talking about the law, laws, legal rules, and the like.'[24] For that reason (amongst others), in this book, in addition to the discussions of legal reasoning and of the role of logic in the law, I sketch theories of legal knowledge, legal science, the structure of laws, the individuation of laws, and of legal subsystems. Furthermore, it should be recognized that such jurisprudential theories, as Dworkin has stressed, are necessarily involved with broader questions of philosophical discourse,[25] relating, *inter alia*, to social, moral, political, linguistic, and logical theory, topics that themselves rest on more basic (yet often unarticulated) metaphysical foundations. It is unduly restrictive to think that building expert systems in law is simply about computerizing legal reasoning: legal knowledge engineering reaches into the very core of jurisprudence and philosophy. All current projects should be examined with

---

[22] *LRLT*, p. 77.
[23] Ibid., p. 229.
[24] *JD*, p. 36.
[25] *TRS*, pp. vii–xv.

this in mind, and all future work should be conducted in the knowledge of this fundamental proposition.

2.3 AN EPISTEMOLOGICAL PROBLEM: LAW AS A SUITABLE DOMAIN OF APPLICATION

So far in this study, I have tentatively suggested how it is that expert systems might reason in law and what theoretical issues are relevant. But a nagging doubt needs to be dispelled, and that is the misgiving evinced by critics to the effect that even if we know what we want an expert system to do, the nature of the legal domain precludes the successful application to it of expert systems technology. The fundamental question of this section, then, is whether the law is a suitable domain of application for the development of expert systems. I tackle this question through consideration of several of the respects in which legal knowledge differs in nature from the knowledge held in most current non-legal expert systems.

It is widely accepted that the ability of human beings to deploy expertise in the solving of problems of any domain is contingent on the possession by them of extensive knowledge of the field of discourse in question. And it is that knowledge, in turn, that knowledge engineers endeavour to embody in expert systems. The suitability of a domain of application for AI work is no doubt dependent to a great extent on the nature (and accessibility) of the knowledge of that domain; and one of the epistemological problems of AI is that of identifying and evaluating the nature of knowledge in given fields with a view to knowledge representation.[26]

Although it has been asserted with some confidence that the potential of expert systems for the legal profession is considerable,[27] we cannot let such optimism obscure one of the observations of Chapter 1: that no expert systems of the sort envisaged have been developed to a stage that renders them of immediate use to legal practitioners. Progress in the field of law has been far slower than in other fields, and in search of an explanation of this fact, it is appropriate to compare briefly the epistemological foundations of successful domains with those of law. In so far as law is concerned, it should again

---

[26] See Sloman, 'Epistemology and Artificial Intelligence' (1979). Cf. Dreyfus, *What Computers Can't Do: A Critique of Artificial Reason* (1972), p. 68.

[27] Waterman, *AGES*, pp. 224–6.

be noted that the question of legal epistemology falls firmly within the bounds of jurisprudence.[28]

In my comparison, I shall focus on two issues: the distinction between public and private knowledge; and the sources of scientific and legal knowledge. (Throughout this book, and particularly in Chapter 3, not only will this account of legal knowledge be clarified considerably, but also many other differences between legal knowledge and non-legal knowledge will emerge.)

Most commentaries on expert systems rely on a distinction between two sorts of knowledge—public and private.[29] The former 'includes the published definitions, facts, and theories of which textbooks and references in the domain of study are typically composed.' However, expertise in any given field, it is argued, invariably involves more than this first type of knowledge and experts are usually possessed of the latter category of knowledge, which 'has not found its way into published literature'. For 'this private knowledge consists largely of rules of thumb that have come to be called *heuristics*. Heuristics enable the human expert to make educated guesses when necessary, to recognise promising approaches to problems, and to deal effectively with errorful or incomplete data.'[30]

I submit, however, that this distinction is inappropriate in relation to legal knowledge, being defective in more than one respect. Notice, first, that although 'public' legal knowledge, appears in the form of legal textbooks, that is, as an orderly presentation, *inter alia*, of descriptive law-statements, such writings are not exhaustive of the category of public legal material. For our formal legal sources—law-formulations—are also to be found in paper and print. While such law-formulations, as I have said, are more sensibly termed legal data, they constitute, in a sense, one higher level of organized public

---

[28] Indeed, in 'What is Jurisprudence' (1978), Tur argued that jurisprudence *is* legal epistemology. Tur here expressly followed Kelsen, much of whose writings were devoted, in Kantian spirit, to explaining how legal knowledge is possible. But for Tur's latest views on this point, see Tur, 'The Kelsenian Enterprise' (1986), and Tur and Twining, *Essays on Kelsen* (1986), p. 33. Also see MacCormick, 'Analytical Jurisprudence and the Possibility of Legal Knowledge' (1984–5), and Singh, *Law from Anarchy to Utopia* (1986), Part III.

[29] See e.g. *BES*, p. 4. This distinction has similarities to the epistemological division between 'knowing that' (public knowledge) and 'knowing how' (private knowledge) that is favoured by philosophers. See e.g. Hospers, *An Introducton to Philosophical Analysis* (1967), p. 143, and generally pp. 143–57, and Ryle, *The Concept of Mind* (1949), pp. 28–32.

[30] *BES*, p. 4. Original emphasis.

material than is manifested in other domains of application. (This difference in the sources of domains is discussed shortly.)

Furthermore, although it is suggested by AI scientists that 'private' knowledge is not to be found in published form, legal heuristics are in fact sometimes set forth in print: in practitioners' handbooks and in internal memoranda within legal practices. Note, for example (in relation to the legal domain of application chosen for the Oxford project—see next section), Sheriff Principal Taylor's remarks in the Foreword to Bennett's book, *A Short Guide to Divorce in the Sheriff Court*:

There is a large field of practice and decision about divorce which is well known in the Parliament House, but with which the solicitor outside Edinburgh will be quite unfamiliar. In this practical Guide, Mr Bennett, who has experience of divorce practice in the Court of Session, passes on this accumulated lore and experience to the solicitors who will be dealing with divorce in the future.[31]

Thus it is not the case that in law, as it is in other fields, that the private knowledge remains untapped in the heads of experts. This heuristic knowledge is often laid out publicly in texts such as the above and, as I have said, semi-publicly in in-office handbooks prepared by experts within legal practices.[32] In sum, then, the public/private knowledge dichotomy is inappropriate in respect of legal knowledge, and in Section 2.5, in the discussion of legal expertise, I shall introduce a more appropriate distinction: between academic legal knowledge and experiential legal knowledge.

The second comparison focuses on the sources of legal and scientific knowledge, but it must be stressed that our concern here is *not* with heuristic knowledge. A recently compiled catalogue of expert systems identifies the following domains of application: agriculture; chemistry; computer systems; electronics; engineering; geology; information management; law; manufacturing; mathematics; medicine; meteorology; military science; physics; process control; and space technology.[33] Examination of the functions of these systems confirms, with the exception of information management, law, and manufacturing, that the vast bulk of the domains are firmly rooted

---

[31] (1984), p. vii.
[32] See e.g. Ross Harper & Murphy, *Sheriff Court: DIVORCE* (1984). (Ross Harper and Murphy is a firm of Scottish solicitors.)
[33] *AGES*, ch. 25.

in the mathematical and natural sciences. For the purposes of this comparison, it shall suffice to confine the discussion to the significant differences between legal knowledge and knowledge of the *natural* sciences (hereafter 'scientific knowledge').[34] It shall further be sufficient, when I talk of knowledge in general, to understand that phenomenon to result from the cognitive appraisal of data within a field of discourse and the subsequent imposition of coherence over that data.

Scientific knowledge is often expressed in the form of scientific laws. Roughly speaking, these laws are formulated as coherent (but, strictly speaking tentative), descriptions of uniformities or patterns in nature, and can serve both explanatory and predictive functions. Those who propound scientific laws are usually presupposing that we can talk intelligibly about an external material world, and that causality is central to that world. The raw datum (the source of knowledge) on the basis of which scientific knowledge is acquired— and over which coherence is imposed—is, therefore, the empirical world in general. In contrast, the sources of legal knowledge—the raw legal data—are, in a sense, to be found in one very restricted sub-set of the physical world (where the notions of cause and effect are of little practical moment), namely, the paper and print that constitute law-formulations. Legal knowledge comes about through intelligent operations on that legal data, such as description and interpretation in the form of law-statements.

Kelsen acutely summarizes the difference between the sources of scientific and legal knowledge when he says that 'nature does not manifest itself in spoken and written words, as the law does'.[35] For the natural scientist, then, his ultimate source is the natural world. That source is not created by human beings, but in some sense is *given* to us, and one of the tasks of the scientist is to *discover* scientific laws. For those concerned with the law, however, their ultimate source has generally been *promulgated* by fellow human beings and

---

[34] A powerful distinction between legal knowledge and mathematical knowledge could also be made, but it seems sensible to focus on the natural sciences, in domains of which the greatest advances in expert systems have been made. The bulk of the medical knowledge in expert systems in medicine is derived from the natural sciences. That this is epistemologically sound is confirmed quite independently (in a very clear discussion of the natural sciences) by Downie and Telfer, in *Caring and Curing* (1980), ch. 4, but their emphasis on the role of the social sciences within medical practice should be noted by medical knowledge engineers.

[35] *PTL*, p. 74.

appears in linguistic form requiring *description* and *interpretation* and not discovery. There are no authoritatively written down formal sources of medicine or of natural science akin to those of law. Still less are the sources of natural science regarded as belonging to a *system* that can be as coherently identified as a legal system can.

What emerges from both my rejection in a legal context of the public/private knowledge distinction and my identification of the different sources of scientific and legal knowledge is surely that the law is a singularly suitable and systematized domain of application for expert systems, where the problems of knowledge acquisition do not seem so urgent. Legal knowledge engineers are, it would seem, more fortunate than their counterparts in other domains, for not only are relevant textbooks available in print for their scrutiny, but, unlike in other fields, the very sources of these materials also appear in organized, published form. Moreover, related legal heuristic knowledge is sometimes available in paper and print in a way that is mirrored in few other domains. Given these epistemological factors, and the fact, as noted in the previous section, that most theorists assume legal reasoning to be, at least in part, a process governed by some principles of rationality, we should now be even more perplexed at the lack of progress in the AI/legal reasoning field.

However, I believe that expert systems in law have not yet been developed satisfactorily precisely because knowledge engineers have to date had insufficient understanding of the idiosyncratic nature of legal knowledge, of which but a brief indication has been given in this section, and a detailed account is offered in Chapters 3 and 4. From these chapters it can be seen that the variety of legal entities that needs to be represented, the difficulty in translating from law-formulation to law-statement, and the complexity and subtle inter-relationships between the resultant units, all suggest it is not possible, without extensive modification and inconvenience, to accommodate legal knowledge within the restrictive frameworks offered by currently available computer programming environments. Yet it should not be assumed because there are no suitable software tools for the development of expert systems in law that the law does not lend itself to this type of computational treatment. The nature of legal knowledge and legal reasoning do not preclude the possibility of building expert systems in law, but impose severe limitations on the range of software tools and techniques that are appropriate for this purpose.

2.4 THE SUITABILITY OF PARTICULAR AREAS OF LAW AND SCOTTISH LAW OF DIVORCE

Given that the law is a suitable *general* domain of application for expert systems research and development, it is appropriate to reflect now on the more specific issue of the suitability of particular branches of the law for the purposes of legal knowledge engineering. In this section, I consider, in the first instance, why it is that tax law seems to be the most promising area. I then offer guidelines concerning choice of legal domain, and introduce the legal domain selected for the Oxford project.

Tax law has been favoured by more leading researchers (those, for example, of TAXMAN, CORPTAX, TAXADVISOR, ATAXIS) than any other legal domain and it is important to assess the significance of this for legal knowledge engineers of today. In an important discussion of the characteristics of future 'consultation law machines', Niblett suggested several years ago that 'a safe prediction is that the first practical machine will give advice on tax law'; and he offered several reasons why this should be so: 'The sources of tax law are statutory and the taxing statutes are construed strictly... Thus the meaning of a taxing statute may be more clearly discerned than the meaning of other legislation... assessment to tax [is] expressed in money terms.'[36] Niblett's analysis raises several very interesting points which I shall examine in turn. With regard to the sources of tax law being statutory in the UK, while it is true that revenue law is primarily based on Acts of Parliament, surely those judicial precedents that bear on the meaning and effect of statutory provisions are also formal sources of tax law? Certainly almost all expert systems in tax law would need to have some case law represented in their knowledge bases; for without knowledge of relevant judicial precedents systems would often be incapable of offering such advice that we would expect of any human legal expert.

Niblett also directs us to the principle that tax statutes are interpreted literally, and refers in this respect to an important passage of a judgment in *Cape Brandy Syndicate* v. *IRC*. No doubt this principle must be partially applicable today or else the notions of 'loophole' and 'tax avoidance' would be rendered meaningless. Yet, in the

---

[36] 'Computer Science and Law: An Introductory Discussion', (1980), pp. 16–17. Cf. Roycroft and Loucopoulos, 'ACCI: An Expert System for the Apportionment of Close Companies' Income' (1985), pp. 127–8.

case of *Mangin* v. *IRC*,[37] Lord Donovan also cited the passage of text that Niblett quotes, but added that the will of the legislator and justice may be of relevance where there is ambiguity, and, further, that the history and motivation behind an enactment may also aid in construction. If this be the case and if we also have regard to several significant cases decided since Niblett wrote the passage under consideration, then it seems that there has been a gradual shift away from a strictly literal approach to construction of tax statutes (at least in relation to certain series of transactions).[38] Consequently, the alleged idiosyncrasy—that tax law, in contrast with other areas of law, is interpreted purely literally—may now no longer be as important a factor in the selection of domains as it once was.

Moreover, it should also be stressed that literal interpretation plays an important role in the construction of *all* statutes. For, whether a piece of legislation (any piece) is construed, in the final analysis, literally, having regard only to the words of the statute, or liberally, in accordance with, say the 'golden' or the 'mischief' rules, there can be no doubt that, *in the first instance*, a literal interpretation must be undertaken. If not, how can the necessity for looking beyond the actual words used to the purpose of the enactment or to the intent of the legislators be assessed? We can only make sense of modes of construction other than the literal method, if we assume that literal interpretation is in some sense, in some cases, insufficient. In other words, literal interpretation is a necessary and logically prior, but not always sufficient, part of the construction process. Therefore, if it is agreed, as Niblett suggests, that an area of law's susceptibility to literal interpretation is a prima facie reason for its suitability as a legal domain of application, then—supplementing this proposition with the above analysis—*all* areas of law are, on the face of it, potentially suitable domains of application.

It follows, for Niblett, that because statutes are construed literally 'the meaning of a taxing statute may be more clearly discerned than the meaning of other legislation'. However, this is not always so.

---

[37] [1971] AC 739.
[38] See the important cases of *W. T. Ramsay Ltd* v. *IRC* [1982] AC 300, *IRC* v. *Burmah Oil Co. Ltd.* [1982] SLT 348, and *Furniss* v. *Dawson* [1983] 55 TC 324, which collectively impinge on the possibility of tax avoidance under certain circumstances. The influence of these cases was considerable in *IRC* v. *Bowater Property Developments* [1985] STC 783, *Craven* v. *White* [1985] 3 All ER 125, and *Ingram* v. *IRC* [1985] STC.

Some tax statutes, it is generally agreed, can barely be understood. As Walker has commented, 'more than any other branch of municipal law tax law is open to the reproach of being utterly incomprehensible by the individuals affected, and even frequently by their legal advisers.'[39] Surely the meaning of many tax statutes is far *less* discernible than that of many other non-revenue legislative enactments. It is not always appropriate to relate the discernibility of meaning of statutes with the manner in which they ought to be interpreted. However, if the incomprehensibility of tax statutes is due to sheer complexity—and not to semantic or syntactic ambiguity—then indeed (but not precisely for the reason Niblett suggests) these portions of revenue law may well be suitable domains. For the complicated rules and the intricate interrelationships between them could all be captured in a legal knowledge base, and the expert system would afford its user a thorough yet manageable path through the law.

The final point that Niblett makes, and rightly so, is that tax law is intimately concerned with monetary concepts, and, therefore, we may add, being numerically orientated, is more amenable to computational treatment than other areas of law.

It might also be added that because tax practice is largely the province of the accountancy profession—a body which seems less averse to technological innovations, and has already made more extensive use of computers, than its legal counterpart—then it is likely that expert systems in law will be developed in the tax law domain. For this last reason, and for those others just substantiated, we can, then, perhaps appreciate the appeal of tax law for knowledge engineers.

The suitability of tax law for the development of expert systems for use today, however, ought not to dictate the direction of current *research*. It is undeniable that all legal knowledge engineers must decide in what area of law they intend their expert systems in law to function. If an expert system is being designed for actual use in legal practice, clearly the motivation behind the construction of such a system in one area of law rather than another (given that the technological difficulties between domains are similar) is the practice's need for such a research facility. Moreover, few practices would embark on the development of a system to be used as a legal tool in the

---

[39] *Oxford Companion to Law* (1980), p. 1207.

knowledge that the technological know-how was simply not available. Tax law may be the domain of the first 'practical' system precisely because in that field much research has been carried out and the technological prerequisites seem to have been satisfied.

However, the choice of legal domain for experimental and theoretical inquiries into expert systems in law is dictated by a wider variety of factors and the successful implementation of a system need not always be the ultimate goal. If indeed tax law is not representative of positive law, as elements of the foregoing discussion indicate, then it is open to question whether experimental research into expert systems in tax law is appropriate, or at least likely to yield fruitful and generalizable results. The successful operation of an expert system in tax law would perhaps be mildly suggestive rather than in any way conclusive of the potential of this new research tool for lawyers. It is surely preferable that research in this field be undertaken with a view to illuminating *all* legal domains of application and not just a particular, almost hybrid, area of law.

Whether a knowledge engineer is constructing an expert system in law for experimental or practical purposes, however, it is submitted that the following guidelines are of use for any legal domain:

1. In so far as any area of law is self-contained, it is desirable that the chosen domain be relatively autonomous, the sources being limited in number and reasonably well defined. The law relating to the taxation of corporations, therefore, would be an inappropriate domain because it might entail, *inter alia*, company law, corporation tax law, value added tax law, and personal tax law—clearly too large a range of legal provisions for expert systems work at this stage of its technological development. The law in Scotland relating to liability for damages caused by animals, on the other hand, is a suitable domain, being a small, identifiable aspect of the law of delict whose sources can easily be located. The identification of a so-called self-contained branch of law and its subsequent severance for the purposes of representing it in a knowledge base raises many problems. It should be borne in mind, however, that these problems are not novel; for this process of 'compartmentalization'—as Dworkin calls it—is and always has been prevalent in legal practice.[40] (On the propriety of dividing the law up, also see Section 4.3.)

2. The chosen legal domain must be one whose problems do in-

---

[40] For an excellent discussion of this concept, see *Law's Empire* (1986), pp. 250–4.

deed require expertise, and not simply brief research, for their resolution. There should be a potentially significant range of difficult problems that can arise within the domain.

3. Intensive coverage of a small legal domain is preferable to superficial coverage of an extensive area of law. This proposition follows from the characterization of expert systems in Chapter 1. I said there that expert systems in law are designed to replicate the performance of legal experts: the knowledge represented, therefore, must be of such a depth, richness, and complexity normally possessed by a human expert. We would, of course, hesitate to call those persons who have a large but none the less shallow familiarity with the law 'experts'.

In relation to this matter it is interesting to note that Mehl suggested, as long ago as 1958, that while a consultation machine designed to answer questions 'over a vast field of law' would undoubtedly be more complex than one that operated in a 'highly specialized field of law', nevertheless, 'according to the exponential law of information, its [the first type's] complexity will increase much more slowly than the volume of legal information which it can handle'. He concluded that 'This means that a machine covering the whole field of law would be simpler and less cumbersome than a series of machines handling separate legal sectors.'[41] As a practical recommendation, however, Mehl's notion of a system embodying the legal knowledge (which is what he means by 'information') of an entire legal system cannot be taken seriously. As can be seen from this book, the practical problems faced in engineering a system to function even in a limited legal domain of application are so numerous that it is likely that the only way 'a vast field of law' could be catered for is through the *networking* of smaller systems. But that is not a job for the near future. (It is likely that networking of expert systems in law will be very important in years to come, because— and this is one of the difficulties resulting from 'compartmentalization'—many legal problems will transcend the divisions of the law imposed by these systems.)

4. A domain in which there is agreement amongst experts over its scope and content is to be preferred to one in which there is no such consensus. This principle makes for systems that can be more readily relied upon (for a knowledge base of inherently contentious content

---

[41] 'Automation in the Legal World: From the Machine Processing of Legal Information to the "Law Machine"' (1958), p. 768.

would be of dubious value). In this connection, it should be added that legal domains in which there seem to be many conflicting legal rules—valid rules that for the same set of circumstances seem to dictate diverging legal consequences—are unsuitable domains of application. (See also Section 4.3.)

5. Legal domains whose problems for their resolution require the use of a great deal of 'common-sense' knowledge are unsuitable for expert systems work. Reasoning in law often involves common-sense reasoning (for instance, judgments about what is 'reasonable'). However, because AI techniques cannot presently cope satisfactorily with common-sense, legal domains of high common-sense content, at present, are not ideal for expert systems development.[42] Such domains can be used, however, if it is deemed acceptable for the user to input common-sense himself during consultations.

Largely in accordance with the five principles above, the legal domain of application chosen to illustrate some of the techniques and findings of the Oxford project, and of this book, is Scottish Law of Divorce. Our particular focus of interest is that aspect of the law pertaining to 'grounds for divorce', and in the course of this book, our domain will be discussed in some detail. The chief formal sources of the domain are legislation (mainly the *Divorce (Scotland) Act 1976*) and a rich body of case law. There is also a wealth of high-quality secondary sources (see Section 4 of the Bibliography of this book). Following our first principle, then, our domain is relatively autonomous, and the sources are indeed limited in number and reasonably well defined. In accordance with my second guideline, it is generally agreed that complex problems arise within this domain and they do undoubtedly require expert attention (particularly in relation to the large body of precedents). If we had confined our scope to statutory material, and broadened our coverage to, say, the entire body of *legislation* relating to husband and wife, the representation of the knowledge would, accordingly, as I suggested in my third principle, fail to constitute expertise. There does, fourthly, appear to be many experts (both solicitors and advocates) in this (relatively conflict-free) area of law amongst whom there is indeed consensus over the domain's scope and content. Finally, faithful to my fifth principle, our selected area does not require a great deal of common-sense reasoning for resolution of problems within its scope.

[42] *BES*, p. 160.

In conclusion, one further and central feature of our chosen domain merits highlight: that it belongs to the Scottish legal system. The law in that jurisdiction falls neatly into neither the category of civil law system nor that of common law system. Rather it manifests features of both these categories of jurisdiction, and in building an expert system in part of Scots Law, some of the problems faced will perhaps be those that will confront legal knowledge engineers working in civil and common law domains alike. The findings, therefore, may be of interest and relevance to both common and civil lawyers, and may bear on the construction of expert systems in law in any legal system.

2.5 LEGAL EXPERTISE AND THE LEGAL EXPERT

Until now in this book, I have spoken rather vaguely of the notions of legal expertise and the legal expert. AI scientists might prefer to replace these terms with such designations as (legal) domain-specific expertise and the (legal) domain specialist, but whatever labels we choose to apply, it is necessary to have a clear picture of what is meant by them. In this section I examine the terms in greater detail, and thereby attempt to indicate what kind of lawyer, for knowledge engineering purposes, might appropriately be called a legal expert. I shall, moreover, offer some guiding principles in relation to constructing a legal knowledge base.

In Section 2.3, it was said that there are significant practical and epistemological differences between legal knowledge and knowledge in other domains. So profound are these discrepancies that they render much that has been written on experts and expertise in non-legal fields of discourse of minimal relevance for the legal knowledge engineer.[43] A fresh analysis is required, therefore, and I shall start this one by introducing a distinction between *academic* and *experiential* legal knowledge. This not only serves to replace the inapposite public/private knowledge division rejected in Section 2.3, but also provides a basis for sensible discussion about legal expertise.

---

[43] e.g. Hawkins, in his detailed paper entitled 'An Analysis of Expert Thinking' (1983), attempts to propound 'a theory of expert thinking'. This exposition, however, relates primarily to expert petroleum geologists, and the epistemological differences between law and petroleum geology severely limit the relevance of that paper for those interested in expert legal thinking.

Academic legal knowledge can be acquired by anyone trained in, or familiar with, the techniques of legal research. The raw data of academic knowledge are the primary and secondary sources of law: that is, law-formulations together with legal commentaries on these materials. Together these can usefully be referred to as 'the repositories of law'.[44] Appraisal, interpretation, and comprehension of these repositories will eventually be productive of academic legal knowledge. Note again that—unlike the 'public' knowledge of non-legal domains—the written repositories may also provide heuristic knowledge. It is academic legal knowledge, generally, that students of the law attempt to acquire, and that teachers of the law invariably possess in some quantity.

Good legal practitioners also have academic legal knowledge. But, in addition, these lawyers acquire what I term experiential legal knowledge, that is knowledge of the day-to-day practical administration of the law. Experiential knowledge is gained not through immersion in the repositories of the law but, as the phrase suggests, from personal experience of the workings of the legal process. And such experience in the practical administration of a legal domain refines and often modifies a lawyer's academic knowledge. Experiential knowledge is generally of two sorts. First, there is heuristic knowledge—the informal, judgmental, experiential, and often procedural, knowledge—which I examine in some detail in Chapter 3. Second, there is what we might term *non-heuristic procedural* knowledge, that is, knowledge about how to go about the administration of the law. I term it non-heuristic because it is not uncertain, informal, or probabilistic in nature. Rather, it consists in sets of algorithmic instructions that indicate essential legal procedures. It is of limited use in legal practice to know academic law thoroughly if that knowledge cannot be correctly deployed by, say, knowing both the correct form to complete or document to draft and the appropriate time to do so. Knowing such matters is having non-heuristic procedural knowledge. (In the next section, I suggest non-heuristic procedural knowledge should be held in legal decision support systems.)

There is, of course, an overlap between academic and experiential knowledge, in that—and this is crucial—experiential knowledge is sometimes articulated in secondary sources of law: in legal textbooks, in practitioners' handbooks, or in 'in-house' materials.

---

[44] This is Walker's term. See *SLS*, ch. 11.

However, the borderline itself might be deemed by some to be unimportant; for it might be thought that a legal expert is simply one who possesses extensive and thorough quantities of *both* academic and experiential knowledge and is capable of solving (usually within a limited domain) difficult legal problems with speed and efficiency. In that case, the legal knowledge engineer is given the formidable job of immersing himself in the repositories of law *and*, through extensive knowledge acquisition sessions, eliciting further—and large amounts of—experiential knowledge from the legal domain specialist. This is perhaps an unassailable sketch of one conception of legal knowledge engineering, but if put into practice would surely confront the general 'bottleneck' problem of knowledge acquisition: sound techniques have not yet been fully developed for the extraction of heuristic knowledge from human experts.[45] It would be greatly preferable, however, if we could avoid the classical problems of knowledge acquisition, and it is suggested that this can indeed be done; and it can be justified through acceptance of and reliance upon the following account of legal expert(ise).

I submit that we can talk meaningfully of a legal expert who is possessed solely of academic legal knowledge, and therefore an expert system can function with academic knowledge alone. (I am not denying that expert systems in the future might usefully have experiential knowledge that is not held in published materials, but am casting doubt on the suitability of that as a current goal.) We need not trouble ourselves with detailed analyses of the general notions of expert and expertise, for they are rather vague and relative notions, whose distinguishing common-sense characteristics do seem fairly uncontroversial: involving high-quality performance of difficult tasks, speed, efficiency, and so forth.[46] Rather, I argue that it is possible to use the term expertise in respect of those who have no experiential legal knowledge, and that such knowledge is not essential for expert systems in law sensibly so-called. And such an argument can be quite easily sustained: for all that is being asserted is that (other prerequisites of expertise being assumed) those who have vast knowledge of areas of law, as found in the written repositories of law, and can deploy that knowledge in reasoning towards legal

---

[45] On the problems of knowledge acquisition, see e.g. Feigenbaum, 'Knowledge Engineering: The Applied Side' (1983), pp. 45–6, and Quinlan, 'Semi-autonomous Acquisition of Pattern-based Knowledge' (1982), pp. 192–3.
[46] For a sound analysis, see *BES*, pp. 41–5.

conclusions, can rightly be called experts. (It can also be argued forcefully that extensive knowledge and understanding of the primary sources *alone*, together with the ability to apply it, may be constitutive of expertise.)

To deny the title 'expert' in some circumstances would be to belittle the knowledge of law that so many non-practising legal academics unquestionably have. An expert system that held the knowledge of some leading academic lawyer would surely be a powerful tool indeed, and its lack of experiential knowledge would by no means render it useless. It must be remembered that expert systems of the sort with which this book is concerned are for use by general legal practitioners: they will use the systems as powerful research tools which will be capable of drawing legal conclusions in specialized areas with which these users have no familiarity. The expertise of the systems, then, will lie not in, say, their possession of non-heuristic procedural knowledge (which the user himself will usually have anyway) but in their profound representation of the substantive law and related heuristics (in so far as the latter are held in secondary sources).[47] Of course, the expert who, as it shall be seen, 'tunes' the system, may be an academic or a practitioner: but if he is the latter, it is his academic knowledge that is of principal use.

My approach to expert systems, then, constitutes a more realistic—if less ambitious—approach to designing legal knowledge bases than that of those who would argue for the full representation of both academic and experiential knowledge. In light of my conception of legal expert(ise), the following guidelines are proposed:

1. In the first instance, the legal knowledge base should be constructed by inputting *only* academic knowledge. Thus at the heart of a legal knowledge base will be the written primary and secondary sources: it will contain the repositories of law.

2. The academic knowledge should be input not by a legal expert but by one of general legal training or knowledge. The time and effort of legal experts are valuable and expensive resources, and there is no reason to waste them by setting tasks that other less qualified persons can perform.

---

[47] In the context of International Private Law, in English courts, in general the laws of foreign jurisdictions are treated as matters of fact, and must be proven by the evidence of a *legal expert* of the relevant legal system. Note that it does now seem, in relation to civil proceedings at least, that the expert need not ever have practised law. See J. H. C. Morris, *The Conflict of Laws*, 2nd edition (London, Stevens, 1980), p. 37.

3. Until suitable 'shells' for expert systems in law have been developed (see Section 4.7), legal knowledge engineering must be carried out (as I have said *research* into expert systems in law must be) in an interdisciplinary manner: by one of computational training and one of legal training. Computer scientists cannot be expected—and, generally, have insufficient knowledge—to be able to engage in the legal research required for building an academic legal knowledge base of intensive coverage (see Principle 3 of Section 2.4). In general, they are no more equipped to carry out such demanding legal work than lawyers are to write computer programs (and this is confirmed by the corruptions of the law held in many of the current programs). And the lawyer too will need extensive guidance from the computer scientist, for a degree of logical rigour will be necessary for which neither legal practice nor legal education has prepared him.

4. Only once the academic legal knowledge base has been developed should the legal knowledge engineers avail themselves of the services of the legal expert (or, preferably, experts). It would be naïve to think that a legal researcher could develop a faultless academic knowledge base. It will no doubt require considerable refinement by legal experts (in a way I shall discuss). Heed must be paid to what has been said by AI scientists: 'It is very easy to be deluded into thinking one knows a great deal about the domain. Remember: the expert became one only after years of training and experience.'[48]

5. The sole function of the legal expert is to 'tune' the academic knowledge base. Tuning is the process by which an expert experiments with a system that is under construction, and refines its knowledge base (and perhaps even its inference mechanism) in light of his own extensive knowledge of the domain.[49] Through extensive interaction with the system—by trying out sample problems (which the expert is singularly qualified to concoct), and by examining the system's explanations—the legal expert will gradually correct basic errors of the original representation (for example, misinterpretations of the primary sources), and modify and refine the knowledge base to reflect his own conception of the domain (perhaps by changing the level of generality of some heuristics or by altering their certainty factors). It is not the prime function of the expert to add great quan-

---

[48] *BES*, p. 165. Their usage of 'experience' need not be equated with my term 'experiential', for my legal expert can be said to have had years of experience of operating with academic legal knowledge.

[49] *CC*, p. 39.

tities of knowledge to the base (although some augmentation is both possible and desirable) but rather to render the knowledge more reliable: in short, to bestow the finishing touches of expertise on the system. Note that the legal knowledge engineer of legal training may act as a useful intermediary between the legal expert and the legal knowledge engineer of computational background, as there will inevitably be communication difficulties at the tuning stage. Moreover, as long as a suitable user interface (see Section 2.7) has been built into the experimental system, the legal expert himself, of course, need have very little knowledge of computer science in general or of expert systems in particular.

In conclusion, three points should be noted. First, the role of the expert in building expert systems in law can be significantly less active than in other domains. Second, the findings of the previous section may be supplemented by suggesting that a legal domain's suitability for knowledge engineering is dependent also on the richness of the written secondary sources to which the engineer has access. Finally, by following my conception of legal expert(ise), the problem that prevents the development of expert systems in other domains, that of knowledge acquisition, can be seen largely to dissolve in a legal context.

2.6 INTERFACING EXPERT SYSTEMS IN LAW WITH DATABASE SYSTEMS IN LAW

Expert systems in law are but one sort of computer system for use within the legal profession. In Section 1.1 I briefly mentioned several others. It would be misleading, however, to examine any one use of computer technology in law in isolation from the others. For lawyers in the future will no doubt combine these various systems into single, large, and powerful word, data, and knowledge processors. Even at this stage, however, I believe it would be advantageous (at least in terms of utility, reliability, resource allocation, jurisprudential propriety, and common sense) if expert systems in law were interfaced with two sorts of database systems in law in particular: legal database information systems and legal decision support systems.

Legal database information systems, such as LEXIS, are simply another medium through which the formal sources of our law—the law-formulations—can be found.[50] In their databases are held, in full text, *inter alia*, large bodies of legislation and case law, and these can be retrieved by the user and presented to him in the same form as they appear in the statute books and law reports. In the knowledge base of an expert system in law, in contrast, is a *representation* of the formal sources of the legal domain of application (together, as I have said and will suggest, with other related knowledge). The representation of the formal sources stands in relation to the relevant law—formulations much in the same position as does a legal textbook—they are *about* (in a way articulated in Chapters 3 and 4) the legislation and the case law. These knowledge bases, then, are themselves a species of secondary source.

Just as it is often considered improper and indeed sometimes incompetent for a lawyer to confine his attention solely to the secondary sources to the neglect and not infrequent ignorance of the primary sources, it would be similarly unacceptable if the user of an expert system in law did not look beyond, but always accepted without further query, the advice offered during a consultation with his system. Thus, it is submitted that it is desirable, jurisprudentially proper, and, many would no doubt suggest, necessary, that the user of an expert system in law has direct access, through the terminal at which he is working with his system, to the primary sources pertaining to his inquiry, that is, to the represented sources. This could be achieved by interfacing expert systems with one or more of the legal database information systems currently in use. It was beyond the scope of the Oxford project to attempt to implement such a proposal, but it is submitted that at that stage in a consultation when the user asks for and is given the citation of the authoritative source of any conclusion offered by the system (one aspect of its transparency), an option to examine the full text of the source cited should be made available. In that way too, the user could in no way justify abdicating all responsibility for interpreting the formal sources to the legal knowledge engineer and legal domain specialist who built the system.

Legal decision support systems could also be fruitfully interfaced with expert systems in law. Such support systems are already available for practising lawyers and they are, in short, no more than sophisticated combinations of word processors and data pro-

---

[50] Some secondary sources, such as law journals, are now held within the LEXIS database, but that material is irrelevant for the purposes of this section.

cessors.[51] They monitor clients' problems from first interview until the disposal of their cases, and perform the bulk of the attendant administrative tasks pertaining to any given series of consultations. Thus, these support systems: draft standard letters, prescribed forms, and relevant documents (all normally in accordance with the particular firm's traditional styles and precedents); record time spent on particular clients, eventually furnishing them with their bills; perform diary functions prompting the user to action when appropriate; and generally act as exceptionally user-friendly checklists. Moreover, information about clients, their problems, and related matters, can all be entered into instruction sheets even by non-legally qualified personnel.

Examination of a description of a commercially available legal decision support system for undefended divorce actions[52] indicates that such a data/word processor could be combined usefully with an expert system in law. The former system mainly acts as a prompt to the lawyer (or his secretary) who has already settled the question of the grounds of divorce (the legal domain of application of the Oxford project, although the jurisdictions are different). The system is designed to perform the necessary administrative jobs—drafting petitions, statements about custody and reconciliation, the various affidavits, and the application for the decree nisi to be rendered absolute—for any divorce situation no matter what the grounds, whether or not there are children, and so forth. Such a system, if developed for use in Scotland, could be interfaced with a version of our system in a way that would result in a system that could assist not only in the above administrative chores, but also in the prior and enduring substantive legal problems. The resultant system, then, would provide legal advice (based on the knowledge of human experts) regarding possible grounds of divorce, and, moreover, would be designed, on the basis of that ability, to produce completed craves, pleas-in-law, writs, and affidavits.

If expert systems in law and legal decision support systems were indeed interfaced as I have suggested, then this would provide further support for my argument of the previous section regarding

[51] See Ruoff, *The Solicitor and the Automated Office* (1984), pp. 55–71. Also see National Law Library, *The Slot Report* (1983), pp. 36–9, particularly in relation to the distinction made between expert systems and legal decision support systems. Sprowl's ABF processor (see Appendix I) can be regarded as constituting an AI approach to the document drafting aspects of legal decision support systems.

[52] See Ruoff, *The Solicitor and the Automated Office* (1984), pp. 60–6.

the nature of legal expertise. I said there that expert systems would only hold such experiential legal knowledge as is held in secondary sources, that is to say, that is academic legal knowledge as well. One objection to that position (in itself not wholly accurate) is that non-heuristic experiential knowledge—knowledge of sets of legal procedures, such as knowing what documents to complete—is frequently not written down for knowledge engineers to peruse. However, such knowledge would be far better suited for inclusion in legal decision support systems (and is in fact so included today). If indeed non-heuristic experiential knowledge is held in decision support systems of the future and not in expert systems in law, then, as long as these systems are interfaced with one another, any objection to the omission of such knowledge from the latter type of system will be rendered nebulous in the extreme.

2.7 THE USER INTERFACE

Fundamental to the successful operation of complex computer installations (particularly IKBS and expert systems), is the way in which human users are able to interact with their machines. The study of this subject—of the man/machine interface, as it is known—has been given extensive attention and support in the UK.[53] An expert system with a vast amount of domain-specific knowledge is clearly of little use unless human beings can, with little difficulty, gain access to that knowledge. It would be ideal, of course, if man could communicate with computers in much the same fashion as he does with his fellow human beings. To that end, AI research is currently being undertaken into natural language processing, speech understanding, and vision and perception, while cognitive psychologists, human factors specialists, and ergonomists are propounding theories of man/machine interaction with a view to recommending optimum interfaces. In this section, I briefly consider some relevant user interfaces that are currently available, I assess their potential for expert systems in law, and, finally, recommend the usage of interactive user interfaces with certain specified features.

Despite extensive research into AI, it must be acknowledged that,

---

[53] See e.g. Department of Industry, *The Alvey Report* (1982), pp. 29–32. Also see Gaines, 'From Ergonomics to the Fifth Generation: 30 Years of Human–Computer Interaction Studies' (1984).

at present, we are unable to program computers to understand natural language: as a result, it is not possible for human beings to communicate verbally with computer systems as they can with one another. (I discuss this matter in greater detail in Section 4.2.) One of the consequences of this fact for expert systems in law is that we will not be able (in the near future, if ever) simply to describe a set of circumstances—the facts of the case—to such systems as we would do to a legal expert: by means both of a connected series of English statements, and appropriate responses to questions asked of us. Although McCarty has suggested that 'for practical purposes ... there are no insuperable obstacles to the development of a legal information system, based on the TAXMAN representation, which could communicate with a lawyer in English',[54] we must be extremely cautious not to infer that he is asserting that the natural language 'front end' envisaged for TAXMAN would be of general applicability for all knowledge-based systems in law. For such an interface would both presuppose semantic and linguistic theories of as yet unknown sophistication, and, moreover, would also demand computational achievements of hitherto unrivalled complexity. It may well be that the conceptual structures of the TAXMAN formalism are such that, within the particular sub-domain of corporate tax law and given a restricted syntax, such semantic, linguistic, and computational matters are simply not relevant. (Yet it seems that the method of communication McCarty has anticipated has not yet been implemented.)

For present purposes, however, if the focus of interest is expert systems in law in general, and not systems peculiar to one particular domain, it is necessary to consider what user interface is most appropriate for any system, given, as I have said, that communication in English is not a realistic candidate. One possibility is to incorporate an interface that, at some stages, requires the user to describe his problem data in an artificial, computer/formal language. As can be seen from Appendix I, this approach was adopted in the TAXMAN, MIT, and Stanford projects (amongst others). There can be no doubt, however, that if our fundamental and motivating aim is to develop a practical aid to legal practitioners, then this option must be rejected immediately as very few lawyers (if any) would be interested in learning, and then communicating by means of, a computer/formal

[54] 'Intelligent Legal Information Systems: Problems and Prospects' (1984), pp. 137–8.

language. Such a tool would be no more than a hindrance. Although I did say in Section 2.4 that the actual implementation of a system is not necessarily the ultimate goal of all research projects in the AI/legal reasoning field, I did not, of course, mean thereby that the feasibility of eventual implementation of a system should be entirely disregarded. On the contrary, practical applications ought to be kept in mind in this field. Assuredly, researchers' expectations of the immediate practical worth of their work will vary vastly, but for those who are concerned (as I am in this book) with inquiring into expert systems in law (in any domain) for use in the conceivable future, surely an interface that requires the user to have extensive computational knowledge is to be rejected.

Another possibility (which cannot always be clearly dissociated from the last one), partially put into effect in some of the Prolog projects, and central to the most sophisticated prototype of the POLYTEXT/ARBIT implementations, is communication through the use of a restricted subset of English. This option demands that the user be thoroughly conversant with the syntactic constraints of the subset in question; otherwise interaction would continually result in some such wearisome computer response as 'SYNTAX ERROR' in respect of all input data not corresponding to the processable grammar. This interface would also seem to be an unlikely nominee as it too would require a degree of preparatory effort on the part of the prospective user that he would probably not be willing to expend. Note that aside from the difficulties I have identified with those systems that require some input in computer/formal language or some restricted subset of English, there is a further disadvantage with systems that accept *only* such input (and do not interact with the user). For, as Sergot argues, the user of such systems would in advance 'have to anticipate the need for all kinds of data just in case they are required'.[55]

The most promising type of user interface—at once computationally straightforward and of immediate practical use—is a purely *interactive user interface*.[56] This demands *not* the input of problem data in one fell swoop at the start of the dialogue, but rather results in an interaction with the computer during which, in various ways, the user inputs data to the system. The user, therefore, simply responds to the requests of the computer. Interactive user interfaces

---

[55] See 'Representing Legislation as Logic Programs' (1985), p. 38.
[56] See e.g. *PRBES*, p. 34.

have indeed been favoured in the majority of the projects surveyed in Appendix I. In their favour also, quite apart from their computational feasibility and their production of 'legal-user-friendly' systems, is the fact that they implicitly implement the preference of those legal experts who say they like to lead consultations, and thereby reduce the potential barrage of irrelevancies that might result from their consultees' untrammelled descriptions of cases.

I suggest that an interactive user interface for expert systems in law should allow, first, the system to ask a set of questions of the user, to which, as I shall show, there are only three possible replies; second, the user to ask certain questions of the system; third, the system to display a series of options on the screen (a menu) from which choices can be made; and, fourth, the system to require the user to input certain basic data at the start of (and, less commonly, during) any dialogue. All four elements of our proposal will be discussed in greater detail in Chapter 6, but the first two topics merit some preliminary attention at this stage.

1. With the exception of questions regarding basic data, to all questions posed by the system, the user may only enter one of the following retorts: 'yes', or 'no', or 'don't know'. During a consultation, the system strives to establish the facts of the instant case as precisely as possible. This is done through the presentation of many questions (and the questions remain relevant through the user's intermittent selections from menus—see Chapter 6). The positive and negative options will be used as linguistic and legal usage (and common sense) dictate, while the 'don't know' reply will be deployed when the user does not feel he has sufficient data or knowledge to answer 'yes' or 'no'. In the latter event, the system may (essentially) break down the question into more comprehensible sub-questions. If the user cannot answer sub-questions in respect of which there are no further sub-questions, then the system asks the user to hypothesize positive or negative replies to these questions (and, later on, is given an opportunity to change these replies). The conclusions that are drawn under these circumstances are what I term *contingent conclusions*, expressed in some such form as, 'If it is true that X, then . . .'. As with human legal reasoning, then, as Walker says, often 'much may have to be left on a hypothetical basis'.[57] Of course, if parts of the law of evidence were incorporated in the system, then

---

[57] *SLS*, p. 453.

uncertain questions of fact might be disposed of through answers to questions based on rules pertaining to the burden of proof. But that would indeed require a sophisticated system (see Section 3.7).

2. At appropriate times during the dialogue, the user can make the following demands of the system. First, he can ask—on the basis of the consultation so far—for an indication of what facts the system has stored as true or false, or what conclusions the system can infer (and the size of response by the computer can be constrained by use of menus). Second, he can ask for an explanation as to how any particular conclusion has been drawn (which will usually be given in terms of the rules used in the inference process). Third, he can ask for citations of the authoritative sources supporting conclusions that have been drawn, or for the rationale (Section 4.4) underlying conclusions for which there is no authority. Fourth, he can inquire why a question has been asked of him, and the system's reply will usually be in terms of the goal (conclusion) or sub-goal (interim conclusion) it is trying to reach. Finally, he can, through use of menus, ask why a particular conclusion has not been inferred; and the system will indicate both those propositions whose truth or falsity has precluded the drawing of some inference, and also the relevant rules involved.

The topic of the man/machine interface is a very complex one: in this section, I have merely outlined some basic requirements for an interactive user interface for expert systems in law. Valuable empirical research could be carried out in this connection to determine with greater precision both the manner in which human legal experts communicate with those who consult them and also the techniques they deploy in establishing the facts of cases before them.

2.8 CONCLUSION

In this chapter I have examined many preliminary matters pertaining to expert systems in law, and have introduced some terminology that not only will be used regularly in the remainder of this book, but serves also to clarify some issues that remain confused in much of the current AI/legal reasoning literature. The vocabulary I have used and will continue to use is rooted in contemporary jurisprudence (a field whose relevance for legal knowledge engineering has emerged from Part One of this book as being substantial).

On the basis of my preliminary analysis of the nature of legal reasoning and identification of the epistemological idiosyncrasies of law, I was able to conclude with some confidence that the law is a particularly suitable domain of application for expert systems research and development. And much of Parts Two and Three of this book will lend further credence to that claim. It was also my purpose to present guidelines for legal knowledge engineers of the future. To that end, I suggested criteria in accordance with which legal domains of application ought to be selected, and, further, on the basis of the discussion of legal expert(ise), I suggested how the division of labour between legal knowledge engineers and legal domain specialists might best be organized.

Finally in this chapter, I advocated that expert systems in law be combined with other computer applications to the law thereby producing more powerful installations, and I recommended, for expert systems in law in particular, the deployment of a specific type of interactive user interface.

PART TWO

LEGAL KNOWLEDGE REPRESENTATION

3

Entities to be Represented in a
Legal Knowledge Base

AI scientists seem to agree that the primary task for knowledge engineers is the acquisition and representation of domain-specific knowledge: while the question of knowledge utilization is regarded as an important matter, it is nevertheless generally conceived as a subsidiary subject (and as a distinct activity in practice). The expert systems literature is also unambiguous on the following point— because expert problem-solving performance in any field is dependent upon extensive quantities of *knowledge*, all expert systems must also contain large representations of knowledge.[1] 'The most powerful systems', it has been said, 'will be those which contain the most knowledge.'[2] In this and the following chapter I shall be concerned, then, with the crucial topic of legal knowledge representation. More specifically, I offer answers to the first two of the 'basic questions' that Winston suggests 'must be answered before any problem solver can be built', namely (1) what kind of knowledge is involved? and (2) how should the knowledge be represented?[3] I address the former question in the present chapter, and defer the latter for discussion in Chaper 4.

In Section 2.3, while considering the epistemological foundations of legal knowledge, I in fact gave a partial reply to Winston's first question. Yet if Winston's challenge is to be met squarely, I must supplement that account with an elucidation of all those entities that

---

[1] *AI*, chs. 2 and 8; *BES*, pp. 4–5 and 56; *CC*, p. 33; *FG*, pp. 9–10 and 54–6; *IS*, ch. 3; *PAI*, p. 4; Barr and Feigenbaum, *The Handbook of Artificial Intelligence*, vol. i (1981), pp. 143–6.

[2] Feigenbaum, 'Knowledge Engineering: The Applied Side' (1983), p. 38.

[3] *AI*, p. 41. Winston also poses two other questions: 'How Much Knowledge Is Required?' and 'What Exactly Is the Knowledge Needed?' These matters clearly relate to the chosen legal domain of application, and must be addressed afresh each time a new expert system in law is being built. Some general guidance on these issues was given in Chapter 2.

ought to be represented in an expert system in law in order that it may function both at the level of a human legal expert, and, more generally, in the manner sketched in Chapter 1. The purpose of this chapter is to articulate such a supplement, which when read together with Section 2.3 presents the theory of legal knowledge underlying the type of expert systems discussed throughout this book.

In Chapter 1, I concluded that none of the projects cited has yielded an expert system that is of practical use to the legal profession. This defect is explicable partly in terms of the nature of the legal knowledge that has so far been input to the systems; the coverage of legal domains has invariably been shallow with emphasis solely on statute law. Yet it is clear to all who have engaged in legal problem-solving that statutes often provide no more than a starting-point for legal research, and recourse to case law and the commentaries of scholars must generally be made. But insufficient examination has been made of the nature of these non-statutory primary and secondary sources with a view to incorporating them in legal knowledge bases; and the entities thought to be necessary and sufficient for legal problem-solving have not been identified. I seek here to fill this worrisome gap in the AI/legal reasoning literature, for unless such an analysis has been undertaken, digested, and implemented by legal knowledge engineers, it is likely that all aspiring expert systems in law will continue to exhibit a trivial level of performance.

The task belongs to legal theory, the foundations of the discussion being based on modern analytical jurisprudence, and, in particular, on works pertaining to legal science, understood in a sense to be clarified in Section 3.1, which deals with the relationship between legal science and legal knowledge representation. In Section 3.2 I discuss statute law, and the way in which descriptive legal science yields statute law-statements. In Section 3.3 I argue it is possible to interpret case law in a fashion that allows us to make case law-statements (analogous in form and content to statute law-statements) consistent with any acceptable theory of *ratio decidendi*. Thereafter, in Section 3.4, I introduce the notion of legal heuristics, and deal with instances of these in the following three sections: in Section 3.5, it is acknowledged that prediction is a central part of the process of legal counselling, as a consequence of which I claim statute law-predictions and case law-predictions are entities to be represented in a legal knowledge base; Section 3.6. introduces the notions of derivations from statute and case law-statements, and generalizations from case law-statements; and in Section 3.7, the topic of legal meta-knowledge is examined. Finally, in Section 3.8, I reconsider the idea of legal heuristics and then make some concluding observations.

3.1 LEGAL SCIENCE AND LEGAL KNOWLEDGE REPRESENTATION

Many legal theorists have written about legal science, and such work seems to bear closely on the topic of legal knowledge representation. Superficial examination of publications pertaining to legal science might indicate that there is radical disagreement amongst leading authors over the province and purpose of that activity. This apparent divergence of views, however, is no more than that pervasive confusion occasioned by theorists putting into service the same label to refer to different phenomena: the lack of consensus over the meaning of legal science, therefore, is largely an instance of terminological discrepancy (see Section 1.6). Three usages of the term legal science can be found. (1) In some texts, writers use the expression legal science where most would simply speak of the study of law (on both a practical and theoretical level).[4] (2) In other works, legal science is used to refer to the theoretical study of law; legal science, on this account is synonymous with jurisprudence, as the latter term is most usually deployed.[5] (3) In still other legal writings, the term legal science denotes (approximately) the task of offering a comprehensive and accurate recasting of the contents of part of a legal system.[6]

In what sense will legal science be deployed in this book? Where there is terminological discrepancy, it is often simplest to stipulate (after clarification) how a term will be deployed, as I shall now do. I am not concerned here with the first sense of legal science. This book, of course, is indeed intimately concerned with legal science in the second sense, although the term jurisprudence is preferred. It is the third usage of legal science—as the recasting of law—that is my

---

[4] See e.g. Walker, *SLS*, pp. 7–9, and *The Oxford Companion to Law* (1980) p. 754. Also see Castberg, *PLP*, ch. 1. On science, see Russell, *The Problems of Philosophy* (1980), p. 90.

[5] See Villa, 'Legal Science between Natural and Human Sciences' (1984), p. 243. Cf. Lloyd, *Introduction to Jurisprudence* (1979) p. 9 n. 32, and generally pp. 6–10.

[6] See e.g. Harris, *LLS*, *passim*; Alchourron and Bulygin, *NS*, *passim*.

concern. Yet it must be stressed that the second and third senses of legal science are connected. Kelsen, for instance, often seems to have used the term in both senses.[7] Recently, Simmonds has clarified this matter. For Simmonds, legal science is 'the systematic and ordered exposition of legal doctrine in the works of juristic commentators' to be distinguished from 'legal theory', although the distinction, he argues, is 'less dramatic than many assume'.[8] For he argues that any clear-cut separation between legal theory and legal science should not satisfy us. It is not difficult to imagine the doctrinal writer being forced to confront questions that are of a distinctly 'theoretical' nature and that would usually and appropriately be considered in works of jurisprudence. For example, should the law be represented as a body of remedies, a set of rules, a system of rights, or a system of duties? . . . the legal scientist . . . must formulate some criteria of appropriateness of representation . . . before we can decide how the law should most appropriately be represented by doctrinal legal science, we must determine criteria of appropriateness: and, to do that, we must investigate the concept of 'a right', 'a duty', 'an interest', and so on.[9]

By using the term 'legal science' here, I shall be referring to that undertaking that is at once descriptive, interpretative, derivative, and predictive, whose function is to present a systematic, explanatory, simple, and yet comprehensive representation of a momentary legal system—that is, a legal system that is valid at one moment in time (see Section 4.5). Legal science, on this analysis, is a pursuit that can be assisted by jurisprudential insight. In providing representations, the overriding purpose of legal science is to *describe* the law, and where, as I shall explain, mere description is inadequate or impossible, to supplement description with interpretation, derivation, and prediction.[10]

The importance of description in legal science is reflected in the works of both Kelsen and Harris. For Kelsen, a particular legal

[7] See e.g. *GTLS*, pp. 162–4, and *PTL*, pp. 70–6, for the use of science in the third sense I have noted, and *GTLS*, p. xiv, where he asserts his pure theory to be a science of law. Perhaps this apparent tension can best be explained in the way that Simmonds relates legal theory and legal science in the quotation in the text. Note that Kelsen also admits that the term 'science of law' can be used in a different way to refer to sociological jurisprudence and sociology of law: *GTLS*, pp. 162–3, and 'The Pure Theory of Law and Analytical Jurisprudence' (1941–2), pp. 50–4. Also see Harris, 'Kelsen and Normative Consistency' (1986), pp. 202–5.

[8] *The Decline of Juridical Reason: Doctrine and Theory in the Legal Order* (1984)' pp. 1–2.

[9] Ibid., p. 6.

[10] Cf. *LLS*, pp. 167–8.

order is a system of norms, which can be described by those engaging in 'legal science', 'normative science of law', or 'normative jurisprudence' as statements known as 'legal rules'. As noted in Section 1.5, his Pure Theory of Law provides the legal scientist with the 'fundamental concepts by which the positive law of a definite legal community can be *described*'. The aim of his general theory of law is 'to attain a scientific exposition of those particular legal orders constituting the corresponding legal communities' and 'to enable the jurist concerned with a particular legal order, the lawyer, the judge, the legislator, or the law-teacher, to understand and to describe as exactly as possible his own positive law'.[11] Likewise, Harris suggests that 'legal science is that activity, widespread in countries with developed legal institutions, whose necessary objective is the systematic exposition of some corpus of legislative materials'.[12] One of the aims of his *Law and Legal Science* is to investigate 'descriptive legal science' or, as he also calls it, 'the primary descriptive activity of legal science'.[13] He is concerned, therefore, with 'the logical status of statements made by legal scientists when they purport to describe the present law on a topic'.[14] For both Kelsen and Harris, then, there is little doubt that description is the 'defining function'[15] of legal science.

However, most analytical jurisprudents, while conceding that legal science is about describing, have recognized that this is not a straightforward matter. For, as Alchourron and Bulygin put it, 'it seems clear that the description of the law is not a mere transcription of statutes and other legal norms, but that it also involves the operation which jurists refer to under the vague term "interpretation" and which fundamentally consists in the determination of the consequences that can be derived from such norms.'[16] In this chapter, following Kelsen and Harris (and most legal theorists) in their identification of description as the central function of legal science, but accepting, as Alchourron and Bulygin do, that there is more to setting out the law than 'mere transcription', I articulate just what those further activities of legal science are.

[11] *GTLS*, p. xiii. Emphasis added. Also see *GTLS*, p. 45, and *PTL*, pp. 71–5. Cf. *LLS*, pp. 35–43.
[12] *LLS*, p. 2.
[13] Ibid., p. 20
[14] Ibid.
[15] *LLS*, p. 11.
[16] *NS*, p. 68.

The relevance of this exercise for legal knowledge engineering is self-evident: the activities of legal science and legal knowledge engineering, it emerges, are substantially the same. While the former expresses its systematic and explanatory exposition in written words to be read by interested parties, the latter holds, available for its users, a similar (if considerably more rigorously formulated) representation, not in paper and print but in computer memory. We may therefore use works on legal science as sources of guidance for building expert systems. Not only are works on legal science of relevance, but so too are all those other jurisprudential writings that address the issue that we have identified as legal science under different headings. For different theorists have referred to essentially the same activity—legal science—by entirely distinct labels. (No doubt this phenomenon has resulted in part from an antipathy, albeit often unarticulated, towards liberal interpretations of *scientific* endeavour.[17]) Table 1 illustrates a selection of terminological divergences.

Irrespective of the diversity of terms used, there is consensus amongst the theorists mentioned in the table over the following. The form in which we find law-formulations—as distinct statutes or case reports—lacks structure, coherence, simplicity, and comprehensibility so that it is desirable for those whose concern is the administration of the law to recast these law-formulations as a body of structured, interconnected, coherent, simple (in so far as is possible), and comprehensible law-statements. The activity of legal science involves, *inter alia*, this transformation.

In this and the next chapter, I avail myself of the arguments that the noted and other theorists have proposed in relation to various aspects of legal science, although it is by no means my purpose to present a complete theory of legal science. Rather, I attend to those specific questions raised by building expert systems in law that have to date been neglected by scholars of legal knowledge engineering. Before proceeding, however, one fundamental assumption—that is defended both explicitly and implicitly in the present work—should be articulated: that *rules* do and should play a central role in legal science, legal knowledge representation, and in legal reasoning. Overwhelming authority for this proposition can be found in legal

---

[17] Hayek, for instance, seems particularly unhappy about Kelsen's use of the term science. See *Law, Legislation and Liberty*, vol. ii (1982), pp. 49–50 and 171–2.

TABLE 1

Theorist	Synonymous Terms for Legal Science
Alchourron & Bulygin	Reformulation of the System.
Bentham	Arrangement of Laws.
Castberg	Legal Dogmatics.
Dworkin	Exposition of the Law.
Golding	Rational Reconstruction.
Harris	Descriptive Legal Science.
Hart	Description; Representation.
Honoré	Restatement of the Law.
Horovitz	Formalisation; Rationalisation.
Kelsen	Normative Science of Law or Jurisprudence; Science of Law; Representation of the Law.
MacCormick	Expounding the Law.
Raz	Description; Representation.
Ross	Description of a Legal Order.
Simmonds	Doctrinal Legal Science.*

* These are the terms used predominantly in *NS*, *OLG*, *PLP*, *TRS*, 'Kelsen and the Concept of "Legal System"' (1961), *LLS*, *CL*, 'Real Laws' (1977), *LL*, *GTLS*, and *PTL*, 'Law as Institutional Fact' (1974), *CLS* and *AL*, *DN*, and *The Decline of Juridical Reason: Doctrine and Theory in the Legal Order* (1984), respectively.

theory,[18] and even a philosopher such as Dworkin, who has questioned the sufficiency of rules for legal decision-making,[19] does nevertheless himself seem to presuppose a predominant place for them, as MacCormick has shown.[20] If this is so, and rules have, as MacCormick alleges, 'logical primacy',[21] then surely it should be sought, in the first instance, to represent legal knowledge in rule form. Moreover, if it is agreed that in all modesty researchers should

[18] Kelsen's continual concern with norms, and Hart's with rules, are eminent illustrations. See *GTLS*, *PTL*, and *CL* respectively. Also note, as two of many possible illustrations, that for Golding, 'the notion of "rule" is somehow fundamental to the analysis of law' (see 'Kelsen and the Concept of "Legal System"' (1961), p. 367), while for Harris, 'the usefulness of rule-based discourse, practices, and values' is 'beyond doubt' (*LLS*, pp. 9–10) and '*the law now in force . . . is exclusively comprised of legal rules*' (ibid., p. 11, emphasis added).

[19] *TRS*, chs. 2, 3, and 4.

[20] *LRSD*, pp. 131–40. See also *LLS*, pp. 158–9.

[21] *LRSD*, p. 140.

devote their energies to designing systems that can solve 'clear cases' as non-judicial agents do, before tackling 'hard cases' of the sort with which judges are regularly confronted, then, as I show in Chapters 5 and 6, the central role of rules for that purpose can scarcely be doubted.

3.2 STATUTE LAW-STATEMENTS

In this book, I use the term 'statute law' to refer to the law held in legal codes, superior legislation, subordinate legislation, and indeed to any written rules and regulations of fixed and determinate verbal form. Statute law has for long been the primary formal source of law in civil law jurisdictions where codes (and legislative supplements) predominate. And in common law countries, since the early nineteenth century, though the practice of promulgating universal codes has not been adopted, extensive portions of legislation have indeed been passed, not only as comprehensive restatements of the pre-existing common law, but often also as the principal means of changing old law and of introducing new legal provisions. Given the great importance of statute law in all legal systems and its increasing relevance for most areas of law, it is clear that most expert systems in law must have knowledge of statute law represented within their knowledge bases. Appendix I shows that the vast majority of the systems surveyed operate on statute law (often to the neglect of case law, as suggested in the following section), although it is likely that most researchers' preference for statute law is rooted in a recognition not of its central role in legal reasoning, but of it being apparently more amenable to computational treatment than case law.

It is not possible, as it is for database systems in law, simply to feed statute law into an expert system in the fixed form in which it is expressed in statute law-formulations, such as Acts of Parliament; for, as Section 4.2 shows, no inference engine could operate on knowledge represented in natural language and no program could currently be written to transform the text into an implementable format. It is necessary therefore to represent statute law within legal knowledge bases as specific types of *statute law-statements*: descriptions of statute law-formulations.

Although statute law today is normally couched in very general terms, making, as Hart has suggested, 'maximal . . . use of general classifying words',[22] this has not always been the sole way of expressing legislative provisions. In the nineteenth century, for instance, as Tapper has pointed out, there was a 'habit of assembling long lists of relatively specific synonyms in statutory sections', although this is no longer current practice.[23] Today's methods have important implications both for pure description of the law, as I discuss in this section, and for deriving rules from statute, as is considered in Section 3.6. (Note that the precise form in which these statute law-statements might be cast is discussed in the next chapter.)

If statute law-statements are to be purely descriptive, which is important both in relation to an expert system's transparency, and to the question of 'derivation' (see Section 3.6), they should be equivalent both in (1) deontic content and (2) generality, to the statute law-formulations that they describe.[24] These two requirements conform with the vast bulk of accounts of legal science, for they simply stipulate that an accurate description of any piece of statutory material must be faithful in *meaning* to the text of which it is a description. Both these restrictions confirm the role of the descriptive legal scientist or legal knowledge engineer as that of reporter of the law who has no business to legislate of his own accord.

More specifically, the principle of *deontic equivalence* requires the legal knowledge engineer, in his rendition of any statute law-formulation, to report all deontic or normative modalities in terms akin to those in which they appear in the primary source, and to desist from imposing his own interpretations where these differ from the original text. Although various synonymous terms can be used to describe the deontic operators that are used in statutory materials to impose obligations and prohibitions, and to confer powers, these must be deployed in a manner that preserves their distinctive normative force (see Section 6.5). Thus where a statute indicates that 'the court must θ', this can usually be rightly described as 'the court is required to θ', or, in conventional notation, 'the court $O(\theta)$'; but not as 'the court is permitted to θ', that is 'the court $P(\theta)$' (although in accordance with most systems of deontic logic these last two

[22] *CL*, p. 121.

[23] *CATL*, p. 115.

[24] My use of the term 'descriptive' should not be construed as understating the frequent complexity of the process of making existential statements about statute law-formulations. No doubt what I term description is often both a creative and an interpretative activity.

propositions are entailed by the others). If a textbook writer did not retain deontic equivalence, he would be universally condemned, for in so doing he would be misrepresenting the law.[25]

The second requirement is that the legal knowledge engineer is expected to pitch his exposition at a level of *equivalent generality* to the object of description: if a rule pertains to a certain act, action, person, or event, then it is precisely that act, action, person, or event (with all its incumbent qualifications, limitations, and so forth) that should be described. We normally assume, in accordance both with the canons of literal interpretation and with common sense, that the terms expressed in any statute law-formulation constitute the upper limit of generality of the categories specified; that is, that the statute means no more than it says. There is, therefore, little room for, and we would invariably reject, any putative description of a portion of statute law that introduced categories wider than those contained in the law-formulation, for we would suppose that such extension would impose duties, or confer powers, not originally intended by the legislature responsible for the original enactment. Even in a legal science whose province exceeds pure description, few theorists find a place for *statute law-generalizations* (although they might allow case law-generalizations—Section 3.6) and it is a category to which no attention is paid in this book. In contrast, most theorists account for statute law-derivations in their theories of legal science, as I do in relation to knowledge representation in Section 3.6.

Most legal scientists tend to make statute law-statements in substantially the same language as the law-formulations of which they are descriptions, and in that way the above requirements are normally met. It is submitted that in representing legal knowledge generally, and in particular when following the methods proposed in the following chapter, this practice be continued in so far as the language of the law-formulations is intelligible.[26]

It is instructive now to examine an example of a statute law-statement, taken from the Oxford project domain of application. (In this example, as in the rest of the illustrations in this chapter, no analysis of the individuation or the structure of laws is offered,

---

[25] See *NS*, p. 80.

[26] Such use of the words of the statute law-formulations would be crucial in the development of a system built with the aid of a shell such as ESP/advisor which 'animates text'. See n. 28 to Ch. 1.

although the basis of one is assumed—see Chapter 4.) The first part of s.1(1) of the *Divorce (Scotland) Act 1976* reads as follows:

[In an action for divorce] the court may grant decree of divorce if, but only if, it is established [in accordance wih the following provisions of this Act] that the marriage has broken down irretrievably.

This portion of text, then, is a piece of statute law-formulation, and can be recast (ignoring for now the pieces within square brackets) as a statute law-statement that is a type of conditional statement:

If and only if it is established that the marriage has broken down irretrievably, *then* the court may grant decree of divorce.

Notice that deontic equivalence is maintained and that the words of the statute have been used regularly. This is an extremely simple example, but of course, as legal scientists through the centuries have discovered, more extensive description of bodies of statute law, accounting for cross-references and so forth, is no trivial enterprise. For statutes are invariably composed not with elegance and immediate intelligibility as goals, but with consistency and completeness in mind. Moreover, problems can arise from statutes that contain ambiguities (syntactic and semantic), for it is difficult to formulate statements of legislative enactments containing such uncertainties. (Indeed, some cases are 'hard' precisely because of such uncertainties—see Section 6.7.)

No doubt, legal knowledge engineers of the future—given the further constraints imposed by their chosen formalisms—will encounter grave difficulties even in the recasting of those statutes that seem to be relatively independent of other legal provisions. But when it is remembered also, as Atiyah has pointed out, that 'very few statutes are self-contained instruments even when they deal with a remote or esoteric branch of the law',[27] then the necessity of representing further relevant sources—and the possibility of still further complexity—looms large. While it may seem beyond dispute, then, that statute law-statements will often be the central entities in any legal knowledge base, it should not be assumed that their identification and articulation is unproblematic. Nor should it be thought that law-statements are exhaustive and sufficient tokens of statute law, for, as I show in Sections 3.5 and 3.6, they may be supplemented with statute law-predictions and statute law-derivations.

[27] 'Common Law and Statute Law' (1985), p. 2.

3.3 CASE LAW-STATEMENTS

Any expert system in law whose domain of application belongs to a common law jurisdiction (or indeed to many other jurisdictions, such as the Scottish legal system), must have the facility for the representation of case law within its knowledge base. One of the critical shortcomings of the vast majority of the projects mentioned in Section 1.4 is the lack of attention that has thus far been paid by their investigators to this question of representing judicial precedents.[28] If an expert system in law is to function at the level of a human expert and to provide useful counsel to its users, surely it must invariably contain knowledge of relevant court determinations. In this section, the question of representing case law (which I take to include the decisions both of courts and tribunals) is discussed and the associated presuppositions of this proposal are articulated.

Judicial precedents are found in the law-formulations that are case reports. Although it is accepted by all in the Scottish legal profession, for example, that judicial precedent is a formal source of Scots Law, there is of course the perennial disagreement over the way in which we ought to identify the rule for which any given case purports to be the authoritative source—this (approximately) is the problem of the *ratio decidendi*.[29] Clearly not every word of a thirty-page judgment of a judge of the Outer House of the Court of Session, for instance, is taken to be the expression of authoritative legal material (unlike the words of statutes); many judgments embrace a complex web of legal history, expressions of moral (personal or popular), social, political, sexual, and religious preferences, portions of descriptive, interpretative, predictive, or derivative legal science, as well, of course, as descriptions of the facts of the instant case and the relevant legal arguments. From such arrays of legal, quasi-legal, and non-legal data, judges, lawyers, legal scientists, legal officials, legal theorists, and citizens have to pluck their interpretations of the rules of law considered to be embedded in the reports. The legal knowledge engineer too is faced with this unenviable task.

The task is clearly an interpretative one: it is an activity of inter-

---

[28] This deficiency was mirrored in the early work on computerized legal database systems. See Tapper, 'Lawyers and Machines' (1963), pp. 136–7.

[29] For an excellent and succinct account of the *ratio decidendi*, see MacCormick, *LRLT*, p. 215, and ch. 8 generally.

pretative legal science. It is not simply a job of shifting words about and recasting them into some canonical form, but a process of scrutinizing and interpreting portions of text in the knowledge that not all of the words before the legal scientist in question are of equal significance, and that in the end he must sift the authoritative *ratio decidendi* from the text leaving the residual *obiter dicta*. The jurisprudential literature on this topic is formidable.[30] Most eminent theorists have contributed to this continuing debate and have propounded a host of conflicting accounts of the *ratio*. On the face of it, it seems unlikely that a consensual account of use to legal knowledge engineering could be derived from that welter of diverging theories, for the identification of the *ratio decidendi* of any case might indeed seem to pose insurmountable practical and theoretical problems. Yet Hart, in an important (and much neglected) passage in *The Concept of Law*, injects a sober and entirely practical contribution to the debate:

Any honest description of the use of precedent in English law must allow a place for the following pairs of contrasting facts. *First*, there is no single method of determining the rule for which a given authoritative precedent is an authority. Notwithstanding this, in the vast majority of decided cases there is very little doubt. The head-note is usually correct enough. *Secondly*, there is no authoritative or uniquely correct formulation of any rule to be extracted from cases. On the other hand, there is often very general agreement, when the bearing of a precedent on a later case is in issue, that a given formulation is adequate.[31]

Hart in effect locates the consensus in this jurisprudential controversy. He does not furnish us with agreement on a conceptual level (but does summarize the problems for us). Rather, he asserts that for any account of judicial precedent to be empirically adequate, it must acknowledge both that there is usually very little doubt over what rule can be derived from any given case report, and, further, that a

[30] Some outstanding contributions to the debate are Goodhart, 'Determining the *Ratio Decidendi* of a Case' (1930), Stone, 'The *Ratio* of the *Ratio Decidendi*' (1959), and Simpson, 'The *Ratio Decidendi* of a Case and the Doctrine of Binding Precedent' (1961). A clear discussion of this topic and a useful bibliography is *LP*, ch. 13.

[31] *CL*, p. 131. See also: Raz's remark that '[i]n the main, however, the identification of the *ratio* of a case is reasonably straightforward' (*AL*, p. 184); and Simpson's contentions that '[t]he tendency has been, however, for the difficulty of the task of determining the *ratio* of a case to be exaggerated. In a large number of instances it is not particularly difficult to arrive at a satisfactory formulation of the *ratio*' ('The *Ratio Decidendi* of a Case and the Doctrine of Binding Precedent' (1961), pp. 168–9).

formulation of such a rule (acceptable for practical purposes) can normally be articulated.[32] Judges in coming to their decisions, lawyers in advising their clients, and legal textbook writers in composing their texts, do indeed seem to ratify Hart's empirical thesis, for if they did not, it would be hard to understand how the common law system could have survived. These people do not memorize, and repeat verbatim, whole case reports, but, it would seem, have recourse to summaries of their legal import in the form of the individuated law-statements that we find in legal judgments, opinions of counsel, and legal texts.[33] No doubt many of the better judgments, opinions, and texts have been composed in the light of a sharpened perception gained from jurisprudential discussions of the *ratio*, and the poorer ones are the worse off for not having this insight. Yet this need not deter us from accepting Hart's account, which I shall indeed adopt as the basis for asserting that it is possible to represent judicial precedents as case law-statements in legal knowledge bases.

Hart's discussion of judicial precedent, however, does require refinement. Given the thesis that we can invariably derive rules from reported decisions and that the task of formulating these rules presents no insurmountable obstacles, cognisance should also be taken of five further points. First, as Harris has pointed out, 'the same precedent may be cited as authority for more than one rule at different levels of generality',[34] an observation few would choose to contest. Second, as MacCormick has said, 'by no means all cases—even "leading" cases—have a single *ratio decidendi*'.[35] Third, the interpretation of any judicial precedent may vary through time.[36] Fourth, some case law-statements must be regarded as being 'provisional', for they denote possible interpretations of law-formulations. Harris suggests this to be true of all interpretations of

---

[32] Cf. Harris, *LLS*, p. 73.

[33] See Honoré, 'Real Laws' (1977), pp. 100–1, Dworkin, *TRS*, pp. 110–12, and Simpson, 'The *Ratio Decidendi* of a Case and the Doctrine of Binding Precedent' (1961), p. 156, all in relation to 'the rule in' *Rylands* v. *Fletcher*. Also see MacCormick's rendition and brief discussion of *Morelli* v. *Fitch & Gibbons* [1928] 2 KB 636, in the course of his worked example of deductive justification (*LRLT*, p. 30), and Atiyah's discussion of *Travers* v. *Holley* [1953] P 246, in 'Common Law and Statute Law' (1985), p. 16. Both MacCormick and Atiyah in these examples manipulate case law as individuated rules. On individuation, see Section 4.3.

[34] *LLS*, p. 159. This accords with the discussion of case law-derivations and case law-generalizations in Section 3.6.

[35] *LRLT*, p. 215. Original emphasis. On multiple *rationes*, see Walker, *SLS*, pp. 393–4.

[36] See Raz, *AL*, p. 185.

precedents, because their 'meaning-content cannot be unambiguously identified'.[37] Some cases, of course, allow of no simple
interpretation and our statements of them should indeed be provisional, probabilistically framed, and supplemented with explanations or justifications of the chosen formulations[38] (for which
purpose the *rationale sub-slot*, proposed in Section 4.4, can be used).
On the whole, however, if Hart's empirical generalizations are accurate, then the provisional facet of case law-statements is peripheral
only; this is reflected in our tendency not to highlight the provisional
nature of our renditions of judicial precedents. It is often not clear
when reading a legal textbook, for example, whether propositions of
law in the text—to which footnote numbers are appended—are indeed statute law-statements or case law-statements, until the citation
in the footnote is examined. Nor is it obvious when lawyers preface
their assertions with words such as 'It is the law that . . .', whether the
eventual proposition is one descriptive of statute law or interpretative of case law. Indeed, to lawyers themselves it often seems to make
no difference. Legal experts, *qua* both interpretative legal scientists
and reasoning agents, do seem to formulate and manipulate provisional interpretations of case law *as if* they were indeed of a fixed
and determinate form akin to statute law-statements. As a result, it
does not seem improper to refer to them, as I shall do here, under the
simple heading of case law-statements.

Fifth, it should not be taken for granted that the entire common
law system can be reduced to a collection of rules (case law-
statements). Simpson has forcefully contended that such a reductionist model misrepresents the common law and is inconsistent with
its development, content, and scope.[39] This is a major issue within
jurisprudence, and I return to it in Chapter 5 in my discussion of the
sufficiency of a rule-based model of law for legal reasoning. An important point, however, must be made at this stage: although the
common law may not be sufficiently represented in terms of rules, it
cannot be doubted that it is invariably possible, desirable, and necessary to interpret individual cases in the form of individuated rules.

---

[37] *LLS*, pp. 91–2. Cf. Simpson, 'The *Ratio Decidendi* of a Case and the Doctrine of
Binding Precedent' (1961), p. 166: 'Case-law rules derived from judicial statements of
law are thus treated by the courts as incomplete things.'

[38] Cf. *LLS*, p. 92. Note that cases may be rendered 'hard' precisely because of the
difficulty of interpreting past decisions (see Section 6.7).

[39] 'The Common Law and Legal Theory' (1973).

This Simpson himself seems to acknowledge in another paper.[40] Case law-statements, we may compromise, are a necessary but not sufficient means of accounting for the common law. The extent to which they are insufficient marks one boundary to the ultimate utility of rule-based expert systems in law.

To summarize: a judicial decision, in the first instance, constitutes a determination of a litigated dispute between two parties. Thereafter, the specific rule that was applied to the particular facts of the instant case is often generalized (some might say induced) by interpretative legal scientists so as to produce a seemingly definitive law-statement (in rule form) of wider application, although a few cases must be expressly interpreted as provisional. There is usually little difficulty in articulating this statement, but a case may be interpreted as being productive of more than one statement, and subject to varying interpretations through time. It seems unlikely, however, that the common law can be reduced only to a system of rules, but rules clearly do have a central role to play in interpretative legal science. As an example of certain aspects of our analysis above, we may take *Donoghue* v. *Stevenson* [1932] AC 562, which related to a particular dispute concerning a decomposed snail, a manufacturer and distributor of ginger-beer in opaque bottles, and a Scottish woman. At one time, the ruling was induced and thought to extend to manufacturers of food and drink, inaccessible receptacles containing such fluids and comestibles, and any consumers of said items. Later, however, on the basis of Lord Atkin's dictum (p. 599), it was taken to apply (approximately) to manufacturers of all those products that do not allow of reasonable opportunity of intermediate examination between distribution and reception by ultimate consumers. At any given point in time, it does seem that most commentators agreed on its scope and on a formulation, but as is shown in Section 3.6, this did not preclude the possibility of further tentative generalization.[41]

---

[40] 'The *Ratio Decidendi* of a Case and the Doctrine of Binding Precedent' (1961), p. 156. See also MacCormick, *HLAH*, pp. 130–2.

[41] The analysis of *Donoghue* v. *Stevenson* given is extremely crude, but is sufficient to illustrate some of my contentions regarding the *ratio*. For a far more detailed discussion of its generality, and for citations of relevant cases bearing on the implications of *Donoghue* v. *Stevenson*, see Stone, *LSLR*, pp. 269–70. It might be, of course, that *Donoghue* v. *Stevenson* is one of the minority of cases where there *is* doubt over its *ratio(nes)*, or indeed, because of its position in the development of the common law, it may be an instance of part of the common law that is not expressible in terms of rules. This would not really affect my thesis for it is an exceptional case, chosen for its notoriety.

Interpretative legal scientists and legal knowledge engineers, then, must formulate case law-statements. To clarify the latter's task, another example is helpful—the case of *MacLennan* v. *MacLennan*, 1958 SC 105. According to Hart, there is no settled method for discovering the rule of law for which any case, and therefore, this case, is authority. Yet, he continues, in most cases—and there is no reason to think that *MacLennan* is not one of that class—there is little doubt. That is patently so. For few lawyers would deny that this case establishes that 'artificial insemination by a donor does not constitute adultery' (the very words used by Lord Wheatley (p. 114) in his judgment). So uncontested does this interpretation seem to be that Clive, the leading commentator on the law relating to husband and wife, parenthetically and in passing summarizes the *ratio*: '(A.I.D. not adultery)'.[42] Such a succinct account by such an eminent commentator implicitly offers support (in respect of one case) for Hart's suggestion. More generally, as I have said, it would be difficult to imagine how the system of precedent could operate at all if Hart is not substantially correct. Hart acknowledges there to be no one correct formulation of rules of law drawn from judicial precedents. The suggestion that there is one uniquely authoritative method of formulation, as I show in Section 4.3, presupposes an ontologically peculiar theory of the individuation of laws. However, reasons can be given for deeming acceptable (or otherwise) any one formulation. Consistent, as I shall argue, with much modern analytical jurisprudence is the conditional statement:

> *If* a married lady has been artificially inseminated by a donor, *then* the court shall not construe that as adultery.

Of course this rendition of the rule is, as Harris stresses, provisional, and it is conceivable that the courts in the future might interpret *MacLennan* as having a wider or narrower scope. Nevertheless, it is a proposition of semantic content similar to the one above that all who we consider to have expertise in this field of law—legal practitioners, academics, judges, and sheriffs of repute— do indeed adopt in their reasoning processes. It is such a proposition, therefore, that should be represented in an expert system in law. As there is no doubt, for practical purposes, that this is a satisfactory interpretation of the case, it is not necessary to attach a certainty factor to the rule. (This would only be done in respect of cases

---

[42] See *DA*, p. 10.

where there is doubt over the *ratio(nes)*, and an explanation would be appended in the rationale sub-slot—see Section 4.4). In representing case law-statements, we must always specify their source, that is, the case report from which the rule has been interpreted, and this will be input to the authority sub-slot—see Section 4.4. Finally, it is necessary to indicate what level of court made the decision and assign it a rank (see Sections 4.4 and 3.7) within the systematic hierarchy of courts.

In this section, I have asserted that it is possible, in certain circumstances, to represent case law as general rules, or, as I have called them, case law-statements. It has not been my purpose to show in detail how this may be done, but merely to produce jurisprudential evidence to support the view that it *can* be done.

The theory of legal science that emerges from this section and the last is a rule-based account, in accordance with which at least part of our law can be reduced to a collection of statements, some of which describe statute law, while others are interpretations of case law. It is such descriptions and interpretations that we have good reason to suspect are brought to bear by human legal experts, together with other entities, in solving legal problems. An obvious question arises in this context concerning the relationship of statute law to case law, but it is one that the jurisprudential literature has not completely exhausted. Atiyah poses it thus: 'Does our law constitute, in some sense, a single coherent, integral body of law, or does it consist of two separate entities, two streams running on parallel lines one of which occasionally feeds into the other, but which are destined for ever to retain their separate identities?'[43] For legal knowledge engineers, the question can be rephrased: can statute law-statements and provisional case law-statements be represented within one legal knowledge base or are two bases required? It is submitted that one knowledge base will suffice. When lawyers engage in legal reasoning, it is undeniable that they recognize there to be distinct 'sources of law', but that very phrase is significant, for it implies there is a unity, law; something that the various sources have in common. Lawyers cast law-formulations into one coherent body of knowledge, albeit drawn from sources that they acknowledge, in their written pleading and oral argumentation, to be diverse. And when reasoning they seem to presuppose, in conformity with a suggestion of Atiyah, that

---

[43] 'Common Law and Statute Law' (1985), p. 1.

'the law does indeed seem to be a seamless web, a huge network of interrelated rules of common law or case law, and of statute'.[44] It is such a network, in part, that may constitute a legal knowledge base, and from it may be drawn, as a human expert might draw from his repository of legal knowledge, all manner of legal conclusions (questions of superiority or ranking of diverse sources being governed by legal meta-rules, as I show in Section 3.7).

3.4 LEGAL HEURISTICS

AI scientists are agreed that expert systems in any domain, in order that they may perform at the level of human experts, must be designed to reason with heuristic knowledge, as well as with the more formal knowledge of the field in question.[45] Underlying this recommendation for the inclusion of heuristics within expert systems is an assumption pertaining to human decision-making by experts, namely, that expert performance in problem-solving by natural persons requires the application not just of the extensive domain-specific knowledge that is held in, say, relevant standard reference sources, but also of the unpublished, experiential, informal, judgmental, and often procedural, rules of thumb that are now commonly referred to as heuristics.[46] When a human expert is confronted with a problem for which he knows no clearly applicable decision procedure, or for which existing procedures are excessively cumbersome, invariably (according to this prevailing decision theory) he has recourse to his store of heuristic knowledge. In this way, incorrect or insufficient information can be handled, informed conjectures can be made, and optimum strategies can be adopted: in short, difficult problems can be solved.

This plausible hypothesis of descriptive psychology has been

---

[44] Ibid., p. 3. Atiyah discusses the many ways in which statutes and cases can interrelate. '[J]udicial exegesis' (pp. 2–3) is particularly important for our purposes, for the form and content of the statute given judicial consideration may well determine the formulation of case law-statements that we deploy.

[45] See, e.g. *PRBES*, p. 1, *BES*, pp. 4, 68–70, *AINM*, pp. 347–53, *IS*, ch. 3, *CC*, pp. 107–9, and Barr and Feigenbaum, *The Handbook of Artificial Intelligence*, vol. 1 (1981), pp. 58–63.

[46] The term 'heuristic' seems to have been introduced to AI by Newell and Simon who themselves borrowed it from Polya. For details on this, see McCorduck, *Machines Who Think* (1979), p. 211.

corroborated in many non-legal domains by those who have undertaken sustained and successful attempts at knowledge acquistion
(see Section 1.2). However, it has less explanatory force in a legal
context. For, as I argued in Section 2.3, heuristic legal knowledge
can often be found in published form, and, moreover, as I hinted in
Section 2.5, it is arguable that legal expertise may, in certain circumstances, be constituted solely by extensive knowledge of the primary
sources alone. Of course, this is not to deny that legal problem-
solving at the level of human experts does indeed often depend on
the deployment of legal heuristics. It simply reminds us once more
that legal problem-solving differs from problem-solving in non-legal
domains. Clearly, then, a crucial task in a jurisprudential inquiry
into expert systems in law, is that of describing, analysing, and clarifying the nature of at least some legal heuristics. That is the purpose
of much of the remainder of this chapter. But before examining
heuristic legal knowledge in detail, it is interesting to note two
sources of evidence, from our legal literature, which suggest that the
prevailing AI theory of decision-making noted above is indeed
applicable to the process of legal reasoning, and, therefore, to building expert systems in law.

First, we should take note of those regular utterances by legal
practitioners alleging that academic legal knowledge (as I characterized that notion in Section 2.5) is not of itself sufficient basis for the
execution of many of the demands of legal practice. Such knowledge, that argument runs, must be complemented with experiential
legal knowledge (Section 2.5) if the successful daily administration
of the law is to result. Lord Denning has also expressed this view:
'The reading of books in libraries—or the attending of lectures by
professors—gives you only a blurred and incomplete picture. In
order to understand what the law is all about, you must see it working in practice.'[47] The second piece of evidence that suggests academic legal knowledge is insufficient for legal problem-solving can
be drawn from our jurisprudential sources: in the writings of the
American Legal Realists, and in works of sociological jurisprudence.
If there is a central theme to American Realism at all, it is that judges
do not come to their decisions solely on the basis of law-statements.
One group of realists—'rule skeptics', according to Jerome Frank
and now to common jurisprudential usage—alleged that those puta-

[47] *The Family Story* (1981), p. 93.

tive legal rules articulated in judicial decisions, that is, those 'paper rules', 'pseudo rules', 'accepted rules', or 'verbally formulated rules' were of no use in assisting the lawyer in the important job (which we acknowledged in Section 3.5) of predicting judicial decisions. For that task, they argued, it was necessary to divine the 'real rules' or 'latent rules' which they maintained were discoverable from patterns in judicial behaviour.[48] The arch rule sceptic, Llewellyn, in fact suggested that these real rules would be more suitably designated 'the practices of the courts',[49] for he maintained that the law was 'what... officials do about disputes'.[50] Although the rule sceptics have been criticized widely and convincingly, when their (often intentionally) extravagant claims are stripped of their excess, and confined to hard cases (see Section 6.7), one residual thesis is now generally espoused by theorists and practitioners alike. That thesis is that in advising clients on difficult questions of law, lawyers must look beyond law-statements, and seek to predict court decisions. When this is done regularly, general trends emerge and informal rules encapsulating these regularities are deployed (often subconsciously, no doubt). In some writings of sociological jurisprudence, we also find suggestions that there is more to the phenomenon of law than the law laid out in paper and print. Pound, for instance, alerted us to the difference between the 'law in books' and the 'law in action',[51] while Ehrlich claimed that a 'juristic science of law' (legal science) must not only detail the 'norms for decision' (law-statements) but also the 'living law'—the social rules that are actually followed by citizens in society.[52] Only on the basis of knowledge of the living law, it has been argued, can informed judgments about current practices and likely enforcement of laws be made. A contemporary analytical jurisprudent, Harris, has reaffirmed the importance for legal scientists of acknowledging social phenomena and social rules beyond law-statements (but has questioned their status as law).[53]

---

[48] See Frank, *Courts on Trial* (1949), p. 73, and Twining, *Karl Llewellyn and the Realist Movement* (1973), Appendix B.

[49] *Jurisprudence: Realism in Theory and Practice* (1962), p. 21. Llewellyn's discussions of 'craft'—the know-how of judges and advocates—is relevant in relation to legal heuristics.

[50] *The Bramble Bush: Our Law and its Study* (1969), p. 12.

[51] 'Law in Books and Law in Action' (1910).

[52] *Fundamental Principles of the Sociology of Law* (1975).

[53] *LLS*, pp. 122–4, ch. 6; *LP*, pp. 241–2.

Both from practitioners and theorists, then, we are left with the impression that effective legal problem-solving presupposes knowledge about the law which extends beyond law-statements, and that experience in legal practice furnishes lawyers with this increased ability to solve legal problems. This in itself is not entirely inconsistent with what was suggested in the analysis of academic and experiential knowledge in Section 2.5. Where the analyses diverge, of course, is over the question of whether experiential knowledge can be found in printed materials. I suggested there to be an overlap between academic and experiential knowledge claiming thereby, and adducing evidence in support, that some of the latter does appear in paper and print. (Moreover, I said that such knowledge as does not so appear is either better suited for inclusion in legal decision support systems (non-heuristic procedural knowledge), or may often be input during the 'tuning' process.) To refuse *a priori* to accept that legal heuristics can be and are sometimes clearly written down is to commit a combination of three fallacies that Twining identifies: 'The Pickitup Fallacy: that the Lessons of Experience are Ineffable and no lessons worth learning can be learned from books'; 'The Unbridgeable Gap Fallacy: it is either impossible or undesirable to narrow the gap between the Law in Action and the Law in Books'; and 'The Law is Law is Law Fallacy (alias Gertrude Stein's Law: any book which includes discussion of a subject-matter other than legal doctrine is Not a Law Book)'![54]

In any event, leaving now the matter of whence the heuristics can be derived, I shall now claim that human legal experts have predictive, derivative, and meta-, legal knowledge, and so too should expert systems in law.

3.5 STATUTE LAW-PREDICTIONS AND CASE LAW-PREDICTIONS

Statute law-statements and case law-statements can be regarded as the *formal* knowledge of the legal domain. They are the non-probabilistic statements of the law: with which we can reason with confidence; of which we have certainty in their truth (within the universe of legal discourse); and whose application by the courts where relevant, we can scarcely doubt. Cast as conditional statements (see Section 4.4) they are of deterministic structure, that is, if

[54] 'Treatises and Textbooks: A Reply to T. B. Smith' (1972–3), p. 274.

their antecedents are satisfied, then their consequents necessarily hold.

The job of the human legal expert, however, may not necessarily be complete once he has indicated to his client or instructing solicitor the apparent legal conclusions that may be reached given his knowledge of statute and case law-statements and a particular set of facts. For any lawyer who offers legal advice—and, therefore, it may be inferred, any expert system in law—is expected, in certain circumstances, to supplement his legal conclusion with some kind of prediction of the court's likely reaction to the facts of any case in the event that litigation ensues. In other words, the advice of the legal expert and the expert system often extends beyond that of pure description of statute law and interpretation of case law to the findings of a predictive legal science. It is significant that consensus in the jurisprudential literature reveals much support for the widespread practice of prediction of the courts by legal advisers. And it should be stressed that it has not just been the American Legal Realists who have emphasized the role of prediction in legal reasoning.[55] Kelsen, for instance, also said that 'the prediction of a future court decision might be considered part of the business of a practical lawyer counseling his client'[56] (although such advice on the Kelsenian analysis would not be within the province of a piece of legal science). Moreover, contemporary jurisprudents such as Summers,[57] Hart,[58]

[55] Holmes wrote: 'The prophecies of what the courts will do in fact, and nothing more pretentious, are what I mean by law ... The object of our study, [Law] then, is prediction, the prediction of the incidence of the public force through the instrumentality of the courts' ('The Path of the Law' (1920), pp. 167 and 173). The realists portrayed lawyers as agents who predict judicial decisions in their quest for legal conclusions, while they regarded judges as those who make instrumental predictions about the effectiveness of rules for society. Also see Frank, *Courts on Trial* (1949), p. 26, and Twining, *Karl Llewellyn and the Realist Movement* (1973), Part I.

[56] *PTL*, p. 89. Cf. *GTLS*, pp. 167–8.

[57] 'Logic in the Law' (1963)—'the reasoning of lawyers who advise clients ... Their job *is* often one of prediction' (original emphasis) p. 256.

[58] Hart did suggest in 1959 that 'where rules are vague, all we can do is to predict what judges will say' (*EJP*, p. 168), and again in 1961 that 'predictions of judicial decisions have undeniably an important place in the law' for '[w]hen the area of open texture is reached, very often all we can profitably offer in answer to the question: "What is the law on this matter?" is a guarded prediction of what the courts will do' (*CL*, p. 143). Of course, he is also renowned for being critical of Llewellyn's suggestion that 'rules are important so far as they help you to predict what judges will do' (*CL*, p. 135, and generally, pp. 135–7). Yet as MacCormick has noted 'Hart and others ignored the caveats and qualifications he [Llewellyn] issued in respect of this statement'. See *HLAH*, p. 174.

MacCormick,[59] and Harris[60] have acknowledged the importance for lawyers of predicting judicial decisions. If human legal experts do as a matter of fact make predictions of court decisions, and, moreover, this practice is welcomed by legal theorists, clients, and instructing solicitors alike, then consonant with the conception of expert systems presented in this book, it is desirable that they too reason with such predictive knowledge, or else they will fail to exhibit expert performance. Predictions of law-statements can be of two types. First, if the statement in question is one of a rule that is addressed to the court itself, then the prediction is that of the likelihood of the court *adopting* the rule as one it should follow. Second, where the statement is not of such a law addressed to the court, then the prediction is that of the likelihood of the court *applying* that rule in its reasoning processes, or at least in its justification of its decision. (Note that although I confine my attention here to prediction of judicial decisions, prediction of the determinations of other officials—such as Inland Revenue inspectors—is often also of great importance.)

In relation to statute law, then, we should, where appropriate, supplement the statute law-statements with *statute law-predictions*: predictions of the probability of a statute law-statement being adopted or applied by the courts. Sometimes this will be necessary when, as Hart has said, the rules are vague.[61] More generally, however, it will be needed when the statute law-statements themselves offer no predictive guidance.[62] It is often the case that a statute law-statement when cast in the form of a conditional statement will only indicate that a particular subject (in our example the court) is, say, obligated or empowered to behave in a certain way. These deontic or normative modalities, however, are not probabilistic, and thus do not guide us regarding the likelihood of adoption or application of the rule in question. Rather they relate to obligation and permission and simply assert the existence of an obligation, or

---

[59] MacCormick, in speaking of the American Realists, has said that '[w]hen, like Oliver Wendell Holmes, they stressed the practising lawyer's need to be able to predict for his client the likely outcome of some case or another, they spoke truly' (*HLAH*, p. 124).

[60] Harris repeatedly notes the utility of predictive information about the law. See *LLS*, pp. 50–1, 82, 123, and 134.

[61] *EJP*, p. 168.

[62] Cf. MacCormick's remark that the American Realists expressed a 'truth when they noted that "black letter rules" are rarely on their own sufficient ground for successful prediction' of 'the likely outcome of some case' (*HLAH*, p. 124).

the conferring of a power.   In order that the descriptive statute law-statement might be of greater informative content, we can supplement it with a probabilistic statute law-prediction indicating the certainty factor (on a scale of 0–1) thus:

> *If* it is established that the marriage has broken down irretrievably, *then* it is probable that the court will grant decree of divorce (0.98).

In other words, it is extremely unlikely that the court will not grant decree if the court holds there to be irretrievable breakdown of marriage.   In another example, where a rule whose consequent describes a duty upon the court to do θ, and the prediction indicates a certainty factor of almost 1 (also on a scale of 0–1) then it provides less surprising information than if it had been a very low factor.   In the latter event, the prediction might reflect, say, borrowing an example of Harris, that 'a newly enacted legal rule would never be applied in practice', in which event, as Harris notes, such information would indeed be useful[63] (and such information would be put into the proposed *rationale* sub-slot: see Section 4.4).

I turn now to *case law-predictions*. Although (provisional) case law-statements, as I suggested in the previous section, are interpretations of case reports, nevertheless they can be treated like statute law-statements, as definitive statements of part of the law. Case law-predictions may be made in two sets of circumstances. First, when it is not possible to formulate a case law-statement in the way I have suggested—that is, in one of those relatively rare instances when a *ratio decidendi* cannot be determined without contention—then a prediction of the court's likely interpretation (and, therefore, adoption or application) must be made. Second, if a provisional case law-statement can be made, it may still be desirable, as I said it was in respect of statute law-statements, to supplement the rendition of the indisputable *ratio* with a probabilistic case law-prediction. This may be appropriate, for example, when it is known what the *ratio* is but it is suspected, perhaps in light of a dissenting judgment or of *obiter dicta*, that the case will not be followed in the future.[64] All case law-predictions, like statute law-predictions, have certainty factors.

The certainty factor of a law-prediction can be estimated or calcu-

---

[63] *LLS*, p. 123.
[64] Such suspicion may come to light from the secondary sources or during tuning sessions.

lated in many ways, and the vast body of literature on prediction of judicial decisions using jurimetric or computational methods might be thought to be relevant here.[65] Yet, as Tapper has shown, many of these methods are open to serious criticism,[66] and we may justifiably question their utility for legal knowledge engineering. It is possible, however, that predictive legal knowledge might, in the tradition of AI, be acquired more effectively from extensive consultation with human legal experts who have great experience of the statute or case law in question,[67] rather than through the application of statistical or jurimetric techniques. Viewed in this way predictive knowledge of the law may be regarded as a form of heuristic knowledge. In any event, it is not my purpose to recommend a particular method of establishing certainty factors, but to stress that expert legal problem-solving often seems to be contingent on the application of statute and case law-predictions, and as such these entities are strong candidates for inclusion in any legal knowledge base.

3.6 STATUTE LAW-DERIVATIONS, CASE LAW-DERIVATIONS, CASE LAW-GENERALIZATIONS

It is possible to imagine an expert system whose knowledge base consists solely of statute and case law-statements. If such a system interfaced with the user in the way recommended in Section 2.7, then it is probable that the questions it would ask would be based on these statements' antecedents, as that is how most contemporary expert systems function. The system might inquire 'Has the marriage broken down irretrievably?', a positive response to which by the user would result in the system asserting that 'The Court may grant decree of divorce'. And, on request, the system would supply the user with the citation of the legal authority that licensed the inference drawn. The number of askable questions, it is clear, would be limited by the number of statements in the knowledge base. Unless the user understood the terms of the statements that are presented during

---

[65] See Tapper, *CATL*, ch. 9, Lawlor, 'Computer Analysis of Judicial Decisions' (1980), and *IJ*, pp. 705–9.

[66] *CATL*, pp. 249–51.

[67] The methods for calculating weights established for SARA (Section 1.5) may be relevant here.

any dialogue, such a system would be virtually useless. Yet a system that contains only law-statements might suffer from just that defect. As noted in Sections 3.2 and 3.3, both statute and case law-statements are invariably cast in very general terms, applying to broad classes of subjects, events, acts, situations, and so forth, in consequence of which any questions generated from a knowledge base constituted by law-statements alone will be posed in correspondingly general language. Such general questions, of course, may be unintelligible to the user, for he may, for example, have no idea what it means for a marriage to have broken down irretrievably, and will, therefore, be unable to *subsume* the particular facts of the instant case under the more general rule, the antecedent of which constitutes the basis of the question just asked. (On subsumption and classification of facts, see Section 5.5.)

With the kind of system I recommend, it is desirable that the user is able to command the system to render any question less abstract, that is, in more concrete or particular (and less general) terms, by the presentation of further questions. This is possible only to the extent that further law-statements are represented, and problems arise when even the most specific law-statements are beyond the comprehension of the user. In other words, difficulties can arise both from the fact that statute law, and, therefore, any statute law-statement, is couched in very general and often not particularly illuminating terms, and also from interpretative legal scientists' tendency to couch case law-statements in similarly broad language. There are, then, serious limitations in having a legal knowledge base composed only of law-statements, for its knowledge is in one sense too abstract and superficial to be useful: the range of askable questions is unacceptably restricted in terms of their complexity and ultimate utility. To avoid this eventuality, I suggest supplementing law-statements, with what can be called *law-derivations*.

Law-derivations, as the name suggests, are neither descriptive statements of statute law, nor are they provisional interpretations of case law, but rather are derivations from statute or case law-statements, arrived at through the application of the techniques of derivative legal science. As such, although they can be derivatively associated with some formal legal source, no legal authority is available which of itself is capable of supporting such a proposition at its specific level of generality, without further explanation. The concept of law-derivations can best be understood through examples, and I shall deal first with statute law-derivations, and then, in far less detail, with case law-derivations.

In countless legal textbooks, many statements that are written as if they are purely descriptive of statutes are, more accurately, propositions that have been derived by the legal scientist from statutes and do not themselves actually appear at the same level of generality or in the same terminology, as any statute law-formulation. These statute law-derivations can be made in different circumstances. For instance, let us imagine, borrowing a classical jurisprudential scenario, that Section 1 of a statute (and a corresponding descriptive statute law-statement), reads: 'If a person takes a stolen vehicle across State lines, then he shall be guilty of...'.[68] We can envisage all sorts of possible derivations from this (assuming that the term vehicle is given no further statutory definition). A writer might allege there to be a statute law-statement to the effect: 'If a person takes a stolen motor-cycle across State lines, then he shall be guilty of...', or he might suggest that 'If a person takes a stolen Sinclair C5 across State lines, then it is likely that he shall be guilty of...'. Neither of these statements are statute law-statements; both are statute law-derivations, and if these were represented in a legal knowledge base, this would be reflected in the system's transparency. In an interaction with a system in this domain, the user might be asked if any person had taken a stolen vehicle across State lines, and might, because he was unsure of what constitutes a vehicle for the purposes of the law in question, request more information (in the form of further questions) about vehicles. If he answered positively to a resultant question that asked if a motorcycle had been taken across State lines, then the system would conclude that that person is guilty. Yet in response to a further request for the legal authority supporting such a conclusion, the system ought not to cite 'Section 1 of...' but ought to explain that the rule which sanctioned the inference was derived from Section 1, and, further, the system ought to present that rule for the user himself to evaluate. There is no such statute law-formulation at the same level of generality that employs similar terminology corresponding to our writer's first statement and so an explicit explanatory connection between the statement and the derivation is needed. In Section 4.4, I refer to such a connection as the *rationale* of a derivation. The other proposition of our writer, regarding the C5, is more obviously a derivation as it is phrased probabilistically in a way that no statute law-statement ever would be. Strictly speaking, all derivations should have a certainty factor, although as in our first example, the derivation might seem so self-evident as to render it superfluous, that is, on a scale of 0–1, of value 1.

All derivations, then, are predictions of a sort; but not all predictions are derivations. For example, statute law-predictions and statute law-derivations, as I have defined them, are not the same type of entity. The former are predictions of the likelihood of certain statute law-statements—that themselves are the result of the processes of descriptive legal science and whose status as accurate representations of the law can hardly be doubted—being adopted or applied by judges as guiding standards or as justifications for their decisions. The latter, however, are predictions of the likelihood of *derivations* being so adopted or applied, but these derivations have not been formulated as statements of descriptive legal science, cannot be affirmed as authoritative and binding representations, but are entities that have been derived through the operation of derivative legal science. By and large, the certainty factors of (non-derivative) law-predictions will be greater than those of law-derivations, as is intuitively obvious.

Statute law-derivations might also be made when past judicial decisions, made under previous but repealed legislation, or decisions from other jurisdictions, provide the basis for rules whose conditions might now be regarded as derivable from current statute law-statements. We might cite these past cases within our explanation of the rationale of the derivation but not as authority for the proposition itself. For instance, the facts of cases relating to behaviour that constituted 'cruelty' for the purposes of the now repealed *Divorce (Scotland) Act 1938*, or constitute 'intolerable behaviour' under the English *Matrimonial Causes Act 1973*, may provide the basis for the antecedents of statute law-derivations pertaining to the behaviour ground under the *Divorce (Scotland) Act 1976*.

Note that statute law-derivations should be distinguished from statements that on the face of it seem to be derived from statutes, but are in truth themselves statute law-statements or case law-statements from different sources and at different levels of generality. For example, although a rule relating to adultery might appear to be a derivation from the statute, it might well be a case law-statement.

This of course will be verifiable during any consultation through the system's transparency facility.

What is the relationship between statute law-statements and statute law-derivations? Harris argues in this respect that 'a derivative legal rule is related to a positive legal rule by a practical deduction' where the former corrsponds to my law-derivation, and the latter to my law-statement.[69] Unfortunately he does not articulate any theory of practical deduction that can assist us here. Kelsen too is unhelpful in this context when, in discussing 'static' systems of norms, he says that 'all the particular norms of such a system are obtainable by means of an intellectual operation, viz., by the inference from the general to the particular', and as an example suggests that 'from the norm "You shall love your neighbour" one may *deduce* such norms as . . . "You shall help him in need"'.[70] It is not at all obvious either in what this intellectual operation consists, nor how his particular deduction regarding neighbours was made. In any event, it is perhaps best to avoid using terms such as 'deduction', and indeed not to regard the process of making derivations as in any sense a formal one, for completeness would then require us to develop an account of the underlying logical, semantic, and linguistic theories in accordance with which such usage and practice could be sustained.[71] It would be less contentious to understand by derivation the informal (often analogical) activity whereby legal scientists and legal experts formulate certain specific rules on the basis of more general rules; doing so in accordance both with our generally acknowledged uses of legal and ordinary language, and with their knowledge and experience of the law. Not only would this conception of derivation be less contentious, but it would also accord with the expert systems ethos, in that the knowledge represented would not be based solely on formal legal knowledge and all that that logically entails. For heuristic rules would also be included. Note that the derivative legal scientists' job of deriving rules, on this analysis, is not dissimilar to the legal reasoning agent's activity of subsuming particular facts under more general rules, and I shall return to this latter topic, and so clarify the former, in Section 5.5.

A further example of a statute law-derivation may clarify the

---

[69] *LLS*, p. 90.

[70] *GTLS*, p. 112. Emphasis added. Cf. Raz, *AL*, p. 147.

[71] But see *LLS*, p. 10, for Harris's use of the terms 'logic' and 'deductive'. Cf. Section 5.1, below.

above analysis. The statute law-formulation contained in s.1(2)(b) (together with s.1(2) itself) of the *Divorce (Scotland) Act 1976* reads as follows:

The irretrievable breakdown of a marriage shall, [subject to the following provisions of this Act,] be taken to be established [in an action for divorce] if [since the date of the marriage] the defender has [at any time] behaved [(whether or not as a result of mental abnormality and whether such behaviour has been active or passive)] in such a way that the pursuer cannot reasonably be expected to cohabit with the defender.

Again the text in square brackets is ignored in casting the above as a descriptive statute law-statement:

> *If* the defender has behaved in such a way that the pursuer cannot reasonably be expected to cohabit with the defender, *then* the irretrievable breakdown of marriage shall be taken to be established.

(Note that this statute law-statement itself clarifies the notion of irretrievable breakdown.) In Clive's commentary on the Act he offers some examples which 'may indicate some of the types of behaviour which *may*, depending on the court's assessment of the whole case before it, be such that the pursuer cannot reasonably be expected to cohabit with the defender'.[72] These are instances of statute law-derivations. For example, he suggests 'physical violence to the pursuer, including attempted and threatened violence'. This proposition has been derived from the Act. Based on his knowledge and understanding of the legal meanings and ordinary uses of the notions of 'reasonable', 'behaviour', and 'expected' that appear in the Act, together with his extensive knowledge and experience of Scots law, Clive has derived a more specific condition of application than the one that can be described through any statute law-statement. It is not itself a description but is rather a prediction of a rule that would be used by the courts and of which any reasoning agent ought to be aware. It might be expressed thus:

> *If* the defender has exerted physical violence *or* attempted to exert physical violence *or* has threatened to exert physical violence on the pursuer, *then* it is possible that the irretrievable breakdown of marriage will be taken to be established. (0.8)

The certainty factor, which from the tenor of Clive's discussion I

---

[72] *DA*, p. 13. Original emphasis.

have estimated *very* approximately on a scale of 0–1, indicates the likelihood of the court establishing irretrievable breakdown given that the defender has behaved in a way stipulated in the antecedent of the rule. Ideally, the factor should be adjusted by an expert during the 'tuning' process, based on his estimation of the possibility of irretrievable breakdown being taken to be established in these circumstances. And if the disjuncts differ in likelihood of application, then they should be represented as distinct rules (see Section 4.4). It is important to note that this kind of derivative knowledge can be found in secondary sources. (The remarks at the end of the previous section regarding calculation of the certainty factor are applicable to law-derivations as well.)

The above analysis applies, *mutatis mutandis*, to the derivation of *case law-derivations* from case law-statements. Although it may seem peculiar deriving from a statement that is itself provisional, it must be recalled that the provisional element of case law-statements is, for all practical purposes, negligible. Human legal experts, *qua* interpretative legal scientists, I argued in Section 3.3, formulate provisional case law-statements and manipulate them as though they are indeed of a fixed and determinate form akin to statute law-statements. They cast these case law-statements in general language, and it is therefore meaningful to talk of deriving entities from them. For instance, as I said, one *ratio* that might be taken from *Donoghue* v. *Stevenson* could be based directly on the words used by Lord Atkin regarding manufacturers of products and consumers (p. 599), and derivations from that might itemize conjectured categories of products or potentially liable persons expected to be held to be within the ambit of that case law-statement. If the account of case law-statements of Section 3.3 is accepted, then there is no obstacle to accommodating the notion of case law-derivations.

The idea of law-derivations, however, may seem radically counter-intuitive. This is probably so because we often conceive of legal reasoning as involving the classification of the facts of the instant case in fairly general terms (stripped of the case's irrelevant idiosyncrasies), and then the subsumption of that classification within the terms of one or more legal rules. That is what might be termed a 'bottom up' theory, in that facts are generalized to coincide with the level of generality of rules. In marked contrast, but unobjectionably so, reasoning with law-derivations, in a sense, presupposes a 'top down' theory: in advance of particular problems, the rules are broken down into more particularized entities, in order that the complexity of the process of classification is minimized (and indeed is partially computer-assisted). This simply constitutes a different perspective on the conventional wisdom. I will return to this matter in Section 5.5.

Case law-statements also yield another possibility, that of *case law-generalizations*.[73] Although I have said that it is usually a relatively straightforward task to determine the *ratio* or *rationes* of any particular case, I did also acknowledge that they might well be extended through time. At any particular moment, then, while a particular *ratio* is generally accepted by the cognoscenti, it is always open to the legal scientist to hazard a guess at how that *ratio* might indeed be developed. He would do so by formulating a case law-generalization: an extension or generalization of the *ratio* whose certainty factor would, according to my theory, be less than that of the case law-statement (if it had one), or else the extension itself would be the *ratio*. For example, as I noted, it might have been thought at one time that the *ratio* of *Donoghue* v. *Stevenson* concerned manufacturers of food and drink only and consumers of same, and a case law-statement to that effect might well have been adopted. At that stage, however, a legal scientist could have generalized that case law-statement and formulated a case law-generalization in terms of Lord Atkin's *dictum*. Again such an entity would be predictive, probabilistic, and heuristic in nature and may be validated later by the court widening a precedent (as is not infrequently done).[74] The intellectual process of judicial widening of precedents, therefore, is akin to that of generalization by legal scientists.

In contrast to the generalizability of case law-statements, it is unlikely that statute law-statements could be generalized by legal scientists, because, as I said in Section 3.2, we normally assume that the terms of any statute constitute the upper limit of generality, and we would not expect the court to extend or develop statutory provisions.

In conclusion, statute law-derivations, case law-derivations, and case law-generalizations may serve in expert systems in law as useful supplements to law-statements, in that they will increase the number

---

[73] These are not the same as Harris's 'generalised legal rules' (*LLS*, p. 92), as Harris has in mind a rule that expresses the combined effect of several rules, whereas I am referring to a generalization of one rule.

[74] On widening rules, see Hart, *CL*, p. 131.

of askable questions, and will provide greater knowledge about the likely range of application of statutes and judicial precedents than law-statements do. They are probabilistic in nature and their certainty factors may be drawn from secondary sources or from human experts. They are, therefore, as I have said, another form of legal heuristic.

3.7 LEGAL META-KNOWLEDGE

The entities considered so far in this chapter constitute what might be termed the first-order knowledge of law: statements, interpretations, predictions, and derivations of the contents of momentary legal systems (see Section 4.5). Involvement in actually constructing an expert system in law reveals—as it has revealed in many other domains—that some of the knowledge that a human expert brings to bear in solving problems is not first-order knowledge directly about the field of law at hand, but is, more precisely, knowledge of a second-order nature, that is, knowledge about knowledge.[75] In law, this can be called *legal meta-knowledge*. Few current expert systems in any domain reason with meta-knowledge, but many leading expert systems researchers firmly believe such knowledge will be central to successful systems of the future.[76] Most of the AI writings on meta-knowledge, however, are fairly speculative and several questions remain unanswered. For instance, there seems to be disagreement over whether meta-knowledge should be represented together with the first-order domain knowledge or in a separate meta-level knowledge base.[77]

In law, there do not seem to have been any serious attempts to include legal meta-knowledge in the current systems, nor indeed have there been any efforts to characterize the notion itself. In this section, I endeavour to remedy this latter defect. It is clear that Part Two of this book, being a jurisprudential—a second order—inquiry into legal knowledge representation, is itself a body of legal meta-knowledge: knowledge about legal knowledge. And systems designed on the basis of this book will (implicitly or explicitly) have such meta-knowledge. That this is desirable was argued in Chapter 1.

---

[75] On meta-knowledge generally, see *BES*, pp. 219–38, and *AGES*, pp. 28–30.

[76] See e.g. *AGES*, p. 29.

[77] Compare *BES*, p. 221, with Goodall, *The Guide to Expert Systems* (1985), p. 101.

However, in this section, my concern is more specifically with *legal meta-rules*, which can be taken to be those rules that prescribe the way in which the other rules (entities) I have mentioned so far are to be used in problem-solving. This accords both with AI usage and with a definition of 'meta-norms' offered by Bing and Harvold in the context of their account of legal database systems in law: 'The term "meta-norm" is . . . used for *all* norms governing a legal decision process. Meta-norms will consequently define or determine the outline of the legal decision process.'[78]

The utility of including legal meta-rules in expert systems in law may become even clearer in the discussion of legal knowledge utilization in Chapter 6: for now, it is sufficient to point out that their deployment results in increased efficiency in manipulation of the contents of the knowledge base during consultations, a reduction in computing resources, and speedier, more skilled, and legally informed, problem-solving performance.

Our legal literature reveals two kinds of legal meta-rule, which may be termed *domain-independent* and *domain-specific* legal meta-rules. I shall look at each in turn. Domain-independent legal meta-rules are those rules that stipulate how and when the rules represented are to be used by the system, no matter what legal domain is in question. Law-statements themselves can be domain-independent legal meta-rules. Statute law-statements describing the *Interpretation Act 1978*, for instance, in assigning meanings to various words often found in statutory source materials, are meta-rules applicable in any legal domain. So too are case law-statements that interpret the common law relating to the construction of statutes. Such *meta-law-statements* might be suitable for inclusion in expert systems of the future. (Note that these same meta-law-statements will probably also be used, in conjunction with other principles of descriptive legal science, in the process of describing and representing statute law in the knowledge base itself.) There are other case law-statements that are also meta-rules peculiar to no particular domain: these are the statements of those rules that pertain to the principle of *stare decisis*. Central to the operation of that principle is the position (in the systematic hierarchy of the courts) of the court which decided the precedent case in relation to the court that is to decide the instant case: for it is on the basis of that relationship that

---

[78] *LDIS*, p. 19. Original emphasis. Also see pp. 35–6.

a precedent can be deemed as binding, or persuasive, or capable of being adopted or, finally, capable of being ignored. The questions of the hierarchical relationship of courts and the force of a prior case are themselves governed by case law, and statements of these cases might be included in any (meta) legal knowledge base as meta-knowledge. This could be done using the 'rank sub-slot' which is introduced in Section 4.4. Note also that meta-rules governing statutory interpretation and *stare decisis* may also be drawn from jurisprudential writings that treat these topics.

Much of the law of evidence can also be described as meta-law-statements. The rules regarding sufficiency of evidence and corroboration, for instance, or those pertaining to the weight of evidence and its evaluation, can all be seen as domain-independent legal meta-rules.[79] These rules determine the operation of rules in any domain by stipulating when facts, written documents, oral testimony, and so forth, may be taken, for the purposes of litigation, to confirm (or otherwise) alleged acts or events. (Of course, it is conceivable too that an expert system could be developed whose first-order knowledge was that of the law of evidence.) But, as Sheriff Stone has recently said, in his *Proof of Fact in Criminal Trials*, 'The law can only go so far in facilitating the decision about facts. At that point, the natural processes, which are the subject of this book, begin.' For, he claims the aim of his book to be 'to provide a systematic and comprehenisve analysis of how facts are proved in criminal trials'.[80] Further, he asserts that he 'explicitly' offers information 'itself based on court experience in various roles over a period of 35 years', acknowledging that 'most advocates assimilate this kind of practical material over a long period, without analysing it'. (The fact that Stone successfully imparts his heuristic knowledge through his book constitutes still further support for my argument that academic and experiential knowledge overlap—see Sections 2.5 and 3.4.) Throughout his work, Stone seems to acknowledge that the (relatively) domain-independent meta-knowledge of how facts are proved cannot be reduced to a set of deterministic rules, but he emphasizes that the relevant factors can indeed be articulated.[81] In turn, if we chose to cast such information probabilistically, heuristic meta-knowledge would result.

---

[79] Cf. *LDIS*, pp. 18–19.
[80] (1984), p. ix.
[81] Ibid., p. x.

Human legal experts might also provide us with legal domain-independent meta-rules of another sort. For instance, experts might suggest, rather obviously, that they never set about predicting how a court may react to a given legal problem until they have surveyed the formal sources, and drawn conclusions therefrom. (No matter how prosaic or commonplace a rule that experts follow might be, it must be represented explicitly in a legal knowledge base if it is to be followed by an expert system.) If we sought to express this as a rule, it would prescribe that the consequences of the applicable law-statements should be provided by the system (where possible) before the probability of the court's adoption or application of the rule is given on the basis of the law-predictions. If such a rule was generally approved by human experts, then it would not be confined to any particular system but to expert systems in general independently of their domain.

Domain-specific legal meta-rules, in contrast, are those rules that stipulate how and when specific entities within a particular legal domain are to be selected by the system. For instance, in respect of the domain chosen for the Oxford project, it is likely that a pursuer seeking divorce because his/her spouse has had sexual intercourse with another could be successful (assuming all other conditions are satisfied) not only under s.1(2)(a) of the Act which deals specifically with adultery, but also under s.1(2)(b) of the Act which pertains to the defender's behaviour at some stage having been such that the pursuer cannot reasonably be expected to continue cohabiting. Yet Clive points out that 'It would normally, of course, be safer to proceed under s.1(2)(a) as the court under that paragraph is not required, or entitled, to consider whether in spite of the adultery the pursuer can still reasonably be expected to cohabit with the defender.'[82] This is another example of a piece of legal meta-knowledge: it is not a law-statement but is a piece of knowledge about law-statements. From this meta-knowledge a meta-rule might be formulated that describes Clive's comment and would be displayed at that stage in a consultation where the user has supplied such responses that render both the adultery and the behaviour grounds capable of being satisfied. The secondary sources of our law are full of such meta-knowledge, and one of the tasks of the legal knowledge engineer of legal training is to survey and identify these

[82] *DA*, p. 13.

sources from which in turn he must compose domain-specific legal meta-rules.

Four final points about my analysis of legal meta-rules should be emphasized. First, in the above discussion I have given examples of the rough content of such rules, and have not sought to cast them in the form in which they would be represented in a legal knowledge base. In principle, they could be accommodated within the structure introduced in Section 4.4, but their precise representational form must be decided by computer scientists who themselves, it should be repeated, have not yet tackled fully all those problems that meta-knowledge raises for knowledge engineering. My chief goal was to show that those entities I have termed legal meta-rules can indeed be divined. Secondly, it will be seen that all those legal meta-rules that are not meta-law-statements, are, like law-predictions and law-derivations, instances of legal heuristics: they are informal, judgmental, experiential, and procedural rules of thumb (about which I shall again say more in the next section). Thirdly, it will transpire, no doubt, that human legal reasoning agents use meta-knowledge beyond legal meta-rules, but that can only be assessed fully once there has been extensive field work in legal knowledge acquisition. Until then, it is wise, as has been done in this section, to concentrate on legal meta-knowledge as it appears in our legal literature. (One matter in this connection that merits prompt investigation is the ability of human legal experts to solve problems when answers to relevant questions do not fall neatly into my 'yes', 'no', or 'don't know' categories. I have in mind the way in which experts come to conclusions even when they have replied 'maybe', 'possibly', or the like, to queries that have arisen. In so doing they frequently use meta-rules of some sort, and so too will expert systems of the future, but the nature of such meta-knowledge today remains unclear.)

Finally, it is crucial to note that some domain-independent legal meta-rules, legal heuristics, are held in the inference engine as well: for, as I said in Section 1.2, the inference engine contains general problem-solving knowledge. This last point will be explained through examples in Chapter 6.

3.8 CONCLUSION

In this chapter, I have suggested various entities that might usefully be represented in the legal knowledge base of an expert system in law in order that it may function at the level of a human expert: and I argued that the legal knowledge engineer is at once, *inter alia*, a descriptive, interpretative, predictive, and derivative legal scientist. I did not give detailed practical guidance regarding the pursuit of these branches of legal science, but focused rather on analysing, clarifying, and classifying different types of legal knowledge. I sought to lay the foundations upon which legal knowledge engineers might now build, by indicating the entities of which they should take cognisance. It might be objected that no principle of 'exclusion' has been propounded stipulating those entities that emphatically must not be included in any expert system in law. Yet surely we know too little of the way in which experts reason in law for such dogmatic rejection to be justifiable (or non-trivial). Only once we have extensive experience of building expert systems in law (in many domains) will it be feasible usefully to proscribe the inclusion of any entities.[83]

It may now be tentatively assumed that law-predictions, law-derivations, and legal meta-rules are the central examples of legal heuristics. Such terminology is in common with all those writings on AI which assert heuristics to be informal, judgmental, experiential, and often procedural, rules of thumb.[84] For the knowledge I term heuristic legal knowledge, not being descriptive or interpretative of any law-formulations, is most certainly *informal* in nature. I have also shown that law-predictions and law-derivations are *judgmental* in character, that is, they express human predictions of likely judicial behaviour. Moreover, their certainty factors are based on the *experience* of the experts or textbook writers who calculated or enunciated them. Finally, the *procedural* legal heuristics are those meta-rules that indicate efficient, promising, and legally acceptable means of solving legal problems, formulated on the basis of extensive experience and knowledge of the particular legal domain of application.

Of course, human legal experts do possess knowledge beyond law-statements, law-predictions, law-derivations, and legal meta-rules. Clearly they have general knowledge of our world: but this is supplied by the user during consultations with the kind of expert systems I recommend and need not be represented explicitly (see Principle 5 of Section 2.4). Human experts also avail themselves of their non-heuristic procedural knowledge: yet I suggested, in Section

---

[83] On exclusion, see *LLS*, pp. 70–81.
[84] See the references in n. 45 of this chapter.

2.6, that such knowledge should more appropriately be held in legal decision support systems.

It is submitted that the need for the representation in expert systems of heuristic knowledge of human legal experts beyond law-predictions, law-derivations, and legal meta-knowledge can only be assessed in the future once we have a great deal more experience of legal knowledge engineering. I am not claiming, of course, that expert systems in law possessing law-statements, predictive and derivative knowledge, and legal meta-knowledge, all taken from written materials and tuning, can *always* perform at the level of human experts. I conclude Part Three by arguing that such knowledge is sufficient for solving both *clear cases of the expert domain* and *deductive cases*, but insufficient, in many respects, for coping with legal problems beyond these categories. But before I can expand upon this, Winston's second question mentioned in the introduction to this chapter—how should the knowledge be represented?—must be addressed. That is the purpose of the next chapter.

4

Analytical Jurisprudence and Legal Knowledge Representation

IN this chapter, I shall consider how the task of actually representing legal knowledge in an expert system might most effectively be tackled. The proposed model of legal knowledge representation is not intended to be sufficiently rigorous for immediate implementation in a computer system, but is conceived as a coherent jurisprudential model that may serve as a point of departure for computer scientists who seek to build expert systems in law. At the same time, it is intended that many classical jurisprudential problems should be addressed and clarified.

In developing techniques for representing legal knowledge, many general criteria—that hold for expert systems in all domains—must be taken into account. The most important of these are outlined in Section 4.1. In Section 4.2, I explain why the activity of representing legal knowledge is currently a human activity and is beyond the capabilities of computer systems of today. In the three sections that follow, I once again adopt the method of considering what guidance jurisprudence can provide for those interested in specific aspects of legal knowledge engineering. In these sections, I am concerned principally, although not exclusively, with statute and case law-statements. In Section 4.3, in deciding into what units law-formulations might best be divided, the question of the individuation of laws is confronted. This leads me, in Section 4.4, to consider the precise structure that these individuated units might have. The interrelationships of these individuated units of defined structure, and the concept of legal system presupposed by my model, is discussed in Section 4.5, where legal sub-systems are represented as decision trees.

In Section 4.6, I contrast my rule-based method of representing legal knowledge with the more ambitious possibility of a conceptual model of law. Thereafter, I argue in Section 4.7 that a shell for expert

113

systems in law may be developed on the basis of the findings of this book. I conclude, in Section 4.8, by summarizing the steps involved in constructing a legal knowledge base.

4.1 GENERAL CRITERIA FOR KNOWLEDGE REPRESENTATION

Although the nature of legal knowledge differs in many significant respects from that of knowledge of other fields of discourse, there are, nevertheless, many matters pertaining to knowledge representation that are of relevance to all knowledge engineers whatever their chosen domain of application. Most importantly, there are generally accepted, domain-independent, criteria for successful knowledge representation. These must be borne in mind no less by *legal* knowledge engineers, and while my proposed methods of legal knowledge representation are largely inspired by writings on analytical jurisprudence, it must be emphasized that they were also developed in the light of the following general criteria for knowledge representation.

1. A knowledge base should be *flexible*, so that extensions to it will not necessitate major upheaval by way of revision.[1] If a knowledge base is kept extendable, experts will be able to tune it without undue difficulty, and, moreover, the construction of an expert system may then be carried out incrementally. In relation to expert systems in law, flexibility is crucial. For this will allow the legal knowledge engineer, without having to build a new knowledge base, to cope with (a) legislative change, or (b) the overruling or modification of judicial precedents, or (c) the addition to a system of neighbouring legal domains.

2. The knowledge represented should be kept *conceptually simple* and as *concise* as possible, as a result of which flexibility can be more easily achieved and inference engines more efficiently designed.[2] Legal theorists have argued for conceptual simplicity in the representation of the law for centuries,[3] and indeed Raz by that very name includes this notion as part of his first guiding requirement for the individuation of laws.[4]

---

[1] *PRBES*, p. 10.
[2] Ibid.; *AI*, p. 23.
[3] For Bentham's thoughts and writings on this matter, see Hart, 'The Demystification of the Law' (1973).
[4] *CLS*, p. 143. On individuation, see Section 4.3.

3. The knowledge should be represented *explicitly* in order not only that the system may exhibit transparency but also so that the experts who are assisting in the design, in the tuning, of a system may examine the knowledge base while it is being incrementally constructed.[5] If this guideline is not observed, then experts would be unable to determine the contents of the knowledge base, and might, therefore, omit crucial knowledge or input material more than once. If *legal* experts failed to include a crucial part of relevant legal knowledge, the system would then fail to solve certain problems within its domain and would consequently be of limited use.

4. A representation should be *complete* both in the sense that it will accommodate, with no lack of precision, all possible assertions of a domain, and in that its coverage of the chosen domain is sufficient for expert performance.[6] A method of legal knowledge representation that could not be used for all types of legal knowledge within its domain would clearly be unsatisfactory. Moreover, a system that offered superficial coverage of an area of law, as I said in Section 2.4, will fail both to perform at the level of an expert and to offer adequate counsel.

5. A representation should facilitate *knowledge acquisition*, that is, it should be designed so as to minimize those problems associated with extracting expert heuristic knowledge from human experts.[7] While a detailed analysis of legal knowledge acquisition is beyond the scope of this book, as shall be seen from Section 4.7, the proposed methods of legal knowledge representation do offer the foundations upon which might be developed a computer system that assists in acquiring even experiential legal knowledge during the tuning process.

6. A representation should be *computable* by some existing procedure, that is, it should be designed in such a way that it can be included as a collection of data structures within the computer system and so that a reasoning mechanism can operate upon it.[8] Although legal theorists' suggestions in the past regarding legal science are extremely helpful in relation to many aspects of legal knowledge representation, none of these was composed with computer science in

---

[5] *PRBES*, pp. 10–11, *AI*, p. 23.
[6] *PRBES*, pp. 17–18, *AI*, p. 23.
[7] *AI*, p. 23.
[8] *PRBES*, p. 9.

mind, and so invariably fail to accommodate this sixth general criterion. In the following sections, I offer a corrective to this shortcoming through a proposed method of representing legal knowledge that implicitly takes this last and the above criteria into account.

4.2 LEGAL KNOWLEDGE REPRESENTATION AS A HUMAN ACTIVITY

In this section I explain why, at present, the process of analysing primary sources with a view to representing the law in a legal knowledge base must be performed largely by human beings. In clarifying what is beyond the current capabilities of computer systems, we may also sharpen our awareness of those aspects of expert systems in law into which research may now feasibly proceed. (The arguments apply, *mutatis mutandis*, to secondary sources as well.)

The formal sources with which we are concerned—legislation and judicial precedent—are expressed in natural language. This form in which we find our sources is neither sufficiently structured nor formal enough to be fed directly into a knowledge base. Discussions of legal knowledge representation, therefore, focus on the techniques to be adopted in restructuring the law so that it can be represented as data structures within computer memory. For the legal knowledge engineer, the object of the exercise is to recast the law into a predetermined framework. In other words, the process is one of reconstructing law-formulations as specific types of law-statements. At present, this task cannot be performed by a computer as it presupposes an ability to process natural language.

Many workers in the field of AI are indeed currently attempting to program computers so that thay can process, 'understand', natural languages. Early work in this branch of AI concentrated on computer translation from one language to another, but most research is now concerned solely with understanding. This work, of course, is of immense significance for if it is successful (to a greater or lesser extent), then we will be able to interact with computers (to a greater or lesser extent), using the medium with which we are so familiar, as opposed to the high-level computer languages or restricted English to which (at best) we are now confined. However, the AI goal of programming computers to understand (in behavioural terms) natural language as human beings can is generally accepted as a very long-term one, although computers can, at present, cope with some very syntactically constrained English statements.[9] It is not necessary for present purposes to detail the difficulties of natural language processing. It shall suffice to say that it involves complexities not just of syntax, but also of semantics: and in determining the meaning of a sentence, just as human beings bring to bear their general knowledge of the world about them, so computers will have to have embodied within them such general representations of appropriate world matters—a formidable task for knowledge engineering. Until the computational problems of representing vast amounts of common-sense knowledge and the linguistic and psychological problems of how it is that we, as human beings, understand natural language, are both understood considerably better, it is barely conceivable that computers will exhibit thoroughgoing AI in this connection.

If computers can process but limited portions of natural language, then there can be little doubt that the descriptive and interpretative activity of legal knowledge representation—entailing, as it must, the scrutiny, analysis, and eventual recasting of legal sources formulated in natural language—cannot be done by the computer alone. It is simply not possible to represent legal sources as statements of pre-determined structure without a more than rudimentary understanding of natural language. Legal knowledge representation is a process for which we currently know no algorithm: for we know no algorithm for processing natural language, and the latter activity is a necessary constituent of the former.[10] However, if legislation were to be drafted with the aid of the computer, as some have advocated, then it might then be possible for such legal sources themselves to be written in a manner that would permit their subsequent and direct translation into a legal knowledge base.[11] Yet the likelihood of widespread computer-assisted legal drafting today remains remote, and, in any event, would have no bearing on the problem of the *ratio*

---

[9] *AI*, ch. 9, *CC*, pp. 24–6, *AINM*, Part III; Weizenbaum, *Computer Power and Human Reason* (1984), ch. 7.

[10] This, of course, as shall be seen in Chapters 5 and 6, presents a difficulty for the thoroughgoing defender of the notion of deductive legal reasoning. The units of the process of legal reasoning clearly are restructured law-statements, and not unanalysed law-formulations. If there is no algorithm (although one might be discovered) for the translation of law-formulations into law-statements, then this suggests that at least one aspect of the process of legal reasoning may not be deductive. The defender, as I shall argue, might retort: in so far as the basic constituents of the reasoning process are law-statements, legal reasoning can be deductive.

[11] See e.g. Kowalski, 'Logic for Knowledge Representation' (1985), p. 6, and Allen, 'Normalized Legal Drafting and the Query Method' (1978).

decidendi which itself involves interpreting case law-formulations as case law-statements. This, too, cannot currently be computerized.[12] In conclusion, although computers might be programmed in some ways to assist in legal knowledge representation, their limited ability to process natural language renders this aspect of legal knowledge engineering a substantially human activity.

4.3 PRINCIPLES OF INDIVIDUATION FOR LEGAL KNOWLEDGE ENGINEERS

I now turn in detail to the question of how we may represent legal knowledge, and the bulk of the discussion in this section will focus on the question of representing primary sources of law. Facing the legal knowledge engineer most patently in this connection is the choice to be made between diverging methods of dividing up and re-structuring the law. For, as Harris has noted:

The law does not announce, on its face, into what units it can most usefully be split up. There is no *given* structure. We may dip into the well of legislative source-materials with conceptually-shaped buckets of many kinds, and we will then bring up rules, standards, laws of any favoured pattern. One of the tasks of legal theory is to give reasons for preferring one bucket-shape to others.[13]

Harris introduces two problems here: those that are discussed by legal theorists under the headings of *individuation* and *structure*. No sharp division between these two notions can be found in the juris-prudential literature, although in the writings of Bentham and Raz distinctions are implicitly assumed, if not explicitly defended. Raz, indeed, goes further than Bentham by stipulating that the problem of structure is not 'identical' with the problem of individuation but that the former is an aspect of the latter.[14] He then even offers an illustration of statements that have the same structure but that are probably not all individuated. Yet he does not seek to identify the

---

[12] It might be that the problem of the *ratio* is closely related to the difficulty of processing natural language; for the success of any attempt to lay down a simple set of rules for the interpretation of judicial decisions may depend on and presuppose an account of how we understand the natural language in which judgments are written.

[13] *LLS*, p. 92. Original emphasis.

[14] *CLS*, p. 73.

precise differences between the problems of structure and individuation. In this and the following section, I adopt a rough distinction between these concepts that is sufficient for present purposes and indeed accords with, but has not been enunciated in, many influential writings on analytical jurisprudence. (It should be stressed that when I talk of structure in this and the next section, I am speaking of the structure of law-statements and not, as I do in Section 4.7, of legal sub-systems and legal systems.)

It is submitted that we may usefully distinguish between the problems of structure and individuation by expecting answers to the former to be *syntactic* in nature, and responses to the latter predominantly *semantic* in kind. For theorists of structure, as is shown in the next section, try to identify the constituents of individual norms and laws, independently of the meaning of these parts. For example, von Wright locates the 'components',[15] while Ross identifies the 'elements',[16] of norms. These commentators, and all others, in their discussions of the structure of *individual laws*,[17] have the following in common: they are concerned chiefly with the syntactic form (1) in which rules are to be found in law-formulations, or (2) into which law-formulations can be recast (as law-statements). And in so far as is reasonable, they all strive to abstract form from content in their proposed accounts. Theorists of individuation, in contrast, are concerned mainly with the semantic content of the constituents of laws. They generally seek to recommend particular principles in accordance with which law-formulations may be divided up into individual laws, invariably doing so, as shall be seen shortly, with particular *purposes* in mind. Such recommendations often do embrace specifications for the structure of their individuated units: the problem of structure, therefore, can sometimes be conceived as one aspect of that of individuation, and, moreover, discussions on the two topics will regularly and legitimately overlap and contain cross-references to one another (as this book's do). The above distinction will be supported in this and the next section through examination both of various writers' theories of individuation and structure and also of my own proposed and closely related principles of individuation and structure. The principles I offer, of course, are composed for legal

[15] *NA*, p. 70.
[16] *DN*, ch. 5.
[17] For present purposes, 'individual laws' may be taken to be synonymous with 'law-statements'. Cf. *AL*, pp. 62–3.

knowledge engineers and not necessarily for all other sorts of legal scientists. First, I shall turn, in this section, to individuation.

The problem of the individuation of laws has not been given extensive jurisprudential consideration over the centuries although it is one which Hart argued as recently as 1970 'still awaits a solution'[18] (contingent on which solution lies a satisfactory theory of legal systems). Individuation, according to all theorists' analyses, pertains to the division of the law into distinct components. It is beyond dispute that it is necessary, for the purposes of description of, or operation with, the law, to break it down into manageable units. What is contentious is the manner in which this should be done. Although detailed principles indicating how we might split up the law can be drawn from legal writings as early as those of Gaius and other Roman jurists, the problem of individuation *per se* was first articulated by Bentham, and only far more recently has it been discussed in further detail by analytical jurisprudents.[19]

The literature on individuation seems to reveal two individuating enterprises: *expositional* and *ontological* individuation.[20] Expositional individuation belongs to descriptive legal science and is that task of dividing the law into distinct laws for the purposes of conveying information about the law. Individuation as an ontological enterprise—involving the division of the law into 'complete' or 'ideal' units in accordance with immutable and transcendent principles of individuation—has been heavily and rightly criticized, by Honoré and Dworkin particularly.[21] The reason that the ontological individuation thesis is untenable and metaphysically unsound is

---

[18] *EJP*, p. 273.

[19] It was Bentham who seems to have been the first to introduce the term 'individuation' to legal theory. See Hart's comments in his Introduction to *OLG*, p. xxxiv n. 5. In what is regarded by Hart (ibid.) as an early draft for a beginning to his *OLG*, Bentham states that by the 'individuation of a law' he means 'the description of that which is to be looked upon as neither more nor less than one entire law' (*OLG*, p. 247). Bentham's work on individuation, however, was largely ignored until the 1960s when Raz revitalized the topic, arguing it to be of 'immense importance to legal philosophy' (*CLS*, p. 70), and continually returning to it in later works such as 'Legal Principles and the Limits of Law' (1972), *AL*, pp. 62–5, and in the postscript of *CLS*. Other relevant writings on individuation are: James, 'Bentham on the Individuation of Laws' (1973); Honoré, 'Real Laws' (1977); Harris, *LLS*, ch. 3; Dworkin, *TRS*, pp. 74–7; Hart, *EOB*, pp. 107, 120–2, *EJP*, pp. 273, 336–7; Singh, *Law from Anarchy to Utopia* (1986), pp. 244–9.

[20] *TRS*, p. 75, and James, 'Bentham on the Individuation of Laws' (1973), pp. 113–15.

[21] See Honoré, 'Real Laws' (1977), and Dworkin, *TRS*, pp. 74–7.

simply that, as the earlier quotation from Harris reminds us, in the law-formulations themselves we are given neither principles of individuation nor units that have already been individuated. Any principles of individuation are necessarily *provided* by the legal scientist or whoever it is that is dividing up the law. The method of division with which the legal scientist provides himself will depend on his purposes in individuating and the notion of completeness of laws will undoubtedly be task-dependent. There is no one overriding purpose of individuation: people choose to individuate for a variety of what seem to be equally respectable reasons, between which we often have no way of assessing their relative importance. Hence it is not meaningful to talk *without qualification* of such notions as ideal or complete laws.

Yet, if one is engaged in descriptive legal science or legal knowledge representation, questions such as 'What is to count as one complete law?' need not always be regarded as ontological or metaphysical conundrums: on the contrary, they may figure as crucial matters to be decided in the selection of an apposite expository strategy—a strategy of expositional individuation. The legal knowledge engineer *must* opt for one particular method of dividing up and restructuring the law, and if, in his quest for this method, he asks what is to count as one law, *for his purposes*, then this query cannot reasonably be interpreted as an inquiry of a metaphysically improper nature. Therefore, when we talk of completeness, we need not be interpreted as positing or presupposing some quasi-Platonic Form Law, but rather we can be understood as talking about completeness of laws given our conception of individuation.

The same line of defence *may* be deployed on behalf of Bentham—he was perhaps talking of ideal, logical, and intellectual units of legal discourse from the point of view of his principles and stipulative definition of individuation, and the fact that laws individuated according to the Benthamite programme are large and clumsy may attest not to an unsatisfactory metaphysical system but to his hankering after meticulous and exhaustive examination and exposition of the law.[22] Raz's position on this matter is perhaps not clear from his writings. From his discussion of Bentham and individuation, and his postscript, in *The Concept of a Legal System*, it is apparent that he would wish to make no untenable ontological presumptions. Yet by introducing, in *The Authority of Law*, what he

---

[22] Cf. James, 'Bentham on the Individuation of Laws' (1973), p. 116.

calls 'laws' over and above what I call 'law-statements' with insufficient clarification of the nature of the former, he still remains open to Honoré and Dworkin's objections. His remarks on 'laws', however, may be understood as an attempt to make sense of the widespread usage of that term, and not as an introduction of a novel and metaphysically peculiar legal entity.[23]

Honoré was surely correct in saying that 'it cannot really be suggested that law consists of units waiting to be discovered by some "empirical" procedure analogous to experiment';[24] if we therefore reject any such suggestions as theoretically untenable, and interpret ontological individuation as task-dependent expositional individuation, it transpires that there need not be an ontological problem of individuation at all.

In any event, the process of individuation merits careful description: individuation is an expository exercise involving the division of law-formulations into smaller units (which are, then, law-statements of a kind), not in accordance with standard subdivisions such as sections or subsections, or catchwords and judgments, but through the application of other criteria, resulting usually in a synthesis of all legal sources relevant to a particular topic. These individuated units can be referred to as complete individual laws without thereby presupposing some untenable legal ontology.

There is, I have said, no one overriding purpose of individuation; people individuate for their own particular reasons and ends. Hence, there cannot be said to be one correct way of individuating. Nevertheless, it is helpful to mention the purposes for which it has been expressly argued individuation ought to be put. In Table 2, I summarize various theorists' suggestions.

(It should be noted, in passing, that individuation as demystification and clarification, for Bentham, involved purging the law of all fictitious entities and replacing them with non-metaphysical notions. This lends some support to our suggestion that Bentham's general account of individuation may best be interpreted as metaphysically sound, as it is unlikely that his conception of the purpose of individuation was expressly and unambiguously an anti-metaphysical one, while his general account remained metaphysically improper.)

---

[23] See *CLS*, ch. 4, and p. 217 n. 15, and *AL*, pp. 62–3. I am grateful to Professor Raz for his clarification of this point.
[24] 'Real Laws' (1977), p. 100.

TABLE 2

Theorist	Purpose or Function of Individuation
Bentham	To demystify and clarify the content of, and increase efficiency in the administration of, the law, as society's chief method of social control.
Hart	To distinguish between separate norms or laws of a legal system, by reference to content, authors, modes of enactment, and date, and in so doing clarify their social function.
James	To reveal, around classes of acts, the structure and content of a legal system in terms of a finite number of individual laws.
Honoré	To describe those real laws that exist in the professional discourse and argument of lawyers and law teachers and that reflect a separate arguable point of law in the legal process.
Harris	To display the fundamental imperative content of positive legal rules, that is, duty-imposing and duty-excepting rules, thereby presenting information about existing legal duties.
Raz	To carve small and manageable units out of the total legal material in order to promote our understanding of laws, their interrelationships, and their normative function.
Dworkin	To describe the legal system of a nation in an illuminating way, in accordance with a chosen strategy of exposition.*

* For these accounts of individuation, see: *OLG*, ch. 14; Hart, *EJP*, pp. 273, 336–7; James, 'Bentham on the Individuation of Laws' (1973); Honoré, 'Real Laws' (1977); Harris, *LLS*, ch. 3; Raz, *CLS*, ch. 4, pp. 140–7, 216–24, and 'Legal Principles and the Limits of Law' (1972); and Dworkin, *TRS*, pp. 74–7, respectively.

All these theorists would surely agree with MacCormick that 'in expounding or operating with law, we need to break the whole mass of legal material into simple but patently interrelated unitary rules'[25] (although MacCormick himself, Dworkin in particular, and many others on some occasions, might also wish to expound the law in terms of non-rule standards—see Section 5.2). Rules, or laws, seem central to individuation: they are the basic units with which all members of the legal profession work. Whether these rules reflect the law's normative function, social function, imperative content, or whatever, will depend on the individuating agent and his particular requirements.

For the Oxford prototype, in accordance with the notion of an expert system in law as an intelligent assistant designed to respond

[25] 'Law as Institutional Fact' (1974), p. 115.

to a set of facts by drawing legal conclusions (see Sections 1.3 and 2.2), we elected for one method of individuating, and of the above theorists, it most closely resembles that of Honoré. It will become apparent that the rules in the system do indeed reflect separate arguable points of law and, in conformity with the ethos of expert systems technology, do reproduce 'the shape of the material with which in teaching, practising, or judging lawyers operate'.[26] I recommend individuating 'in such a way as to make clear the issues involved in fixing their [laws'] scope rather than their functions'.[27] I make this recommendation in light of the particular activities and needs both of legal knowledge engineers and of users of our envisaged expert systems in law; accepting thereby Raz's comment that ['t]he concept of a law should be moulded in the way best designed to serve the activities and needs of the people who are concerned with the law'.[28] (Note, however, that the account of structure proposed in the next section is flexible enough to allow also for rules that indicate the social or normative functions of laws, and so forth, and so rule-based expert systems could be designed to advise on these matters, if that were required.)

The following, then, are indications of the principles of individuation, recommended for legal knowledge engineers, followed in the development of the next section's theory of structure, and, as Appendix II indicates, adopted in the construction of the Oxford prototype system. (They are to be read together with the general criteria for knowledge representation given in Section 4.1, and in conjunction with the findings of the following section.)

1. Law-statements, law-predictions, and law-derivations should be represented as rules, to which I refer as *legal productions*. The structure of legal productions is described in the next section.

2. All legal productions should be represented as specific types of *rules of inference*: rules that stipulate what (a) may, or (b) must, or (c) may not, or (d) will probably, or (e) will probably not, be inferred from given premises (data, facts, interim legal conclusions, that are taken to be axiomatic).[29] Just as, in logic, rules of inference are used to state what may be inferred from one or more statements of speci-

---

[26] 'Real Laws' (1977), pp. 99–100.

[27] Ibid., p. 108.

[28] *CLS*, pp. 142–3.

[29] Cf. Ryle's discussion of (not necessarily legal) laws as 'inference-tickets', in *The Concept of Mind* (1949), p. 117. Also see Gottlieb, *LC*, ch. 3.

fied structure, then in law, legal productions serve a similar (but not identical) purpose.[30] Although the recommended theory of structure would allow it, legal productions should not be cast as behaviour-guiding norms directed at citizens. Rather, they should be conceived as directions to legal reasoning agents in general, whether they be human beings or expert systems in law. When embodied in legal knowledge bases, legal productions direct expert systems' lines of reasoning. This principle echoes the theories of Kelsen and Ross that hold all genuine legal rules to be directions to legal officials.[31] There are, however, important differences. My theory does not insist that the rules are addressed to legal officials: rather they are formulated as guides for any agent who is seeking to assess the legal consequences of given data. I am not committed, therefore, to a sanction-based theory of law, with all the incumbent problems that such a model brought for Kelsen and Ross.[32] The reasons for this principle of individuation, and the consequences of its adoption, will be seen far more clearly from Sections 6.4 and 6.5.

3. Following Honoré (but in conformity with the limitations laid down by the previous principles), legal productions should resemble the units with which lawyers operate in their reasoning activities, as these are reflected in legislative materials, judgments in case reports, written and oral pleadings, and secondary sources. (The generality or particularity of the productions, therefore, will be dictated largely by the terms of the repositories of law.) In that way, as Raz would want, legal productions will not deviate from the ordinary, common-sense concept of a law,[33] and, moreover, will tend to be 'relatively self-contained'.[34] Note in this connection that a great deal of the repositories of law are indeed expressed as rules of inference for reasoning agents. A large proportion of sections within statutes, for instance, are formulated in terms such as 'It shall be established that...' (or the equivalent—see Section 6.5), and our renditions of *rationes*, and our phraseology in secondary materials, also follow this practice.

---

[30] Note Goodall's remark that 'expert systems are sometimes described as using "rules of inference" (their rules) to prove theorems from axioms (the given data about a problem)' (*The Guide to Expert Systems* (1985), p. 80).

[31] See e.g. Kelsen, *GTLS*, pp. 45–9, 58–61, and Ross, *DN*, pp. 90–2. My ideas also bear similarities to some of Raz's remarks on 'the legal point of view' (*AL*, pp. 112–13, 140–3).

[32] See e.g. Hart, *EJP*, pp. 299–300, Harris, *LLS*, pp. 102–6, and Raz, *CLS*, ch. 4.

[33] *CLS*, p. 142, 'Legal Principles and the Limits of Law' (1972), p. 832.

[34] *CLS*, p. 144.

4. Following Raz, in so far as the law-formulations allow, legal productions should be of a manageable size.[35] This is not really relevant for the user of an expert system, from whom the representation is hidden (apart from when it is revealed through the transparency facility), but is an essential rule of thumb for the human activity of representing legal knowledge. The likelihood of error when describing the law in terms of large, complex units is far greater than when using small, modular, manageable productions that exhibit 'conceptual simplicity'.[36] Moreover, if productions are of a manageable size, this will facilitate flexibility: it will be easier to alter a small part of a knowledge base than a larger one, as there will be fewer related productions with which to cope. In the words of Raz, there will be 'simplicity of identification'.[37] (In accordance with this fourth guideline, for example, it will be seen that the proposed structure of legal productions, introduced in the following section, precludes the possibility of inclusion within one production of alternative conditions of application whose qualifications are not the same as those of the principal condition. If this possibility was not eliminated, vast, unwieldy, and erroneous productions could well result.)

5. Following Raz, there should be clear indications of all the relationships that hold between legal productions.[38] This matter is discussed more fully in Section 4.5. For now, it will suffice to note that the task of the legal knowledge engineer is to build a knowledge base of interrelated legal productions whose connections are central to the operation of the inference mechanism. Further, explicit expression of the interrelationships at the design stage greatly facilitates satisfactory development of the knowledge base, and is essential at any later stage when alteration to the knowledge is required (that is, it promotes flexibility).

6. Following Raz, conjunctive and exceptive qualifications (as I call them in the following section), are contained in separate legal productions, *but*, in accordance with the previous principle, are related to the legal production(s) which they qualify.[39] In contrast to Raz, then, and in sympathy with Bentham, although the qualifi-

[35] 'Legal Principles and the Limits of Law' (1972), p. 832.
[36] *CLS*, p. 143.
[37] Ibid. For a relevant anticipation of the question of *flexibility*, see *OLG*, p. 236, where Bentham discusses 'making amendments without inconvenience'.
[38] *CLS*, p. 145.
[39] 'Legal Principles and the Limits of Law' (1972), pp. 831–2. See also Harris, *LLS*, p. 94.

cations are fully expressed in distinct productions, their *conclusions* (see next section) are nevertheless included within the productions they qualify.[40] In this way, I suggest we can avoid Bentham's alleged 'logical indigestion' that results from 'massive, clumsy, repetitive' units of law,[41] we can acknowledge the intimate connection between laws and qualifications to which Bentham points us, and we may implicitly reject (as Dworkin does) Raz's suggestion that such qualifications are laws that conflict with the laws to which they are exceptions. We thereby endorse Dworkin's claim that the question involved is no more than one of expository strategy.[42] Note that the problem of contradictory productions cannot be disposed of in this fashion. This is an issue over which there is radical disagreement in jurisprudence[43] (largely for reasons both of current philosophical insolubility and of disagreements over relevance), but it is one which need not be entered at this stage of research and development into expert systems in law. For, in accordance with Principle 4 of Section 2.4, a legal domain which apparently contains conflicting rules (as I defined them) is not currently a suitable legal domain of application. (In the future, it will need to be settled whether the legal knowledge engineer should (1) strive to maintain a conflict-free knowledge base, or (2) explicitly represent all those conflicts that seem to appear in the sources.)

7. No (reductionist) attempt should be made to reduce all legal productions to deontic statements of some putative single atomic modality. My structure allows the representation of several classes of deontic phrase within legal productions. In order that the inference mechanism may function—see Section 6.5—it is necessary to assign a normative category to each production. The possible categories are obligation (O), permission (P), and prohibition (Ph),

---

[40] *OLG*, chs. 10, 14; and *EOB*, p. 121.

[41] James, 'Bentham on the Individuation of Laws' (1973), p. 113. But note that because the full representation of legal knowledge is not perused by the user during consultations, Raz's limiting requirements regarding laws that are over-repetitive or redundant are not relevant—see *CLS*, pp. 142–3, and 'Legal Principles and the Limits of Law' (1972), pp. 831–2.

[42] *TRS*, p. 77.

[43] See Harris, *LLS*, pp. 81–3, and 'Kelsen and Normative Consistency' (1986); *CLS*, pp. 172–3, and 225; *EJP*, pp. 324–34; *PTL*, pp. 320–47, *GTLS*, pp. 363–88, *ELMP*, chs. 10–12; Munzer, 'Validity and Legal Conflicts' (1973). For a discussion of Kelsen's views on this matter, see Hartney, 'Hans Kelsen's Theory of Norms' (1985), pp. 36, 123–6, and 205–34, and Weyland, 'Idealism and Realism in Kelsen's Treatment of Norm Conflicts' (1986).

understood in a restricted sense that I identify. The consequence of the anti-reductionism (again, as is shown in Section 6.5) is that it is possible to avoid being committed to any one school of deontic logicians in relation to such questions as whether or not permissions are reducible to obligations.

The principles of individuation introduced and outlined above can be fully understood only in light of, and should be re-examined after scrutinizing, the proposed inference mechanism and the theory of structure. I look at the former in Part Three, and turn to the latter in the following section.

4.4 THE STRUCTURE OF LEGAL PRODUCTIONS

In this section, which should be read in conjunction with the last, I discuss the question of the syntactic form of individuated productions. My concern with structure, however, goes beyond that of statute and case law-statements, and it is necessary to provide a structure appropriate for all the entities identified in Chapter 3, and not just for those that describe the formal sources of law. In the first instance, I summarize, in tabular form, various jurisprudents' theories of the structure of norms and laws. It is beyond the scope of this book to examine all these accounts in detail: rather, I am concerned at this stage simply with the actual syntactic form that they recommend so that consensus might be identified at that level.

There can be little doubt that there is indeed here a remarkable degree of consensus amongst the theorists mentioned. Although it may seem from casual perusal that, on the contrary, there is profound disagreement, most of the divergences are simply terminological discrepancies. Yet, it should be clear that none of the theories of structure in Table 3 is of itself sophisticated enough to constitute the basis of a coherent model of law for the purposes of legal knowledge representation: none is sufficiently detailed; none was formulated in accordance with the general criteria of knowledge representation (or their equivalent) identified in Section 4.1; and none takes account of all those entities identified in Chapter 3. (Remarkably, Bentham's theory is at once the oldest and yet most developed.) However, if these theories are synthesized, noting the respects in which some are more acceptable than others, and this is done in the light both of the general criteria of Section 4.1, and of the entities noted in Chapter 3, then a satisfactory and useful structural model emerges. I introduce this, in abstract form, in Table 4, and discuss it in some detail in the remainder of the section. Note that an extended elaboration of the use of the proposed model is given in Appendix II to this book, in which I present a formalization of some of the law-statements that describe part of Scottish Law of divorce.

It must be borne in mind that I am not suggesting that mine is the only way that laws may be structured for the purposes of expert systems in law.[44] But my theory does have sound bases both in jurisprudence and AI, and, moreover, as the Oxford prototype system confirms, is of significant practical value.

TABLE 3

Theorist	Antecedent	Consequent
Allen	Antecedent set of conditions.	Deontic obligation, forbidden, indifference, or permission operator; descriptive part.
Bentham	Object: an act of some sort or other, being the object of a wish or volition on the part of the legislator. Qualifications: limitative or exceptive circumstances.	Aspect: a wish or volition of which such act is the object.
Eckhoff	Operative facts.	Legal consequences.
Gottlieb	Protasis: in circumstances X; times, place, persons, other rules.	Apodosis: Y is required prohibited or permitted (character).
Harris	The conditions under which the deontic operator applies to the positive or negative act-situation.	An ought or may deontic operator.
Kelsen	1. Delict. 2. Conditions; temporal limitations, spatial limitations.	Sanction. Individual; command, permission, authorization; manner of behaviour; action or omission.

[44] Cf. Dworkin's comment that 'lawyers use rules and principles to report legal information, and it is wrong to suppose that any particular statement of these is canonical' (*TRS*, p. 76).

Table 3—*continued*

Theorist	Antecedent	Consequent
MacCormick	Operative Facts.	Legal Consequences.
Olivecrona	Ideational element or ideatum: certain conduct (agendum) in a certain situation (requisitum).	Imperantum.
Raz	Norm-subject; norm-act(ion); performance condition.	Norm-character.
Ross	Those which specify the action-idea: subject; situation; theme.	Those whose function it is to indicate that the action-idea is presented as a pattern of behaviour.
Stone	Legal conditions: norm-addressee; given act or omission (behaviour).	Legal consequences: deontic modality—obligatory; prohibitory; permissory.
Tur	X [factual situation] is.	Y [legally determined consequence] ought to be.
Twining and Miers	Protasis: content; condition; subject; and occasion.	Apodosis: character.
von Wright	Condition of application; authority; subject; occasion.	Content and character.
Wasserstrom	Antecedent: particular kind of relationship, activity or person.	Legal consequences that ought to follow.*

* These theories of structure are, for example, found peppered throughout 'Analysis of the Logical Structure of Legal Rules by a Modernized and Formalized Version of Hohfeld's Fundamental Legal Conceptions' (1985) (amongst other theories), *OLG*, 'Guiding Standards in Legal Reasoning' (1976), *LC*, *LLS*, *GTLS* and *PTL*, *LRLT*, *Law as Fact* (1971), *CLS*, *DN*, *LSLR*, 'Positivism, Principles and Rules' (1977), *How To Do Things With Rules* (1982), *NA*, and *JD*, respectively.

The general structure proposed in this section, consistent with all of the theories of structure presented in Table 3, is that of the conditional statement, of the form 'If *p*, then *q*' where *p* is called the *antecedent* or *protasis*, and *q* the *consequent* or *apodosis*. (The terms antecedent and consequent shall be used in this book.) More specifically, the structure is that of the *compound* conditional statement. Borrowing a term from AI, and thereby avoiding the associations with certain legal theorists that the use of words such as rules,

TABLE 4

LEGAL PRODUCTION NO.	:

LOGICAL OPERATOR :
ANTECEDENT
1. *Principal Condition of Application* :
   Temporal Limitation(s) :
   Spatial Limitation(s) :
   Authority + Rank :
   Rationale :
   Legal Addenda :
2. *Alternative Condition(s) of Application* :
   Temporal Limitation(s) :
   Spatial Limitation(s) :
   Authority + Rank :
   Rationale :
   Legal Addénda :
3. *Conjunctive Qualification(s)* :
   Temporal Limitation(s) :
   Spatial Limitation(s) :
   Authority + Rank :
   Rationale :
   Legal Addenda :
4. *Exceptive Qualification(s)* :
   Temporal Limitation(s) :
   Spatial Limitation(s) :
   Authority + Rank :
   Rationale :
   Legal Addenda :

CONSEQUENT
5. *Deontic Phrase* :
   Obligation :
   Permission :
   Prohibition :
6. *Predictive Phrase + Certainty Factor* :
7. *Conclusion(s)*
8. *Relationship* :

norms, and principles, would no doubt cause, I shall refer to such statements of the structure described as (*legal*) *productions*. (It should not be inferred thereby that the type of expert system I propose in this book is a 'production system' in the specific sense in which computer scientists use that term.)

The components or elements of the productions that I have identified shall be called *slots* and *sub-slots*, and when these (sub-)slots are filled, I shall speak of their *contents*. Some (sub-)slots, for example the logical operator slot, may be filled with only one of the predetermined alternative contents, while others may be filled with any relevant propositions or pieces of text.

When restructuring a legal domain, it is not always possible, and on some occasions not desirable, to fill all the (sub-)slots or to use all the possible contents of the slots. For instance, if a rule has no exceptions or qualifications, the appropriate slots may be left unfilled; or, again, if the rule in question is a simple meta-rule of antecedent-consequent form, then perhaps only the principal condition and conclusion slots will be filled. Moreover, it is intended that the proposed structure should be able to accommodate any of the theories of structure tabulated previously (and others, no doubt), and also any of the theories of individuation mentioned in the previous section. For example, if we chose to implement Tur's theory of structure in an expert system, we would leave many slots unfilled, and the *permission* normative category sub-slot would never be filled. I shall now examine the slots in turn.

The logical operator slot, which resides beyond the production's antecedent and consequent, can be filled only by two of the logical operators associated with the propositional calculus, namely, the conditional and bi-conditional operators. These are known as 'sentence-forming operators on sentences',[45] and are symbolized as '$\Rightarrow$' and '$\Leftrightarrow$' respectively. These symbols belong to a standard notation, and when translated into English are usually taken to represent 'if...then...' and 'if and only if...then...'. There are other renderings of these symbolic expressions. Stone, for instance, would seem to translate them as 'always if' and 'always and only if', calling these the logical constants (that is, logical operators) of extensive implication and equivalence.[46] Whatever English rendering of these symbolic expressions is preferred, however, it *must* be stressed that their translation into natural language is only approximate: for their meaning is conditioned by mathematical laws and not by linguistic usage.[47] Although the translation is necessarily approximate, for the purposes of building legal knowledge bases the casting of the law as legal productions of 'if... then...' or 'if and only if... then...' structure, symbolized as above, will suffice.[48] Disregarding for now all the other slots I have identified, the following two examples, from the Oxford project domain of application, illustrate the use of the two possible contents of the logical operator slot:

> The marriage has broken down irretrievably $\Leftrightarrow$ The court may grant decree of divorce
>
> The defender has committed adultery $\Rightarrow$ It shall be established that the marriage has broken down irretrievably.

Turning now to the antecedent of the legal production, there are four possible categories of slots here, attached to each of which are five further sub-slots. The role of the four slots can perhaps best be understood from the following logical expression, where P, A, C, and E stand for principal condition of application, alternative condition of application, conjunctive qualification, and exceptive qualification, respectively, and disjunction is symbolized as '$\vee$', conjunction as '$\wedge$', and negation as '$\neg$'.

$$(P \vee A) \wedge C \wedge \neg E \Rightarrow consequent$$

An approximate translation of this expression into English would be: 'if P or A, and C and not E, then *consequent*'. Note that the qualifications are to both conditions, something that is far clearer from the formal expression. There can be more than one alternative condition, conjunctive qualification, or exceptive qualification, as the following representation indicates:

$$(P \vee A \vee A^1 \ldots A^n) \wedge C \wedge C^1 \ldots C^n \wedge \neg E \wedge \neg E^1 \ldots \neg E^n$$
$$\Rightarrow consequent$$

In the principal condition of application slot, a (positive or negative) proposition, statement, word, or series of words (hereafter a 'proposition') is inserted which specifies an act, action, event, situa-

---

[47] See Ayer, *The Central Questions of Philosophy* (1973), pp. 184–5.
[48] Cf. *BL*, p. 60.

tion, or state of affairs. Such a condition can be a 'brute fact', or may be a more or less 'institutional fact' (see next section) that constitutes what is called, in Part Three of this book, an *interim legal conclusion*. It is only possible for a production to be used in a line of reasoning if the principal condition is satisfied. When it is satisfied (together, where appropriate, with any other conditions, qualifications, and limitations), then, as shall be seen, the system may move on to the consequent of the production (see Section 6.5). Where a production has only one condition, the principal condition slot is used. Where there are (positive or negative) alternative conditions, the alternative condition(s) of application slot(s) are deployed. Often it will be clear—either from a statute, the judges' *dicta*, or the practice of lawyers—which condition is the principal condition and which are the alternative conditions. Where it is not, an arbitrary selection can be made: in that event, it is simply a matter of exposition.[49] Alternative conditions may only be put into the same production as the principal condition if all these conditions share the same qualifications (but not necessarily the same temporal or spatial limitations). If they have different qualifications, then a separate production should be used. (This can be justified in terms of the fourth principle of individuation stated in the last section which pertains to maintaining productions at a manageable size.) Qualifications to the conditions are put into the conjunctive qualification(s) slot(s) and the exceptive qualification(s) slot(s) as appropriate. Both conjunctive and exceptive qualifications are propositions that reduce the ambit of the production by stipulating that further conditions either must, or must not, hold. The use of an antonym could clearly render a conjunctive qualification an exceptive qualification or vice versa.[50] The use of these four slots is amply illustrated in Appendix II, from which it can be seen that the conditions and qualifications can be related to one another using the standard operators of propositional logic.

Attached to *all* propositions belonging to one of the four classes mentioned above are five further sub-slots. The scope of any con-

---

[49] See Bentham's discussion of 'principal' or 'leading' provisions: *OLG*, p. 124.

[50] The principal and alternative conditions together with conjunctive qualifications can be equated with what Hohfeld called '*affirmative* operative facts', while exceptive qualifications correspond to his '*negative* operative facts'. See *Fundamental Legal Conceptions* (1919), p. 32 (original emphasis). The proposed conjunctive qualification is functionally equivalent to Bentham's limitative qualification. See *OLG*, p. 115.

dition or qualification may be limited in terms of (1) time (or occasion) or (2) space. In the former event, for instance, as when a condition applies only since, say, the date of the marriage (or at one point in time), the first sub-slot, the temporal limitations sub-slot, is used. In the latter, usually in relation to matters of jurisdiction, the second sub-slot, the spatial limitations sub-slot, is employed.[51] If the temporal and spatial limitations sub-slots of all the productions in a series that constitute a line of reasoning remain unfilled, then, strictly, this implies that the productions are relevant at all times and in all places.

Where appropriate, the citation of the authoritative source of the attached proposition should be inserted in the authority and rank sub-slot of a legal production.[52] For instance, in the authority and rank sub-slot of the first example given above, we would input 's.1(1) of The Divorce (Scotland) Act 1976', while in the same sub-slot of a legal production that expresses a case law-statement, we would insert the citation of that case. This sub-slot contributes to the expert system's transparency for it makes authority available for any conclusion that the system draws. Of course, the antecedent of a production is not always simply a single proposition, and many productions will contain a principal condition, alternative conditions, together with several qualifications, attached to each of which will be a filled authority and rank sub-slot. To illustrate this, consider subsection 1(2)(a) of the 1976 Act: 'since the date of the marriage the defender has committed adultery', which proposition is preceded in the Act by 'The irretrievable breakdown of a marriage shall ... be taken to be established ... if'. The production might tentatively be drafted as follows:

LOGICAL OPERATOR: conditional
1. PRINCIPAL CONDITION OF APPLICATION: the defender has committed adultery
Temporal Limitation: since the date of marriage
Authority and Rank: s.1(2)(a)
5. DEONTIC PHRASE: it shall be established that
7. CONCLUSION: the marriage has broken down irretrievably

---

[51] On temporal and spatial limitations, see Kelsen, *PTL*, pp. 10–15, and *OLG*, pp. 72–5.
[52] On the specification of the source of authority, see *LLS*, p. 21, and *OLG*, pp. 18–30.

Yet, in accordance with the sixth principle of individuation of Section 4.3, within this production we must also relate the above rule to any exceptions, such as that in s.1(3): 'The irretrievable breakdown of marriage shall not be taken to be established . . . by reason of subsection (2)(a) of this section if the adultery . . . has been condoned . . .'. Thus the draft of the above production may be extended, acknowledging that the authoritative source of the exception is different from that of the simple rule above:

---

4. EXCEPTIVE QUALIFICATION: the adultery has been condoned
Authority and Rank: s.1(3)

Note that the proposition 'the adultery has been condoned' also appears in the conclusion slot of a distinct production which stipulates under what conditions, qualifications, and so forth, that conclusion might be inferred: and the two productions will be expressly related through the relationship slot. (The above example further illustrates the sixth principle of individuation of the previous section.)

In the same sub-slot as the authority is input, an indication of the rank of the authority is also required; for which purpose a simple numerical value scale would suffice.[53] Because lawyers do not attach equal force to all authoritative legal sources—for instance, *rationes* from higher courts are often rightly regarded as being more persuasive than those of lower courts—then this may be reflected in the form of meta-knowledge within an expert system (see Section 3.7). Where more than one authority supports the same conclusion, for instance, based on its meta-knowledge of ranking, the system might present the citations in order of force.

However, as noted in Chapter 3, for not all of the entities that we would be advised to have in our knowledge base will there be a formal source that expresses the semantic content of the production at the same level of generality. For legal knowledge engineers will derive (and generalize) law-derivations (and law-generalizations) from statutes and case reports. On these occasions, the inclusion of a citation within the authority sub-slot would be inapposite, and the rationale sub-slot would be used. In this latter sub-slot should be inserted a justification or explanation of why the particular produc-

---

[53] *LLS*, pp. 70–3.

tion has been formulated together with the citation of the authority from which it has been derived or generalized. This sub-slot may also be used to justify the formulation of a particularly controversial provisional case law-statement, in which event both the authority and rationale sub-slots will be used, with appropriate cross-references. Moreover, the rationale behind law-predictions may be input to this slot. Generally, the rationale sub-slot is central to the transparency of the expert systems I recommend.

The fifth and final sub-slot, the legal addenda sub-slot, is a catch-all slot into which background information or information that is not appropriate within a logical formalism may be put. An instance of the latter can be found in s.1(2)(b) of the *Divorce* (*Scotland*) *Act 1976*, as the following example shows:

The defender has behaved in such a way that the pursuer cannot reasonably be expected to cohabit with the defender [principal condition] *whether or not as a result of mental abnormality and whether such behaviour has been active or passive* [LEGAL ADDENDA] ⇒ It shall be established that the marriage has broken down irretrievably [consequent]

Information that may be relevant and that ought to be available during a dialogue with the system, but that defies inclusion in all other slots, may be inserted in the legal addenda sub-slot.

With regard to the consequent of the legal production, this has four slots. In the deontic phrase slot will be inserted the deontic verb (or equivalent) and the verb phrase used in the statute or *ratio*, or expressed in the secondary sources, as the case may be. A possible content of this slot would be 'it' shall be established that'. Although there is a wide range of normative vocabulary, I argue in Section 6.5 that any deontic verb can be regarded, in functional terms, as sub-sumable under one of the three normative categories: obligation (O), permission (P), or prohibition (Ph). And so the deontic verb (or its equivalent) must be categorized by marking or filling one of the appropriate normative category sub-slots that are attached to the deontic phrase slot. This is done for the purposes of the deontic inference mechanism described in Section 6.5.

Predictions and derivations can also be accommodated within the proposed structure, and in the predictive phrase and certainty factor slot should be input the relevant predictive phrase—for example, 'it will probably be established that'—together with the certainty factor which indicates the likelihood of the legal production in question being adopted or applied by the court. The certainty factor is fundamental to the operation of a system that reasons with uncertainty under some probabilistic calculus. Note that if certainty factors are included in accordance with the proposed structure, then alternative conditions should only be held in the same legal production if they share the same conclusion *and also* if they are conducive to the same certainty factor.

In the conclusion(s) slot should be inserted the proposition(s) (positive or negative) that may, must, may not, will probably, or will probably not be inferred, if the various conditions, qualifications, and limitations are satisfied. The content of this slot may vary according to the type of production being represented. For instance, if the production is a law-statement with a filled obligation normative category sub-slot—a rule stipulating perhaps that under certain conditions, 'it shall be established that...'—it is usual to find a single proposition in the conclusion slot. By elaborating sufficiently detailed antecedents, lawyers (and legal knowledge engineers) tend to phrase such rules in ways that are unambiguously dispositive of the circumstances to which they apply. On the other hand, sometimes when the production is a law-statement with a filled permission normative category sub-slot—perhaps a discretionary rule conferring a power on a judge to implement one of a range of options—there will be more than one proposition filling the conclusion(s) slot, each one corresponding to one of the available options. It is likely, however, that when computer scientists are building expert systems in law, they will break down some productions with multiple conclusions into separate, conjunctive rules. For instance, they might represent the rule 'P(a $\vee$ b $\vee$ c)' as the following conjunction of rules: P(a) $\wedge$ P(b) $\wedge$ P(c). This would be a fruitful approach for those writing in Prolog, because the extended Horn clause logic implemented in Prolog cannot accommodate rules with disjunctive conclusions.[54]

Finally, as can be seen from Appendix II, the content (or part of it) of the conclusion(s) slot invariably appears within the content of one or more of the (sub-)slots of the antecedents of other productions and in this way the productions are interrelated, the 'address' (the 'legal production no.' together with the slot no.) of the related productions being filled in the relationship slot. The conclusion(s)

54 See Sergot, 'Representing Legislation as Logic Programs' (1985), pp. 8–11.

slot, then, is fundamental to a chain of reasoning, as can be seen from the following section.

4.5 LEGAL SUB-SYSTEMS AS DECISION TREES

Just as a legal textbook writer does not attempt to systematize an entire legal system but focuses on a particular branch of the law, so too the legal knowledge engineer must also identify the legal sub-system (as I shall refer to it) that he intends to embody in his expert system. Having already proposed a method of individuating the law, and then structuring the resultant units together with legal heuristics, it is now appropriate, in this section, to address the issue of the general configuration of legal sub-systems. The legal knowledge engineer does not simply enter a series of discrete and unrelated productions into the computer memory, but must systematize them within a predetermined, rigorous (and yet flexible) framework that itself establishes often complex logical interconnections between the individuated units. Using jurisprudence once more as the point of departure, I shall now recommend a particular model of sub-system: the decision tree. This model is the foundation of the computational model of legal reasoning developed in Part Three. Several questions must be considered in relation to legal sub-systems. First, what is meant by legal systems and legal sub-systems? Second, is the legal sub-system represented in a legal knowledge base a 'momentary' or a 'non-momentary system'? Third, in what ways are the knowledge base's constituents—the productions—related to one another? Fourth, what guidance can jurisprudence offer for the development of a decision tree as a representational model for the universe of legal discourse?

In relation to the meaning of 'a legal system', Raz has said that it 'is not a technical legal term', but one that 'is primarily used in thinking about the law, not in the actual use and application of the law'.[55] In other words, the concept of a legal system is nowhere legally

---

[55] *AL*, p. 78. See also Golding, 'Kelsen and the Concept of "Legal System"' (1961), p. 355: 'there is no privileged sense of the term "system"'. Note that the problems of the 'unity' and 'identity' of legal systems (*AL*, ch. 5) are beyond the scope of this book, mainly because my concern is with very small parts of legal systems over which there is no doubt regarding their status as authoritative sources—see Section 2.4 on suitable legal domains of application.

defined for us, and jurisprudents must offer characterizations of the notion as appropriate for particular purposes. It is helpful here to follow the jurisprudential taxonomy proposed in Section 2.1, and to be aware that the sources of legal systems are linguistic *legal system formulations*, about which we make existential *legal system statements*. The term legal system is often taken to refer to such formulations or statements. However, the ontological status of propositions containing 'legal system' not being used in one of these senses is problematic, and the discussion, in Section 2.1, of the two irreconcilable legal ontologies can be consulted in this context.

The taxonomy can also be applied to the concept of 'sub-system', which is an identifiable, and (relatively) separable part of a legal system (formulations or statements). (On the substantive content of legal sub-systems for expert systems in law, see Section 2.4.) Legal sub-systems can vary in size, some being so small as to reflect, consonant with Section 4.3, a separate point of law; while others, in contrast, will contain large bodies of interconnected rules. Generally, however, when I speak of legal sub-systems in this book, I shall be talking of the content of legal knowledge bases: all those legal productions—statements, derivations, predictions, and so forth—that may be represented in a legal knowledge base. It is possible, of course, for a knowledge base to contain more than one sub-system.

With regard to the second question, there seems to be general agreement amongst those analytical jurisprudents who have addressed the matter that a useful distinction can be drawn between the notions of momentary and non-momentary legal systems.[56] Although the division is implicit in many writings of the past, it seems first to have been given explicit formulation by Raz, who defines a momentary legal system as one that 'contains all the laws of a system valid at a certain moment'[57] and non-momentary legal systems as 'legal systems existing in a period of time'.[58] One of the many jurisprudential questions that arises from the development of expert systems in law is whether the productions represented in the legal knowledge base are descriptions of, provisional statements about, derivations or predictions of, momentary or non-momentary legal sub-system formulations.

[56] Raz, *CLS*, pp. 34–5, pp. 189–97, *AL*, p. 81; Alchourron and Bulygin, *NS*, pp. 88–9; Harris, *LLS*, pp. 42–3 and pp. 111–15.
[57] *CLS*, p. 34.
[58] Ibid., pp. 184–5.

The idea of a momentary legal system (as law-formulations) is straightforward enough: at any given point in time we can identify, in accordance with some rules of identity of legal systems, all and only those formal legal sources that may establish or confirm the validity and authority of any rules or principles derived from them. These sources together constitute a momentary legal system: a collection of linguistic formulations. Statements of legal science are primarily *about* such momentary legal systems. The same is true of the productions represented in any legal knowledge base. Of course, as was established in Chapter 3, neither legal scientists nor legal knowledge engineers indulge solely in description: they also interpret, derive, and predict. Yet the fundamental basis of these descriptions, interpretations, derivations, and predictions ought to be the collection of valid formal sources that are the legal system formulations. No doubt, explanations and justifications of productions may require reference to non-momentary legal systems. Ultimately, however, it is the function of an expert system in law to offer meaningful advice on what the law, according to one or more human experts, would seem to be or would be held by officials to be, at one moment in time. It may be concluded that a legal knowledge base should contain a description of part of those law-formulations that make up a momentary legal system, together with interpretations, derivations, predictions, and meta-rules, based on these formulations.[59]

The third question concerns the relations that hold between productions within a legal knowledge base. What kind of structure may the legal knowledge engineer impose on the law-formulations in constructing his legal sub-system? The considerations to be borne in mind are by no means identical to those to which legal scientists must have regard: for as well as seeking to present the law in a readily comprehensible manner, the legal knowledge engineer must also represent a sub-system in a fashion that accords with the general criteria of knowledge representation outlined in Section 4.1. Yet writings on the problem of the structure of legal systems from the point of view of legal science often do relate closely to the knowledge engineer's task of structuring legal sub-systems. This can be appreciated on reflection on Harris's brief outline of two fundamental questions that confront the legal scientist who reflects on the structure of legal systems: 'Has the law described by legal science an

---

[59] Cf. *LLS*, p. 67.

essential structure? If so, in what does the essentiality consist?[60] One of the most fertile sources of insight into the question of the structure of a legal system is the work of Kelsen.[61] He distinguishes between a 'static' and a 'dynamic' theory of law: 'According to the first alternative, the object of the theory of law is the law as a system of valid norms—the law in its state of rest. According to the second, the object of the legal theory is the process in which law is created and applied—the law in motion.'[62] This distinction is echoed by Raz when he distinguishes between 'genetic' and 'operative' structure of legal systems.[63] He argues that in systems of genetic structure, the relations are genetic, that is, they relate to laws authorizing the existence of other laws. Such a system will indicate what laws are valid at any point in time and what powers exist for the future creation of laws. Corresponding approximately with Kelsen's dynamic theory of law, it is understandable that Raz thinks 'it is tempting to say that the genetic structure is the structure of non-momentary legal systems' whereas of the operative structure, on the other hand, he says ['w]e should like to consider it as the structure of momentary systems' as it is concerned with existing laws and their effects.[64] Consonant with one contemporary jurisprudential dichotomy, then, it can be said that legal knowledge engineers are concerned with the operative structure of legal sub-systems.

Further jurisprudential insight can be gleaned from another of Kelsen's divisions: between static and dynamic norm systems.[65] Both are hierarchical systems of norms, at the root of which tree-like structure there lies a basic norm. The norms of a static system are considered to be inherent in their basic norm, and can be derived from it in the way that the particular can be derived from the general. There is a presumption, or it is self-evident, that the basic norm of a static system has binding force. A typical static system, Kelsen argues, is one of natural law. In contrast, the norms of a dynamic system regulate the process by which the law is created and

---

[60] Ibid., p. 70.
[61] As Golding says, 'In attempting to formulate a fairly precise use (or set of uses) for the term "legal system" and to explicate the various facets of the concept of legal system, one naturally turns to the works of Hans Kelsen'. See 'Kelsen and the Concept of "Legal System"' (1961), p. 355.
[62] See e.g. *PTL*, pp. 70–1, *GTLS*, p. 112, pp. 122–3.
[63] *CLS*, pp. 183–5.
[64] Ibid., p. 185.
[65] *GTLS*, pp. 3 ff, 112–13, 399–401, and *PTL*, pp. 195–8.

applied. The basic norm of a dynamic system, according to Kelsen's theory, is both one of the reasons for the normativity and validity of all norms of the system, and, moreover, is the definitive basis for the unity and identity of the system.[66] A legal system is a dynamic system of norms. A combination of the two systems is also possible.[67] Indeed, according to Stone, 'actual legal orders often (if not usually) provide a mixture of static and dynamic elements'.[68] Neither of these normative systems is conceived by Kelsen as being constituted by norms chained together at the same level, but, rather, they are both made up of norms arranged at different levels in a hierarchy.[69] That is his model of all normative systems, whether static, dynamic, or a combination of the two. It is such a hierarchical structure that I recommend for knowledge bases of expert systems in law.

It is clear that expert systems in law for use by legal practitioners will not function on the basis of a Kelsenian static system, for that kind of system, as Kelsen defines it, is a system of morality or the like. Note too that although it is essential for an expert system in law to be able to offer authority for any conclusions drawn or inferences made, identification of the chains of validity of individuated rules is not their primary function given both the characterization of expert systems in law offered in Section 1.3, and the discussion of validity in Section 2.1. Rather, these systems are to be designed to assist human beings in arriving at legal conclusions and solving legal problems based on the represented knowledge. While Kelsen's models of dynamic and static systems individually do not provide us with a sufficiently coherent model to implement in a legal knowledge base, they do furnish us both with a sensitivity to the types of systems that might be candidates for inclusion in expert systems, and also with an awareness that a legal sub-system (as formal sources) once subjected to the processes of legal science (in all its forms) is an entity whose constituents are related to one another in a way not immediately apparent from perusal of law-formulations.

I have argued in this chapter that the knowledge base of an expert system in law might most suitably be rule-based. I have noted in this section that eminent legal theorists have advocated that norms be structured hierarchically, but, as Raz has observed in connection

---

[66] But see Raz, *AL*, chs. 5 and 7, and Stone, *LSLR*, ch. 3.

[67] *PTL*, pp. 197–8.

[68] *LSLR*, p. 106.

[69] *GTLS*, pp. 123–4, *PTL*, pp. 221–3.

with Kelsen, this might be done as a tree diagram or as a pyramid.[70] The pyramid model, however, as Raz suggests, is less flexible, in the ordinary non-AI sense, than the tree diagram, in that it imposes a rigidity and uniformity on all systematized rules that the latter need not. It is also less flexible, in the AI sense, for, as will become apparent, a branch of a tree can be removed, replaced, or inserted with relative ease, whereas the pyramid may require extensive adjustment in order to accommodate change and yet retain its characteristic form. I conclude, then, that the tree model is to be preferred.

Although a tree diagram as a means of representing parts of legal systems is no innovative image for jurisprudence,[71] and it can be deployed as a means of representing both static and dynamic systems, neither has its full potential been exploited by legal theorists, nor has the nature and contents of such trees been fully clarified. In this respect, AI can contribute to jurisprudence by providing novel and precise terminological conventions regarding what are generally referred to as *decision trees*.[72] Invariably the junctions on such trees are referred to by AI scientists as *nodes*, while the connections between the nodes are known as *branches*. Branches that connect nodes directly connect *parents* with *children*, so that the *root node* has no parents, while the nodes at the other extreme—the *terminal nodes* or *leaves*—have no children. A node is an *ancestor* of a node that is its *descendant* if the former is placed closer to the root than the latter and there are branches connecting the two. Inserting the children of a node is spoken of as *expanding* the node: unexpanded nodes are called *open* nodes, and nodes once expanded are said to be *closed*. (It is assumed that any tree under discussion is inverted, with the root at the top.)

In the tree shown in Figure 1, therefore, where letters denote nodes and lines stand for branches, (a) is the root node, (d), (e), (f), (j), (k), (l), and (m) are terminal nodes or leaves. Further, (c) is the parent of (g) (which is, of course, the child of (c)), and (g) is an ancestor of (h), (i), (j), (k), (l), and (m). Using this terminology, in a Kelsenian 'dynamic' normative system, for instance, all nodes denote norms, the root norm is the basic norm, the branches of the tree represent chains of validity, all children derive their validity from their ances-

---

[70] *CLS*, p. 99.
[71] See e.g. Baker, 'Defeasibility and Meaning' (1977), p. 46, and Raz CLS, ch. 5, particularly pp. 99 and 113.
[72] *AI*, pp. 89–90.

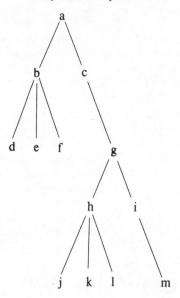

FIG. 1

tors, and so forth. Yet, as AI research has shown, the decision trees created by the systematization of antecedent-consequent rules are unlike this Kelsenian model in several respects.[73] Rather, they are known as 'and/or' trees, whose nodes denote propositions or statements or words (and not norms or rules) and whose branches represent some logical relationship. They can be represented graphically as shown in Figure 2.

The introduction of the arcs allows us to distinguish graphically between 'and' and 'or': the former is denoted by the inclusion, and the latter by the omission, of an arc. This can be understood in the light of an explanation of the tree in Figure 2. If we let (a) stand for some proposition whose truth (or falsity) we seek to establish, then that tree can be taken to represent how (a) may be inferred: (a)'s children indicate that if (b) *or* (c) are true, then (a) may be inferred. In turn, (b) may be inferred if (d) *and* (e) *and* (f) are true, and so on. The inclusion or omission of arcs, then, determines the application of the conjunctive and disjunctive operators respectively. This tree could

---

[73] See *AI*, pp. 186–9, and Barr and Feigenbaum, *The Handbook of Artificial Intelligence*, vol. 1. (1981), pp. 38–40.

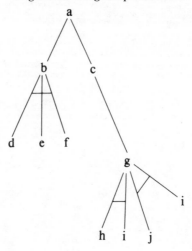

be summarized as a set of rules:

    (1) $(h \wedge i) \vee (j \wedge i) \Leftrightarrow g$, or, more elegantly, $(h \vee j) \wedge i \Leftrightarrow g$.
    (2) $g \Leftrightarrow c$.
    (3) $d \wedge e \wedge f \Leftrightarrow b$.
    (4) $b \vee c \Leftrightarrow a$.

It can be seen from this—and this is crucial—that the consequents of some rules function as the antecedents of others.

The development of a legal knowledge base can be regarded as the systematic and controlled growth of a sort of 'and/or' decision tree, while legal reasoning, I shall argue, consists, in part, in the *searching* of such a tree (see Part Three). A *legal decision tree*, as might be expected, is constituted by nodes that are connected by branches. The nodes themselves can contain both filled slots of legal productions together with their respective filled sub-slots. Note that the nodes are *not* rules, but propositions (with related data and limitations). Legal productions are embodied in decision trees in the following way. All nodes that are not terminal nodes, that is, all nodes that have been expanded, hold propositions that fill the conclusion(s) slots (hereafter 'conclusion' slots) of legal productions. Attached also to any node that holds a conclusion slot are the deontic phrase and predictive phrase + certainty factor slots, which are relevant only when that slot is functioning *qua* a conclusion slot, and not *qua* one of the (sub-)slots of an antecedent (see Part Three). Generally, the left-most child of a generation within a legal decision tree holds a principal condition. The alternative conditions and conjunctive and exceptive qualifications may be identified within a tree by looking to the inclusion or omission of arcs (but it must be remembered, as was said in the last section, that alternative conditions belong to the same production as a principal condition only if they share the same qualifications). In the last diagram, then, if that were taken to be a legal decision tree, (h) denotes the principal condition, (j) the alternative condition, (i) the qualification (conjunctive or exceptive), and (g) the conclusion.

I shall refer to the most basic production of any sub-system as the *foundation rule*: cast in the specified structure, the conclusion of the foundation rule will usually appear in the final determination of a distinct part—a legal sub-system—of any expert system. That conclusion slot is of course the root node of the legal decision tree. The antecedent of the foundation rule will be that interim legal conclusion or cluster of interim legal conclusions whose satisfaction renders the foundation rule applicable. As we travel down the tree (through the law-statements to the legal heuristics) the nodes will have slots that tend to be filled with progressively less technical language. The root node will generally be an extremely abstract legal conclusion expressing the result of the concatenation of many other propositions, whose relative positions in the hierarchy will frequently dictate whether their slot is filled in more or less 'institutional' terms. The terminal nodes (the antecedents of what may be termed the system's *primitive rules*), in contrast, will often be slots filled with the language of everyday discourse, of 'brute fact': indeed it might be argued that a legal knowledge base is not complete until its terminal nodes are interpretable through the use of an ordinary dictionary.[74] Yet, as long as the users of expert systems are general legal practitioners, it is surely necessary for the terminal nodes to hold only propositions understandable to that agent, bearing in mind, as emerges from the following two chapters, that any terminal node can be presented as the most specific askable question. If the users were laymen, then the case for developing a decision tree whose terminal nodes were cast in ordinary, dictionary-interpretable language, could then be much more forcefully canvassed.

[74] *LLS*, p. 26. *OLG*, pp. 158–9. On the brute/institutional fact distinction and its relevance for law, see MacCormick, 'Law as Institutional Fact' (1974), and MacCormick and Weinberger, *An Institutional Theory of Law* (1986), particularly the Introduction.

The conception of legal sub-systems implicit in the representational form of the legal decision tree posits one fairly straightforward logical relationship between the entities discussed in Chapter 3, when they are cast as legal productions: they are internally related[75] to the extent that every legal production (with the exception of the foundation rule) has a conclusion slot that appears in one or more (sub-)slots of other productions' antecedents, and, moreover, every legal production (with the exception of the primitive rules) has one (or more) antecedent (sub-)slot which appears in another production's (or other productions') conclusion slot. Thus, every legal production is internally related to at least one other production within the sub-system; and the relationship slot expressly indicates these internal relations.

It is interesting to note that although the standard jurisprudential hierarchical model of a legal system as a tree diagram whose nodes are rules was rejected in favour of a decision tree whose nodes hold propositions that are parts of rules, nevertheless the final model constitutes a return to a commonly accepted jurisprudential position in so far as the relationships between the antecedents and consequents of connected productions are concerned. When Stone suggests that 'the legal consequences referred to in one norm may become part of the legal conditions of a different norm',[76] or when Gottlieb points out that 'the rules governing matrimonial domicile apply to married persons, but the existence of a state of marriage is itself dependent upon yet other rules',[77] or again when MacCormick asserts that 'a proposition stating the "legal consequence" of one rule may in turn state the "operative fact" of another',[78] then all these theorists, and many others[79] can be taken to be endorsing the idea of chaining rules together in a way compatible with my proposed representation (and with the methods of knowledge utilization outlined in Chapters 5 and 6). None of these theorists, however, has offered a model of legal system that will coherently sustain the type of interrelationships envisaged between compound conditional statements, and this section's proposal is conceived as a remedy for that defect.

The fourth and final question about legal sub-systems asks what

[75] On internal relations, see Raz, *CLS*, pp. 6, 114, 140–1.
[76] *LSLR*, p. 200.
[77] *LC*, p. 39.
[78] *LRLT*, p. 45.
[79] e.g. Horovitz, *LL*, pp. 151–60, and Ross, 'Tu-tu' (1956–7). Also see Honoré, 'Groups, Laws, and Obedience' (1973), pp. 9–10.

guidance jurisprudence can give to those who seek to cultivate legal decision trees. Beyond the general advice in Section 2.4, and the more specific recommendations in this chapter regarding individuation and structure, one further reminder, based on remarks by Golding on rational reconstruction, may be useful.[80] The content and detailed structure of a particular legal sub-system (and indeed of legal productions) can be discovered only after extensive examination both of the primary and secondary sources, and of the fruits of the tuning process. The recommendations regarding structure, individuation, and legal sub-systems given in this book indicate only the general features that the legal knowledge engineer should expect his knowledge base to exhibit. Therefore the task of filling the slots and relating their contents to slots of other productions in a fashion consistent with the suggested principles of individuation, can, as Golding has said of rational reconstruction, 'only be done in... [a] piecemeal, step-by-step fashion'.[81] As the academic legal knowledge base is being constructed (see Section 2.5), and even during tuning, the productions and relations will no doubt be subjected to continual revision, as novel features of the sub-system and of experts' activities are exposed. Legal knowledge representation, therefore, is a piecemeal and incremental process. And the proposed structure of legal sub-systems as decision trees, in conformity with the first and fifth general criteria of knowledge representation that were identified in Section 4.1, is sufficiently flexible to allow for this fact, and, moreover, it facilitates legal knowledge acquisition.

4.6 RULE-BASED AND CONCEPTUAL MODELS OF REPRESENTING LEGAL KNOWLEDGE

In this book, I have advocated a rule-based model of representing legal knowledge, in contrast to other workers in the field who have recommended quite different methods of legal knowledge representation, known as 'conceptual models'. In this section, I examine the idea of including such conceptual models of legal domains in the

---

[80] 'Kelsen and the Concept of "Legal System"' (1961), pp. 384–6.

[81] Ibid., p. 384. Note that Golding is concerned with rational reconstruction largely as a way of exposing hierarchical relationships of validity. The general point of the necessity of a piecemeal approach, however, is still illuminating for the purposes of this section.

knowledge bases of rule-based expert systems in law, and recommend that all expert systems have a rule-based model at their core which will cope with the solving of many clear cases. This model—which will be a heuristic model—must be supplemented by a conceptual model if hard cases are to be solved by expert systems in law of the future. In this discussion, I will be required to discuss many matters relating to legal reasoning that are more properly the province of Part Three. My lack of rigour here in dealing with topics of legal reasoning, such as clear and hard cases, will be remedied in the following two chapters. The principal concern at this stage, it must be stressed, is that of how to *represent* legal knowledge: I clarify the possible role of a conceptual model in the process of legal knowledge representation and reflect briefly on what we might expect a conceptual model to be like.

The distinction between rule-based and conceptual models of legal knowledge representation was first introduced to the field of AI and legal reasoning by McCarty in 1982.[82] Following the recommendations of a prominent AI researcher, P. E. Hart,[83] who had advocated the employment of 'deep' over 'shallow' systems (terms to be explained) in the general expert system domain, McCarty suggests, as noted in Section 1.5, that 'the most critical task in the development of an intelligent legal information system, either for document retrieval or for expert advice, is the construction of a *conceptual model* of the relevant legal domain'.[84] Unfortunately, McCarty never makes it absolutely clear in what a conceptual model consists, mainly because he offers the reader an example of such a model (in TAXMAN) rather than providing a more general account of this approach to the representation of legal knowledge.

As Appendix I illustrates, instances of rule-based models abound. The model recommended so far in this book is also rule-based but I have perhaps gone further than previous researchers by proposing a structure of greater complexity and flexibility that is applicable to any legal domain. Moreover, I have provided principles in accordance with which the law might best be individuated, and have articulated the underlying theories of legal knowledge and legal science

[82] 'Intelligent Legal Information Systems: Problems and Prospects' (1984). McCarty refers to what I call rule-based models as 'propositional' models.

[83] 'Directions for AI in the Eighties' (1982).

[84] 'Intelligent Legal Information Systems: Problems and Prospects' (1984), p. 126. Cf. Sharpe, 'Logic Programming for the Law' (1984).

presupposed by the model. The underlying principle of any rule-based model however is straightforward. A body of law is reduced to a set of rules of a certain structure and these rules are related in some systematic representation. The problem data are *matched* against the antecedents of the rules, which are then *fired*, and the consequents of these, in turn, fire other rules. There are many ways in which the computer can search through the rules (see Sections 6.2 and 6.3): but, ultimately, the process is one of matching the data propositions to the knowledge base propositions.

However, it is easy to envisage a system that contains thousands—possibly hundreds of thousands—of rules, and, in law, this is to be expected in the future if the system is to offer profound coverage of a not insignificant domain. In order that the vast body of rules can be searched more efficiently, it is necessary to employ *heuristic search strategies* (see Section 6.3), which render the knowledge base manageable by including in the inference engine some rules of thumb that allow human experts to manipulate large bodies of rules. Yet even that refinement will not contend with one fundamental shortcoming of those 'shallow' rule-based systems: that if the data proposition does not exactly match the knowledge base proposition (of any of the rules' antecedents) then no rules will be fired and thus no conclusion or advice will be offered by the system. As McCarty points out, 'the phrase "without court appearance" would fail to match a phrase reading "without a court appearance" '.[85] Note that this remark refers only to systems whose interface requires the facts of the case to be described in computer/ formal, or restricted natural, language. McCarty's suggestion does not bear, in this respect, on those systems that have the interactive user interface recommended in Section 2.7, because the intelligent human user would not be affected by such linguistic differences: he would match his problem data with the antecedent of a relevant rule without worrying about the failure of his formulation to correspond exactly with the system's rule.

More generally, however, purely rule-based systems can cope only with problems for which they have explicitly represented and applicable rules: in other words, they have limited intelligence. And this limitation affects systems whatever the nature of their user interface. For, even in respect of systems with interactive interfaces of the sort

---

[85] 'Intelligent Legal Information Systems: Problems and Prospects' (1984), p. 147.

I advocate, the use of purely rule-based representations will undoubtedly restrict the form and number of possible questions that the systems may pose. It must be stressed that if the system does ask apposite questions (or, with the other interfaces, if there is indeed an exact match between the input and represented statements), then these rule-based systems may in fact be of great utility. The rule-based model is not of *no* use, but is of *limited* use as a basis for legal knowledge representation. Its utility lies in the solving of many clear cases, those, in the words of H. L. A. Hart, 'in which there is general agreement that they fall within the scope of a rule'.[86] A system with an interactive user interface akin to that described in Section 2.7, as I argue in Section 6.6, will solve clear cases: when the problem data will fall clearly within the scope of the slots of the antecedent of productions, which are recast as the questions. (In Section 6.6 the notion of clear cases is analysed in some detail.) And systems with the other interfaces will be more likely to respond successfully in clear rather than hard cases, for it is more probable that problems of clear cases will be formulated in ways that the legal knowledge engineers had anticipated. Of course, in the latter type of system, a poorly formulated data description may be fatal, and to grapple with this eventuality, and to design systems to solve hard cases, it would seem necessary to develop knowledge bases with conceptual models of the relevant legal domain.

The problems raised by the inherent limitations of rule-based systems are not exclusively those of legal knowledge engineers; Michie and Johnston level the same charge at MYCIN and PROSPECTOR that I have made against rule-based systems. They ask, as I did: 'What happens when a rule-based system encounters a situation for which it has no rules? It has run out of know-how. What it needs is the ability to work out a way of patching the gap.'[87] Their solution to this general problem of building expert systems (one that accords with P. E. Hart's recommendations) is to develop 'causal' models of the domain of application. McCarty's corresponding solution in law is to develop deep conceptual models. How might these rule-based and conceptual models relate to one another? Michie and Johnston's suggestion seems convincing:

An expert system needs to be able to follow heuristic rules most of the time,

---

[86] *EJP*, p. 106.
[87] *CC*, p. 167.

responding quickly and using little in the way of computing resources. Then when a situation arises to which none of the rules applies it should be able to bring into play a causal [conceptual] model of the domain, which will be slow and expensive but capable of reaching a solution.[88]

Restricting attention now to systems with the interactive user interface of Section 2.7, it might be expected that a rule-based model will lie at the core of such expert systems, while the conceptual model will provide the means by which the systems are able, in effect, to reason in (some) hard cases. (Section 6.7 discusses the different types of hard cases.) It is clear, according to the layout proposed by Michie and Johnston, that the two models coexist but are separable. Thus, at the outset, we might build a purely rule-based model and refine this later through the addition of a conceptual model. (But it must be emphasized again that a purely rule-based model may well be of great use on its own, for instance, for solving clear cases of the expert domain—see Section 6.6.)

So far, few attempts have been made to develop conceptual models of areas of law. McCarty, deBessonet, Meldman, and Hafner in their work, for example, move towards such an approach, but their results are not universalizable in so far as they do not seem to be offering any coherent guidance regarding the development of conceptual models in other legal domains.

The crucial question in this section does not relate to what defects in rule-based systems conceptual modelling overcomes, but is this: what might a conceptual model be like? It is clear that its function will be to fill the gaps in rule-based legal knowledge bases (see Section 5.8), but it is far less clear, on a general level, what the nature of the representational form will be. It is tentatively submitted (in the light both of relevant writings on AI and legal reasoning, and on expert systems in general), that a conceptual model in law will consist of a theoretical representation of the specific area of law in question involving a model of its characteristic reasoning processes, the structure of its legal statements, and denotations of all the central entities involved. Descriptions of the relations between all the components will also be encoded, for which purpose a rich theory of deontic logic will be required (see Section 6.5). These conceptual models will probably be specific to their domain of application, and

---

[88] Ibid., p. 171. But note that P. E. Hart is less sure about how such models would operate in conjunction: 'Directions for AI in the Eighties' (1982), pp. 13–14.

will not be generalizable. For example, a conceptual model relating to part of the Scottish law of Delict may involve some abstract representation of that sub-domain, perhaps in the form of a semantic network (which is one promising medium for the development of conceptual models). The general nature of delict will be embodied in such a model, accounting for the essential elements, namely: first, a wronged party who has suffered loss or injury; second, some act or omission that constitutes a breach of duty; and third, a causal link between these first two elements. The model might also include general clarifications both of these three elements and of the relationships holding between them, thus affording the user of an expert system access not simply to a body of rules, but also to the underlying theory of delict which may be of use in the absence of clearly applicable rules. Such a characterization, however, reflecting as it does that the literature on conceptual models in law is rather vague, confirms that the development of such models constitutes perhaps the most challenging jurisprudential assignment yet formulated.

Yet it may well be premature to take up the challenge today, for there are both theoretical and practical factors that tell against the development of conceptual knowledge bases. As can be seen from Chapter 2 and this chapter, from the point of view of actually representing knowledge, the legal domain is quite different from, and seemingly more complex than, most other domains of application. Moreover, while current legal theory, being carried out now within a rule-based paradigm (as I argue in Section 5.2), offers guidance for rule-based modelling, it has little to say directly about conceptual modelling. It emerges indisputably from the literature that there is irreconcilable disagreement over what goes on when legal reasoning agents cannot subsume their problem data under a particular rule or set of rules, and it does seem that these disagreements are currently philosophically insoluble (pertaining often, in relation to judicial legal reasoning, to the political role of the judiciary). Any conceptual model, therefore, will not be based upon consensus in jurisprudence, but will necessarily embody a contentious and tendentious theory with which many will find fault. From a practical perspective, building a conceptual model of a legal domain promises to constitute a formidable task. In accordance with the third principle of individuation, I suggested that productions should resemble the units with which lawyers operate in their reasoning activities (Section 4.3), and

I have pointed to the written materials which might be examined for this purpose (Section 2.5). There are no direct counterparts to these repositories in respect of the constituents of conceptual modelling. The task of developing a conceptual model, therefore, is one for which there is reliable and unequivocal help available neither from legal theory nor from the primary or secondary sources of law.

Given: (1) the theoretical and practical objections just noted; (2) the fact that rule-based and conceptual models are probably separable; (3) that a rule-based model lies at the core of any system; and (4) no useful rule-based model has yet been developed that is used today by lawyers, it would be most fruitful for the legal profession if research and development in this field currently concentrated mainly on rule-based legal knowledge representation.

4.7 TOWARDS A SHELL FOR EXPERT SYSTEMS IN LAW

Expert systems researchers have developed invaluable software tools for knowledge engineers known as *shells*[89] or *skeletal systems*.[90] These programs render the knowledge engineer's job considerably less onerous by providing him with a ready-made inference mechanism upon which to construct his expert system, thereby removing the need for him to design, and write the code for, his own inference engine. Shells are created by removing the domain-specific knowledge of an existing expert system and leaving the inference sub-system, which can then, in turn, be applied to a different problem domain. Perhaps the best known skeletal system is EMYCIN (for Essential or Empty or Engine MYCIN), which resulted from the removal of the blood and meningitis infections diagnosis rules from the expert system MYCIN.[91] By combining EMYCIN—the residual inference engine—with a collection of rules pertaining to pulmonary function, it was possible, without having to design a new reasoning mechanism, to build PUFF (amongst others), an expert system that diagnoses breathing disorders. Moreover, TAXADVISOR, the system for federal tax planning (see Section 1.4 and Appendix I), was also developed using EMYCIN. There are other shells that are also relevant for legal

---

[89] See e.g. Hammond and Sergot, 'A PROLOG Shell for Logic Based Expert Systems' (1983).

[90] See e.g. *BES*, p. 286, and *AGES*, p. 83.

[91] See Feigenbaum, 'Knowledge Engineering: The Applied Side' (1983), pp. 42–3.

knowledge engineers, amongst which are: APES, in which some of the Prolog Projects' programs were run (Section 1.4 and Appendix I); CRYSTAL, upon which DPA was built (Section 1.4 and Appendix I); ESP advisor, which was designed for the purposes of 'animating' text and might be useful for statute law; and xi, on which an employment law system has been developed.[92]

Not only can the basic inference mechanism of a previous expert system be retained through the use of shells, but other beneficial features of the original system, such as its user interface and its transparency, can also be transferred. However, skeletal systems do need to be used with caution as the reasoning mechanisms of systems designed to perform one particular task are not always suitable for the performance of others, although inference mechanisms within the same general domain—for example, medical diagnosis—are generally transferable.

It is submitted that one of the most important goals of researchers in AI and legal reasoning should be the development of a shell for expert systems in law. Such a tool would not only afford the general benefits noted above but would also encourage legal knowledge engineers to concentrate on their particular legal domain of application and not to be hindered by any computational and jurisprudential difficulties that others have overcome. The shells currently available are unsuitable for expert systems in law. EMYCIN demands the casting of rules as 'attributes', 'objects', and 'values': this rule-type is clearly at odds with the third principle of individuation of Section 4.3, in that it would require us to compile rules that deviate from our ordinary, common-sense concept of the units with which lawyers normally reason. We ought not to be restricted by rule structures that were designed for non-legal purposes. APES, CRYSTAL, and ESP, although useful, are also not absolutely ideal for representing the law, as they can comfortably accommodate neither the entities identified in Chapter 3 nor the idiosyncrasies of legal productions identified in this chapter.[93]

Our Oxford prototype, however, does provide the basis for a shell for expert systems in law. If the user interface, and the inference mechanism described in Chapters 5 and 6, are retained, and the divorce law productions are removed from the knowledge base, then

---

[92] See n. 28 to Ch. 1.
[93] Relevant here is the work on a 'toolbox' for expert systems in law as part of the 'Datalex Project', being conducted largely by Alan Tyree at the University of Sydney.

we are indeed left with the basis of a skeletal system in law. In its favour are the facts that the system was originally designed for the domain of law, and it was developed on the basis of shared jurisprudential assumptions about reasoning with rules. Moveover, in accordance with the fifth general criterion for knowledge representation noted in Section 4.1, such a shell could be adapted to facilitate knowledge acquisition, by developing an interactive computer system capable of generating a knowledge base from a body of legal productions alone.[94] The task for legal engineers in that event would simply be to articulate a body of productions: these could be translated by the computer into a legal knowledge base, and human experts could then tune that academic knowledge base. However, given also that human experts undertook to learn our proposed structure of productions, it is even conceivable that they could directly input their non-academic experiential legal knowledge.

A final favourable feature of the Oxford system as the foundation of a shell stems from the articulation in this book of the underlying jurisprudential assumptions of the proposals: members of the legal profession may now evaluate the merit of further expert system development through shells in a way that was not previously feasible when writings in this field were of predominantly computational orientation.

4.8 CONCLUSION

In this chapter and the previous one, I have addressed the central issue within the field of expert systems in law: legal knowledge representation. In Chapter 3, I identified those entities that ought to be represented within a legal knowledge base, and, in this chapter, I have suggested in what way, and in light of what factors, the actual representation of these entities might proceed. Taken together, these two chapters both provide guidance for anyone building expert systems in law, and, moreover, reveal the underlying jurisprudential theories of legal knowledge, legal science, individuation, structure, and legal sub-systems that will be presupposed through any implementation of the recommended methods of representing legal knowledge. It has not been my purpose to recommend or evaluate

---

[94] See *AI*, pp. 189–91, and *CC*, p. 52.

particular programming languages for the implementation of our proposals: that is for computer scientists to do.

Although, as I said in Section 4.5, legal knowledge representation is a piecemeal activity, from the findings of the last three chapters an appropriate strategy can be discerned, and it is summarized in the following plan of the steps to be taken in representing legal knowledge:

1. Selection of a suitable legal domain of application/legal subsystem, and recruitment of legal expert(s). See Sections 2.4, 2.5, and 4.5.

2. Scrutiny of both the primary and secondary sources. See Section 2.5.

3. Isolation and informal description of the relevant statutory source material. See Sections 3.1 and 3.2.

4. Identification and informal description of the relevant judicial precedents. See Sections 3.1 and 3.3.

5. Synthesis of the relevant secondary sources and formulation of informal and very tentative legal heuristics. See Sections 3.4–3.8.

6. Gradual cultivation of the legal decision tree constituted by individuated legal productions of specified structure. At this stage, the academic legal knowledge is input to the system (law-statements first, and then the legal heuristics), and this may be done with a computer scientist, or by means of a shell. See Sections 2.5, 4.1, 4.3, 4.4, 4.5, and 4.7.

7. Tuning of legal knowledge base by legal expert(s). This can be done manually through scrutiny of a written knowledge base, or with the assistance of the computer where an inference engine has been designed or a shell is being used as a means of testing the knowledge base. The expert will adjust certainty factors, correct errors and inconsistencies, and even add new knowledge. See Sections 2.5, 3.4–3.8, and 4.7.

8. Design of interface of expert system with database systems in law. See Section 2.6.

Steps 1 to 5 have been followed by legal scientists in the past, and it can reasonably be expected that their demands can be fulfilled. Step 7 seems quite unlike any other legally orientated activity, and it is difficult to anticipate all the problems that will arise at this stage, although AI writings on knowledge acquisition and tuning in general do suggest that the tasks involved are by no means trivial.

Step 6 is open to many of those criticisms that have been levelled in the past at the activity of translating law-formulations into some formalism using a particular logical notation or diagrammatic form. In 1973, for instance, Tapper foresaw grave problems for Allen's techniques of normalization that seem to be equally relevant for the legal knowledge engineer.[95] He pointed both to the heavy reliance there must be on the skill of the normalizing agent, and to the extensive responsibility we must grant to the analyst upon whom the ultimate accuracy of all translations must depend. Although the same objections may also be directed at the legal knowledge engineer, and, of course, the same defences as Allen has offered may be marshalled in his defence, two further points may be made.

First, because, as I argued in Section 4.2, legal knowledge representation is necessarily a human activity, we are faced with the choice between that of expert systems in law built by human beings upon whose skill we rely and upon whom great responsibility is bestowed, or that of no further research and development into expert systems in law at all. It is submitted that the former option is preferable. As long as the potential pitfalls of representing legal knowledge are borne in mind, then legal knowledge engineering may proceed tempered always by a welcome caution. Misgivings such as those of Tapper's should not be construed as prejudicing the entire expert system enterprise but as highlighting potential problems. Secondly, if academic legal knowledge bases are tuned and many legal knowledge engineers and legal experts work together on the same legal sub-systems, then we shall be less dependent on the skill of single analysts, more able to share responsibility, and far more likely to represent legal knowledge thoroughly, accurately, and efficiently.

[95] *CATL*, pp. 95–8.

PART THREE

LEGAL KNOWLEDGE UTILIZATION

5

The Possibility of a Deductive Legal
Inference Engine

ALL expert systems require inference engines so that conclusions can be drawn from problem data on the basis of their knowledge bases. The inference engine of an expert system contains general problem-solving knowledge, and AI scientists refer to the issue of designing this mechanism as the problem of knowledge utilization. The topic of what may be called *legal knowledge utilization*, then, relates to the nature of the inference engines which allow expert systems in law to use their legal knowledge in the processes of legal reasoning and legal problem-solving. In this chapter and in Chapter 6 I address this subject and seek, once more from a jurisprudential perspective, to expose the implications and limitations of *deductive* inference engines for expert systems in law. Although the discussion is related specifically to the theory of legal knowledge representation developed in the two preceding chapters, the findings are nevertheless fairly generalizable, being relevant for all rule-based expert systems in law that have similar user interfaces to the one recommended in Section 2.7.

In this chapter, I examine some well-known jurisprudential arguments that cast doubt on the possibility of legal reasoning being an exclusively deductive activity; and I assess their relevance for expert systems in law with deductive legal inference engines. I start in Section 5.1 by examining the notion of logic, and its role in the law. In Section 5.2, I discuss how Dworkin's ideas about legal principles affect the feasibility of deductive legal reasoning, while in Section 5.3 I show that human judgment is required whenever a legal conclusion is drawn. Whether legal rules can be formulated or selected, and the facts of a case classified, with the help of logic is considered in Sections 5.4 and 5.5 respectively. Section 5.6 is devoted to the implications of the open texture and vagueness of legal and natural language for legal reasoning, and Section 5.7 deals with the question of implied exceptions being inherent in all legal rules. Based largely on the rest of the chapter, Section 5.8 highlights the nature of the gaps in any rule-based legal knowledge base, and, in the final section, Section 5.9, concluding observations are made.

5.1 LOGIC, LEGAL REASONING, AND DEDUCTIVE LEGAL INFERENCE ENGINES

For many centuries, man has sought to formalize the activities of drawing logical inferences and of engaging in rational thought: indeed it is to the achievement of these goals that much of the study of logic has been devoted.[1] The feasibility, in recent years, of realizing the related objective of mechanizing the process of *deductive* reasoning is, of course, directly attributable to the advent of computer technology.[2] Many AI scientists, in particular, have been concerned with this matter as it is clear that all expert systems must be programmed to execute at least a rudimentary type of logical reasoning. The notions of logic and deductive reasoning will of course strike a responsive chord in the ears of any legal theorist who has considered both the problems of, and the literature that has been devoted to, the nature of legal reasoning and its relationship to the field of logic. In the context of building expert systems in law, it is clear that these classical questions once more fall for consideration. Yet the theorist of legal knowledge engineering is concerned not only with propounding a theory of legal reasoning but also with implementing it in an expert system. It is necessary, therefore, that the proposed account of the processes of legal inference should be sufficiently rigorous as to be of practical use to a computer scientist whose charge is to develop a working system.

In the first instance, it is desirable—for the purposes of a jurisprudential discussion of legal knowledge utilization—that the terms 'logic' and 'deduction' (and variants thereof) be analysed and clarified, for, as shall be seen, in respect of these concepts the legal

---

[1] For both a historical account of attempts to mechanize logical and mathematical reasoning and an indication of the logical and mathematical limitations to which this activity is subject, see Shepherdson, 'The Calculus of Reasoning' (1983), pp. 3–17.

[2] On the mechanization of deductive reasoning, see Robinson, *Logic: Form and Function* (1979), particularly ch. 1. For an indication of progress in this field, see Robinson, 'Logical Reasoning in Machines' (1983), pp. 19–36.

reasoning literature is fettered both by terminological discrepancies and theoretically untenable arguments. Like the terms 'jurisprudence' and 'philosophy', the term 'logic' does not allow of a simple and straightforward account of its nature and scope. For the purposes of this book, however, no detailed enquiry into the foundations of philosophical logic is required and several quotations from influential logicians will provide a satisfactory indication of our concern with the subject. Logic has been characterized variously as: 'the systematic study of the fundamental principles that underlie correct, "necessary" pieces of reasoning . . . as these occur in *proofs, arguments, inferences,* and *deductions*';[3] 'the study, by symbolic means, of the exact conditions under which patterns of argument are valid or invalid';[4] 'the study of consistent sets of beliefs'.[5]

For present purposes, then, the main issues of the study of logic can be taken to be: the validity or soundness of arguments; and the structure and principles of sound, consistent, and valid reasoning patterns and processes. Logicians, it should be understood, seek to develop formal logical systems, such as the predicate or propositional calculi, in order to provide precisely defined, abstract, and purely formal canons or standards, compliance with which while reasoning we can be confident will yield valid arguments. Such formal logics, if Haack is followed in construing that category liberally, embrace not only the 'traditional' Aristotelian syllogistic logic and the 'classical' propositional and predicate logics, but also 'extended' logics such as deontic logic, modal logic, and imperative logic, and 'deviant' logics such as fuzzy logic and many-valued logics.[6] Together these systems provide a variety of ways in which inferences can be drawn in diverse fields of discourse. They have flourished recently as objects of study now that AI scientists have come to recognize their utility for their purposes.[7] Formal systems are expressed in formal languages and consist of sets of axioms (statements for which no proof is required) and/or rules of inference (rules which stipulate what may be inferred from statements of specified logical structure). The inference engine of an expert system

---

[3] Robinson, *Logic: Form and Function* (1979), p. 1. Original emphasis.
[4] *BL*, p. 5.
[5] Hodges, *Logic* (1977), p. 13.
[6] *PL*, ch. 1. Note that, unlike Haack, I exclude 'inductive logics' from the list. By doing so my usages of 'logic', 'deduction', and 'deductive logic' are more comprehensible.
[7] See Turner, *Logics for Artificial Intelligence* (1984).

necessarily implements some formal logical system, and my concern here is to consider the nature and implications of formal logical systems that might be thought to provide the fundamental principles applicable to the process of drawing legal inferences.

As well as 'logic', the term 'deduction' is central to this discussion, and it is useful to characterize it (albeit very roughly) at this stage. Deduction involves reasoning from given premises to a conclusion that necessarily follows from the application to these premises of the canons of some formal logical system. We might say of a valid deductive argument that the assertion of its premises cannot logically be accompanied by a denial of its conclusion without contradiction. Deductive inference, as I have said, can be mechanized by computer.

The connection between deductive logic and the law and the nature of legal logic is a well-documented area of jurisprudence. However, the ambiguity of the term 'logic', with its various connotations and collocations, has itself, no doubt, promoted a greater wealth of commentary from legal theorists than was warranted. Indeed much confusion has been occasioned by the fact that jurisprudents have, in one or more of the following ways, equated the term 'logic' with: (1) reasoning in general; (2) particular types of reasoning procedures; (3) rationality; (4) common sense; (5) the syllogism and syllogistic reasoning; (6) classical systems; (7) the study of both classical and non-classical systems.

These terminological discrepancies render the search for consensus rather difficult but if the field of inquiry is confined to one particular usage, and this is deployed together with the above clarification of the notions of logic and deduction, this greatly simplifies the task. When I talk of logic, and variants thereof, I shall be concerned with deductive logic within traditional, classical, extended, and deviant formal systems. However, problems can arise through the use of 'logic' even in this restricted sense. For there are several ways in which a lawyer or legal theorist may wish to use logic: (1) to present, clarify, and demonstrate an argument of legal theory;[8] (2) to justify *ex post facto* a legal decision that may or may not have been reached through non-logical means;[9] (3) to select factual and legal premises, and to draw legal conclusions from them.

---

[8] See e.g. Dworkin, 'No Right Answer?' (1977), and Raz, *AL*, ch. 4.

[9] On deductive justification of legal decisions, see *LRLT*, chs. 2 and 3, and *JD*, *passim*.

(On the legal conclusion/legal decision distinction, see Section 6.7.) In this book, I am, of course, concerned with this third usage (unless otherwise indicated). The focus of study, then, with a view to building expert systems in law, is the use of deductive logic in the selection of premises and the drawing of legal conclusions, that is, in legal reasoning (Section 2.2): and on this topic a great deal has been said by legal theorists in the past.

It might be thought that we must ignore that vast bulk of writings on logic and the law from the Enlightenment until the 1950s which—with notable exceptions such as those of Bentham and Hohfeld—is undeniably fettered by what might be called the *syllogistic fallacy*: the erroneous equation of traditional Aristotelian logic with logic in the wider sense discussed above. This error affects the works not only of opponents of the use of logic in legal reasoning, but also of the proponents of deductive legal inference techniques. Antagonists—such as Holmes and all those who allegedly were revolting against formalism,[10] and Lloyd[11]—launched misdirected assaults when they focused only on the legal syllogism, because in so doing they failed to address the question of the possibility and desirability of the employment of other more sophisticated non-traditional logics in legal reasoning.[12] However, promoters of the use of logic in legal reasoning from that era—such as Beccaria,[13] Brumbaugh,[14] Lucas,[15] and Walker[16]—in confining their logical weaponry to the syllogistic form, also presented a weak case, for

---

[10] The aphorisms of Holmes are frequently cited in support of rejection of the use of logic in the law. See e.g. *The Common Law* (1968), pp. 5 and 244; *Lochner* v. *New York* 198, US 45, 76 (1905), Holmes J. dissenting; *Collected Legal Papers* (1920), pp. 184, 239, and 280. Both Cohen and Dewey, however, recognized that Holmes was referring only to the syllogism: see 'The Place of Logic in the Law' (1916), and 'Logical Method and Law' (1924), respectively. On the revolt against formalism, see *IJ*, p. 679. There were many lawyers in this camp, e.g. Pound (see his 'Mechanical Jurisprudence' (1908)), Llewellyn, Frank, and indeed the bulk of the American Legal Realists. Outside the USA, Germany's Jhering, France's Geny, and England's Salmond, Paton, and Allen, also fall into this category. Formalism has many synonyms in jurisprudence: mechanical jurisprudence, deductivism, slot-machine jurisprudence, literalism, legal fundamentalism. For a particularly thorough discussion of formalism and legal theory, see Summers, *Instrumentalism and American Legal Theory* (1982), ch. 6. Also see Hart, 'PSLM' (1958).
[11] 'Reason and Logic in the Common Law' (1948), p. 474.
[12] Cf. Guest, 'Logic in the Law' (1961), p. 181.
[13] *On Crimes and Punishment* (1746), p. 15.
[14] *Legal Reasoning and Briefing* (1917), ch. 2.
[15] 'Logic and Law' (1919).
[16] 'The Theory of Relevancy' (1951), p. 14.

they did not reveal the full potency of deductive logic for legal reasoning.

Yet even if it is accepted, as an eminent logician has suggested, that 'predicate calculus is to syllogism what a precision tool is to a blunt knife',[17] no one ought to reject too quickly all the observations of the above commentators: much of their material is pertinent whatever logical system one has in mind, and pertains not exclusively to the intricacies of formal logic, but more generally to lawyers, their research and reasoning habits, and those of their activities that seem to be beyond the province of *any* calculus. Logicians and computer scientists of today could no doubt make nonsense of many past jurisprudents' comments on formal logic and the law, but excessive attention to the logical minutiae might well obscure our view of salient and valuable observations about the legal process that fall far beyond the scope of any logician's knowledge and experience. It is submitted, therefore, that despite their logical infelicities, many fairly old jurisprudential works will provide useful guidance for legal knowledge engineers. This is particularly so if they are read in conjunction with writings of such contemporary theorists as Allen,[18] Gottlieb,[19] Hart,[20] Harris,[21] Horovitz,[22] Jensen,[23] MacCormick,[24] Tammelo,[25] Wasserstrom,[26] and the various deontic logicians (see Section 6.5). These not only reflect an upsurge of interest by legal writers in formal logic, but also often refer to and clarify the older pieces to which I have referred.

Pervading the jurisprudential literature are objections to the notion of deductive legal reasoning and sustained attempts to counter these charges. Much of the remainder of this book is devoted to the identification, analysis, and clarification of these objections and their implications, and formulation of replies to them in so far as they are appropriate in relation to the design of inference engines for

---

[17] *BL*, p. 169.
[18] See e.g. 'Analysis of the Logical Structure of Legal Rules by a Modernized and Formalized Version of Hohfeld's Fundamental Legal Conceptions' (1985). (This paper is co-authored by Saxon.)
[19] *LC*.
[20] 'PSLM' (1958).
[21] *LLS*.
[22] *LL*.
[23] *The Nature of Legal Argument* (1957).
[24] *LRLT*.
[25] *Modern Logic in the Service of Law* (1978).
[26] *JD*.

expert systems in law. Some of these objections, in light of expert systems technology, allow of fairly straightforward retorts, while others highlight the limitations of rule-based expert systems in law. Still others present profound problems that will demand extensive research in the future. Many of them, it should be noted, overlap.

Although it may seem that there is radical disagreement amongst legal theorists over the possible role of deductive logic in legal reasoning, it often transpires that these are disagreements over relevance. Few (if any) theorists deny that logic can perform *some* function in legal reasoning: the divergence of views relates to the *extent* of its applicability and desirability. My concern now is with pinpointing consensus over the possibility of deductive legal reasoning (on the basis of which expert systems work may proceed); but in so doing I shall also expose errors and misconceptions in several analyses.

The potentiality of deductive logic in the legal reasoning process will be seen to mark the limits of the intelligence and utility of expert systems in law of the conceivable future.

5.2 THE ARGUMENT FROM PRINCIPLES: EXPERT SYSTEMS AND NON-RULE STANDARDS

An account of legal inference compatible with the theory of legal knowledge representation developed in Chapter 4 will necessarily speak of the manipulation of production rules as being central to the activity of legal problem-solving. However, such a *rule-based* model of legal reasoning is clearly open to the criticism, now familiar to all contemporary jurisprudents, that, in coming to legal conclusions and decisions, legal reasoning agents often receive insufficient guidance from rules and, therefore, both do, and ought to, apply non-rule standards. This argument can be detected in many early writings, and has been rigorously defended by modern writers such as Eckhoff[27] and Sartorius.[28] But no writer has propounded a more sustained and sophisticated critique of the idea of legal reasoning as a deductive, purely rule-based activity than Dworkin, who for

---

[27] See e.g. 'Guiding Standards in Legal Reasoning' (1976), pp. 205–19.
[28] See e.g. 'Social Policy and Judicial Legislation' (1971), and 'Bayes' Theorem, Hard Cases, and Judicial Discretion' (1977).

twenty years has been casting doubt on the thesis that the law is a system of rules, and upon whose own work a substantial secondary literature has now emerged.[29] In this section, I consider what bearing Dworkin's theses have on the enterprise of building expert systems in law. As will become apparent from my reply to the Argument from Principles, it is not necessary here to enter this jurisprudential debate at length: a brief sketch of the central matters will suffice.

Dworkin argues that lawyers and judges, while solving legal problems, as well as reasoning with rules, often also have recourse to non-rule standards that he terms 'principles'. He uses this term in a generic fashion so as to embrace all 'principles, policies and other sorts of standards' used by lawyers; indeed to denote 'the whole set of these standards other than rules'.[30] Dworkin draws 'a logical distinction' between rules and principles, claiming that while 'both sets of standards point to particular decisions... in particular circumstances... they differ in the character of the direction they give'. In the terminology of AI, Dworkin would claim rules to be non-probabilistic in nature (as I said myself of law-statements), whereas principles, he would suggest, are probabilistic. For he says rules, replete with their exceptions, 'are applicable in an all-or-nothing fashion', and when valid the answers they supply 'must be accepted',[31] whereas a principle simply 'states a reason that argues in one direction, but does not necessitate a particular decision'. Principles therefore have a 'dimension of weight' (functionally equivalent to my 'certainty factor') that all rules lack,[32] and, moreover, can conflict and be balanced against one another in a way that deterministic rules cannot. Finally, principles are standards expressed at a far higher level of generality than rules. In sum, Dworkin says that 'all that is meant, when we say that a particular principle is a principle of our law, is that the principle is one which officials must take into

---

[29] See *TRS, A Matter of Principle* (1985), and *Law's Empire* (1986). Some important secondary commentaries on Dworkin are: Cohen (ed.), *Ronald Dworkin and Contemporary Jurisprudence* (1984); Harris, *LLS*, pp. 160–4; Hart, 'American Jurisprudence through English Eyes: The Nightmare and the Noble Dream' (1977); Raz, 'Legal Principles and the Limits of Law' (1972); Tapper, 'A Note on Principles' (1971); Tur, 'Positivism, Principles and Rules' (1977).

[30] *TRS*, p. 22. Eckhoff points to Dworkin's generic use of 'principles' as a source of confusion amongst critics: 'Guiding Standards in Legal Reasoning' (1976), p. 206.

[31] *TRS*, p. 24.

[32] Ibid., p. 26.

account, if it is relevant, as a consideration inclining in one direction or another'.[33]

Through examples, Dworkin shows how judges in concrete cases actually do deploy principles in their decision-making, and his conclusion is that any theory asserting the law simply to be a system of rules is both descriptively and normatively inadequate. Correspondingly, the legal knowledge engineer who is sympathetic towards the Dworkinian analysis might be dissatisfied with *purely* rule-based expert systems in law. Yet he would not find support in Dworkin's writings for the commencement of a programme for the representation of legal principles within a legal knowledge base. For Dworkin points out that for all principles there are a wealth of counter-instances in which their application is not appropriate because of their relative weight, and these counter-instances 'are not, even in theory, subject to enumeration'.[34] In other words, even although we can, as Tur has shown,[35] cast individual principles in the form of conditional statements, we cannot itemize all their exceptions. With legal productions, in contrast, we can include within the proposed structure (see Section 4.4) the vast bulk of any production's exceptive qualification propositions (which themselves, as I have said, are usually the conclusion slots of other productions). Note also that Dworkin would seem to want to reject the very idea of formalizing an entire legal system or sub-system (that is, consisting both of rules and principles): for in a later essay, in commenting on his earlier work, he states: 'My point was not that "the law" contains a fixed number of standards, some of which are rules and other principles. Indeed, I want to oppose the idea that "the law" is a fixed set of standards of any sort.'[36] And in a still later paper, he says: 'I did not mean, in rejecting the idea that law is a system of rules, to replace that idea with the theory that law is a system of rules and principles. There is no such thing as "the law" as a collection of discrete propositions, each with its own canonical form.'[37] Therefore, the Argument from Principles claims, *inter alia*, that: (1) there is more to legal reasoning than deduction from rules; and (2) any attempt to formalize the contents of a legal system is misconceived. It must be

---

[33] Ibid.
[34] Ibid., p. 25.
[35] 'Positivism, Principles and Rules' (1977), pp. 56 and 61.
[36] *TRS*, p. 76.
[37] Ibid., p. 344.

recognized, of course, that Dworkin's theory has not commanded universal support. Harris, for example, has argued that information of a descriptive legal science 'can be supplied exclusively in terms of rules, and references to a principle which may have been instrumental in the creation of a rule or exception to a rule will be redundant',[38] while others have cast serious doubt on whether his rules/principles distinction is indeed the logical dichotomy Dworkin avers it to be.[39] Wherein, it might well be asked, lies the consensus in this aspect of jurisprudential discourse? It is submitted that even in this controversial debate there is a substratum of agreement to be found, upon which legal knowledge engineers might build their expert systems.

'Legal positivism' according to Dworkin, 'provides a theory of *hard* cases' involving judicial discretion and interstitial legislation, which he rejects in favour of his own theory according to which 'it remains the judge's duty, even in *hard* cases, to discover what the rights of the parties are, not to invent new rights retrospectively'.[40] Hard cases, for Dworkin, are those litigated disputes: 'when no settled rule disposes of the case';[41] when 'reasonable lawyers and judges ... disagree about legal rights';[42] and 'when no settled rule dictates a decision either way'.[43] As I show in Section 6.7, there are many ways in which a case might be hard. However, what about clear cases where there is indeed a settled rule under which the facts of the case can be *subsumed* (see Section 5.5)? In answer to this question, we find consensus between Dworkin and the legal positivists who argue for rule-based models of legal reasoning. For, as Harris has said, 'Dworkin does not challenge the conventional positivist assumptions about the decision of legal questions in clear cases by the application of valid rules',[44] and indeed, his rights thesis 'presupposes' the 'model of rules' concept of law he would have us reject.[45] In other words—those of MacCormick—'Dworkin has added to, rather than subverted, the "ruling theory" which he thinks

---

[38] *LLS*, p. 67.
[39] See e.g. Tur, 'Positivism, Principles and Rules' (1977), Raz, 'Legal Principles and the Limits of Law' (1972), and Tapper, 'A Note on Principles' (1971).
[40] *TRS*, p. 81. Emphasis added.
[41] Ibid., p. 81.
[42] Ibid.
[43] *TRS*, p. 83. Also see pp. 359–63.
[44] *LP*, p. 173.
[45] *LLS*, pp. 158–9.

so inadequate', and there does indeed seem to be implicit in Dworkin's writings, as in *all* theorists' arguments, a recognition that 'there is a certain sense in which the "rules" have logical primacy'.[46] It would seem that there is general agreement that what goes on in *clear* cases—and those in that class decided both by judicial and non-judicial legal reasoning agents—is uncontroversial: so much so that no one has offered a detailed explanation of what it is that makes a legal dispute a clear case. No jurisprudential disputes have raged over clear cases. And most writers do seem to conceive of reasoning in clear cases as quasi-deductive in character. Dworkin himself has said that 'in easy cases legal rights can be deduced, in something close to a syllogistic fashion, from propositions reported in books that are available to the public, and even more readily available to lawyers the public can hire'.[47] All legal theorists, it is submitted, operate within a rule-based paradigm:[48] they share the background assumption that clear cases can be solved through the application of rules. But they disagree over both what does and ought to happen where the legal rules seem to have gaps (see Section 5.8) or where they seem to dictate conclusions contrary to principle or purpose (see Section 5.7), or when they seem to be silent. Moreover, theorists disagree over the significance of the role of deduction in the solving of clear cases.

What is clearly lacking in the jurisprudential literature is an articulation of the concept of clear cases (as expressly distinguished from hard cases) and a theory of the resolution of clear cases. Throughout this and the following chapter I seek to remedy that deficiency, and provide an account of clear cases based on jurisprudential consensus.

For an expert system in law to remain jurisprudentially impartial, that is, for it to embody no contentious theories of law or legal reasoning, I argue, it must reason only with rules—within the current jurisprudential paradigm. In consequence, there will be no facility for reasoning with non-rule standards. This, of course, may not trouble those theorists who conceive of the law as a system of rules peppered with gaps and indeterminacies, into which interstices, in

---

[46] *LRSD*, p. 140.
[47] *TRS*, p. 337.
[48] On the concept of 'paradigms', see Kuhn, *The Structure of Scientific Revolutions* (1970).

hard cases, the reasoning agent necessarily injects various extra-legal standards.

But for followers of Dworkin who argue there to be principles of law, or of Simpson who claim there to be non-rule standards of common law (see Section 3.3), this inherent limitation of representational scope deserves justification (although one need not be taken, simply in virtue of offering a reply, to be espousing any particular theory). I said in Section 1.3 that expert systems in law ought to be for the use of general legal practitioners, who when confronted with legal problems beyond their own fields of competence, may use computer systems as assistants rather than referring their cases to other lawyers. But Dworkinian principles, and principles of the common law, are domain-independent legal knowledge, and as such should have been inculcated into such lawyers during their education and training. Competent lawyers should not need to engage in research to acquire such knowledge but should be familiar with it anyway: it is not domain-independent knowledge (other than meta-knowledge) that it is conceived expert systems will embody, but rather domain-specific, 'technical' rules with which only specialists are now conversant.

The Argument from Principles, then, even if cogent, does not prejudice the development of expert systems in law as I have characterized them. I now proceed, therefore, with only rule-based systems in mind.

5.3 THE ARGUMENT FROM ACT OF WILL

The importance of the Argument from Act of Will resides in its clarification of the operation of logic and, crucial for present purposes, in its provision of the bases of the Argument from Legal Rule Choice (see Section 5.4) and the Argument from Particularity of Facts (see Section 5.5).

In crudest form, in relation to deductive legal reasoning, it can be summarized thus: the activity of legal reasoning ultimately presupposes an *act of will* and the presence of clearly applicable rules and the facts of some case do not lead to *any* conclusion unless a reasoning agent does indeed draw the inference. Hart captures the thrust of the argument in his comment that 'rules cannot provide for their own application, and even in the clearest case a human being must apply them'. He makes this claim having noted that 'rules cannot claim their own instances' (see the Argument from Legal Rule Choice), and 'fact situations do not await the judge neatly labelled with the rule applicable to them' (see the Argument from Particularity of Facts).[36]

The techniques of logic, like expert systems, are tools of human beings and require human thought and action in order that they can operate. If a conclusion is arrived at through deduction this means that *someone* has used the techniques of deduction to draw their conclusion. This point might seem painfully obvious. Yet a failure to recognize its analogue in the context of computer use lies at the root of the widespread fear of the new technology. For computers are the slaves, and not the masters, of their human users.

A fuller statement of the Argument from Act of Will, from Kant's *Critique of Pure Reason*, raises other issues that are clearly of relevance to the design of expert systems. Kant said that 'judgement' is 'the faculty of subsuming under rules; that is, of distinguishing whether something does or does not stand under a given rule (casus datae legis).' He continues:

General logic contains, and can contain, no rules for judgement. For since general logic abstracts from all content of knowledge, the sole task that remains to it is to give an analytical exposition of the form of knowledge [as expressed] in concepts, in judgements, and in inferences, and so to obtain formal rules for all employment of understanding. If it is sought to give general instructions how we are to subsume under these rules, that is, to distinguish whether something does or does not come under them, that could only be by means of another rule. This in turn, for the very reason that it is a rule, again demands guidance from judgement. And thus it appears that, though understanding is capable of being instructed, and of being equipped with rules, judgement is a peculiar talent which can be practised only, and cannot be taught. It is the specific quality of so-called mother-wit; and its lack no school can make good.[50]

Given that expert systems apply production rules to the facts of cases in accordance with some logical calculus, Kant's version of the Argument from Act of Will reminds us that in every interaction with

---

[49] 'PPL', p. 106. For another rendition of this argument, see Gottlieb, *LC*, ch. 5, especially pp. 67–9.
[50] *Critique of Pure Reason* (1929), pp. 177–8.

these systems there must be some ultimate *human* judgment without which the system is unable to offer any guidance. This act of will and judgment, I show in Section 5.5, determines the applicability of one or more legal productions to the instant case and must be executed beyond the confines of any formal logical system. He is surely correct in insisting that such human judgment is an instinctive process but, as this book suggests, perhaps he and others have underestimated the utility of these other rules, of which Kant talks, in the activity of actually making a judgment. In the terminology of Chapter 3, in the knowledge bases of expert systems in law, these rules are legal heuristics: predictive, derivative, and meta-, legal knowledge formulated as legal productions. Given a sufficiently extensive representation of these legal heuristics, the necessity for the involvement of 'mother-wit', at a technical legal level, can be suppressed to a tolerable minimum.

The Argument from Act of Will, then, in relation to expert systems in law with the interactive user interface described in Section 2.7, alerts us to the fact that legal conclusions can never be drawn by computer systems in the absence of some initial human judgment. Moreover, it cautions us that if expert systems are to be truly useful assistants, legal knowledge engineers must seek to represent such a sufficiency of legal heuristics that will render any human involvement relatively passive. These matters will be dealt with in more detail in the following sections.[51]

5.4 THE ARGUMENT FROM LEGAL RULE CHOICE

Gottlieb, in *The Logic of Choice*, introduces the Arguments from Legal Rule Choice and Particularity of Facts in the following passage: 'It is always possible to formulate a major premise (rule) and a minor premise (facts) of a judicial syllogism so that it entails a necessary conclusion. But this conceals the fact that the hard problem in a legal decision consists in the adoption and formulation of such

---

[51] The Argument from Act of Will might be thought to be attributable to Kelsen, by whom norms were regarded as the meanings of acts of will (see e.g. *ELMP*, pp. 229, 240–2). Kelsen's views in this respect, however, also bear on the question of the logic of norms, and I deal with that matter, and with some of his views, in Sections 6.4 and 6.5.

premises.'[52] And the hard problem to which Gottlieb refers cannot be resolved by deduction, it is often argued, because, as Guest admits, 'logic does not purport to determine the content of the premisses on which it works; nor does it purport to decide from which premisses we should begin or in any way disable our choice'.[53] The Argument from Legal Rule Choice asserts, therefore, that legal reasoning cannot be deductive because one central aspect of the process involves choosing the legal premise in what, *ex hypothesi*, is necessarily a non-deductive manner. In consequence, it might be said, expert systems will be of no help in the selection of legal productions applicable to any set of problem data.

It is instructive at this stage to consider what is perhaps meant by the extremely vague propositions that legal reasoning can or cannot be deductive. A weak version of the deductive theory asserts no more than Gottlieb concedes, namely, that we can always (or at least sometimes), so arrange our legal and factual premises in a fashion that yields a conclusion that follows, by the canons of some formal logical system, as a matter of necessity and that can therefore correctly be termed a deductive argument. In the context of expert systems, this *weak thesis* confirms the possibility of generating legal conclusions from the application of a body of production rules to a set of facts. Yet some antagonists of deductivism in law, while not rejecting the weak thesis, put forward the Argument from Unimportance (see Section 6.6) which states simply that this role of deduction is relatively insignificant. More than this, they say that deduction plays a role only in one aspect of the legal reasoning process, for that activity also involves, the critics argue, the selection of premises. A stronger thesis, then, must claim that an important and significant part of the process of premiss selection (both legal and factual) can be, and is, executed on a deductive basis.

It is only a stronger thesis, therefore, that provides an answer to the Argument from Legal Rule Choice. There are, however, three discernible versions of the Argument from Legal Rule Choice, which must each be addressed in turn. First, there is the claim that the individuation of laws—for the purposes of their subsequent inclusion in a deductive argument—is not itself a process in which formal logic can have a major role, or at least is a process for which we have de-

---

[52] *LC*, p. 17.
[53] 'Logic in the Law' (1961), p. 178.

veloped no suitable logical apparatus.[54] I corroborated this claim earlier when, in Section 4.2, I argued that legal knowledge representation is a human activity. I said there that no computer systems (and, therefore, no logical processes) can be used, on their own, to derive legal rules embodied in the formal sources of law, because of their inability to process natural language. In other words, legal science (in all its various aspects), cannot be executed through the application of deductive logic, and legal reasoning in so far as it involves the formulation of legal premises cannot be represented as an entirely deductive process. In respect of expert systems, it can be concluded only that legal knowledge representation is not a deductive activity. But this does not tell against a deductive legal inference engine.

Secondly, there is the suggestion that 'in many cases competing major premises [legal rules] are advanced and it is not possible to use syllogistic reasoning to determine which... is the applicable one'.[55] Where there is more than one applicable legal rule, it is asserted, logic cannot be of use in the process of *conflict resolution* (as it is known by AI scientists). It is necessary to be aware, however, of what might be taken to be two different types of conflict. On the one hand, we might say there is a conflict where two (or more) valid rules seem to apply to the same circumstances but point to different legal conclusions: and I have already said that a legal domain containing such a conflict is not suitable for current expert systems development (see Sections 2.4 and 4.3). Those theorists, like Harris,[56] who believe that legal scientists should describe the law as a non-contradictory field of meaning, would in any event argue that there are conflict resolution strategies for such apparent conflicts (and, for our purposes, comparisons of certainty factors may be of use in this respect).

On the other hand, we might also speak of a type of conflict where there are two (or more) valid rules that seem to apply to the same general circumstances (although they have different antecedents) and also seem to dictate the *same* conclusion. Such rules, in a sense,

[54] When Gottlieb talks of the 'formulation' of premises, we can take him to have this version of the argument in mind (in so far as legal premises are concerned). See *LC*, p. 17.

[55] Gottlieb, *LC*, p. 18. Also see Stone, *The Province and Function of Law* (1968), pp. 138–9, and Horovitz, *LL*, p. 140.

[56] *LLS*, pp. 81–3. Also see Harris, 'Kelsen and Normative Consistency' (1986), p. 220.

compete within one another. Although the presence of these rules in the knowledge bases of some (non-legal) rule-based expert systems is taken to constitute 'redundancy',[57] this term is entirely inapposite in respect of expert systems in law. For, as I argue in Section 6.3, a competent lawyer will explore many possibilities, and will welcome the support of a range of different rules for any single conclusion he could be called upon to justify. Such supporting rules are far from redundant. This second type of conflict is illustrated in Section 3.7, in respect of adultery and behaviour rules, during the discussion of domain-specific meta-rules. Although, because of the type of expert system involved, it was unnecessary for the purposes of the Oxford project to use the quoted suggestion of Clive as the basis of a conflict resolution strategy, it could be so used in other systems to direct the most promising line of *search* (Sections 6.2 and 6.3).

It is crucial to note that if conflicts (of whatever sort) between legal productions can be resolved by some acceptable *resolution meta-rules*, then it is clearly within the power of deductive inference engines to implement such rules.[58] The second version of the Argument from Legal Rule Choice, therefore, is considerably weakened by the existence of acceptable conflict resolution search strategies. Moreover, there is now good reason to believe that a stronger deductive thesis is tenable, in that logic can sometimes be used to assist in the selection amongst competing legal premisses.

The third version of the Argument from Legal Rule Choice is the contention that, even where there is no question of conflict, rules cannot 'provide for their own application', in the words of Hart.[59] In some respects, this aspect of the Argument from Legal Rule Choice seems akin to the Argument from Act of Will, in that it is being suggested that human beings must apply rules, for a rule cannot 'itself step forward to claim its own instances'.[60] There is an overlap here, but the latter argument is best seen as referring to the initial human judgment that must be made at the start of any line of reasoning, whereas the former pertains to the manner in which any production is *fired* (see Section 6.2). I shall now show that this firing

---

[57] On redundancy, see Suwa, Scott, and Shortliffe, *An Approach to Verifying Completeness and Consistency in a Rule-Based Expert System* (1982). On this second type of conflict, see *AI*, pp. 174–6.

[58] Cf. Sinclair, 'Legal Reasoning: In Search of an Adequate Theory of Argument' (1971), p. 841.

[59] 'PPL', p. 106.

[60] Hart, *CL*, p. 123.

can be part of a deductive process (in contrast to the exercise of 'mother-wit').

A legal production, of the sort introduced in Section 4.4, is a compound conditional statement of the form 'If p, then q' where the antecedent p stipulates the conditions of the production's application (and the qualifications to these conditions), and the consequent q directs the reasoning agent as to the legal implications (or likely implications) of the satisfaction of p. Consider now the following production:

$$K \wedge L \wedge M \wedge \neg N \Rightarrow R$$

If K, L, and M hold, and N does not (a user says 'yes' three times, and 'no' once, respectively, in reply—on the basis of the instant case—to questions regarding the truth of K, L, M, and N), and given the further rule of inference 'if p, then rule that has p as its antecedent is applicable',[61] then as a matter of formal logic, R may be inferred and is necessarily a relevant or applicable consequent. Moreover the production itself is relevant to the case at hand. More generally, a legal production can be formulated so that it has, as its antecedent, precise conditions and qualifications. When these are satisfied it can meaningfully be claimed that the complete production (complete in the sense that it consists both of antecedent and consequent) provides for its own application ('triggering off...its own application', in the words—perhaps surprisingly—of Gottlieb[62]) and this operation can be called deductive. In other words, given a collection of facts or interim conclusions, and our additional rule of inference, we are committed by logic to the application of certain rules from which, in turn, a final legal conclusion can eventually be deduced.

Furthermore, if rules of this structure are represented in expert systems then it can be expected that when they are presented, via their users' responses, with an array of facts and/or interim conclusions, they will select the appropriate rules. My replies to the second and third versions of the Argument from Legal Rule Choice, then, promote what might be called the *strongish* deductive thesis. A

---

[61] This rule of inference, held in all rule-based systems, has a similar effect to the widely accepted rule of inference, *modus ponens*, which states that for any statements P and Q, from P together with '$P \Rightarrow Q$' we may infer Q.

[62] *LC*, p. 39. Cf. Eckhoff's explanation of Dworkin's account of rules, in 'Guiding Standards in Legal Reasoning' (1976), pp. 207–8. Note then that, on this analysis, Dworkin's treatment of reasoning with rules accords with the *weak* deductive thesis.

stronger one still emerges in the next section, from my riposte to the Argument from Particularity of Facts.

5.5 THE ARGUMENT FROM PARTICULARITY OF FACTS: CLASSIFICATION AND SUBSUMPTION

In the previous section, it was seen that some writers consider the central but non-deductive aspect of legal reasoning to be the process of premiss selection. The Argument from Particularity of Facts is a variant of that claim and asserts that the process of determining the factual premisses—the facts of the case—is necessarily a non-deductive one. Jensen, in *The Nature of Legal Argument*, has framed the charge as follows:

The problem in a great number of cases may be expressed symbolically thus: All *S* is *P*, but the crucial question is just whether the conduct of the defendant (or of the plaintiff or of the accused) is *S*. In other words, the problem is one of classification rather than one of deduction.[63]

And in respect of classification, Hart has noted that

fact situations do not await us neatly labelled, creased, and folded; nor is their legal classification written on them to be simply read off by the judge. Instead, in applying legal rules, someone must take the responsibility of deciding what words do or do not cover some case in hand, with all the practical consequences involved in this decision.[64]

Or, again, as Gottlieb says,

The main philosophical objection to regarding legal reasoning as a species of deductive reasoning is that the heart of the question in legal reasoning is the classification of particulars. If one gives a term a certain interpretation, then a certain conclusion follows, but logic cannot help classify particulars.[65]

This argument has recently been reaffirmed by Detmold, who in doing so addresses the concern of this book directly. For he stresses

---

[63] (1957), p. 16. Also see Wilson, 'The Nature of Legal Reasoning: A Commentary with Special Reference to Professor MacCormick's Theory' (1982), pp. 278–9, and 280. Wilson follows Jensen, Hart, and Gottlieb, in developing the Argument from Particularity of Facts, but her attack on MacCormick is misplaced, for MacCormick defends the *strongish* and not the *strong* deductivist thesis.

[64] 'PSLM', pp. 63–4. Also see Golding, 'Kelsen and the Concept of "Legal System"' (1961), pp. 380–1.

[65] *LC*, p. 17. Note Gottlieb's implicit vindication of the *stronger* thesis.

that beyond general legal rules 'ever present and available for hard decision, are particulars', and yet insists that 'what is ultimately beyond the grasp of a computer is not complexity, but particulars'.[66] The facts of *any* case are very complex, he points out, and he refers us in this respect to (although is not entirely convinced by) Hampshire's thesis of the inexhaustibility of description according to which any situation has an inexhaustible set of identifiable features, only the few salient of which we express (or even notice) when explaining events in our world. How then can deductive logic or expert systems be used to classify the complex web of facts of even the clearest of cases?

To answer that question, it is necessary to have a clearer understanding of the process by which legal reasoning agents classify facts, and, as it is often said, *subsume*[67] them under the more general categories established by the law: this is the process of factual premiss selection that precedes the drawing of legal conclusions.

The facts of any case can always be characterized in a vast number of different, highly specific ways: and, because the facts involve acts, events, and circumstances that hold in particular points in time and space, they are, to that extent, unique. The antecedents of legal rules (law-statements), in contrast, invariably have temporal and spatial scope beyond single, identifiable points in time and space. Moreover, their conditions and qualifications are expressed in terms of categories of a higher level of generality than those used in any adequate description of the relevant facts of a case. When a lawyer is confronted with a collection of data, the legal consequences of which it is his task to divine, he must, on the basis of his experience and knowledge, analyse the data, eliminate what he considers to be irrelevant, and assemble the residue in some orderly fashion. And it

---

[66] *The Unity of Law and Morality: A Refutation of Legal Positivism* (1984), pp. 261 and 15, respectively. For a critique of Detmold's arguments in this respect, see Susskind, 'Detmold's Refutation of Positivism and the Computer Judge' (1986).

[67] On classification and subsumption, see: Hart, *CL*, pp. 121–4; Paulson, 'Material and Formal Authorisation in Kelsen's Pure Theory' (1980), pp. 175–7; Guest, 'Logic in the Law' (1961), pp. 193–4; Alchourron and Bulygin, *NS*, pp. 31–4; Gottlieb, *LC*, pp. 43–7; Castberg, *PLP*, pp. 52–68; Walker, *SLS*, pp. 439–41; Horovitz, *LL*, pp. 68–72; Golding, 'Kelsen and the Concept of "Legal System"' (1961), pp. 380–1; Wilson, 'The Nature of Legal Reasoning: A Commentary with Special Reference to Professor MacCormick's Theory' (1982), pp. 278–9; MacCormick, *LRLT*, pp. 95–7; Kelsen, *ELMP*, pp. 246–7; Detmold, *The Unity of Law and Morality: A Refutation of Legal Positivism* (1984), pp. 14–17 and 260–1; Harris, *LLS*, pp. 84–92 (subsumption as a logical principle of legal science). Much of my discussion is based on a synthesis of these writings.

is the legal implications of the residual, specific data that he will identify through the application of more general legal rules to them. Of course, such a model is an over-simplification, as the processes of analysis, elimination, assembly, and identification will not normally progress linearly but will interact and have mutual impact: together we often refer to these processes as those of classification and subsumption. It is clear, then, that subsumption involves bringing the particular under the general, and in so doing thereby classifying the particular, but the precise nature of this operation requires further elucidation. (This clarification, as I said in Section 3.6, will also shed light on the relationship between law-statements and law-derivations.)

Let us take the example of the rule forbidding 'motor vehicles' to be driven through a public park and the case of X driving his 'saloon car' in that park (assuming no outlandish circumstances). Reasoning agents no doubt would deem that rule applicable having 'subsumed' the facts within the terms of the rule, or, more precisely, the term 'saloon car' under the heading 'motor vehicle'. The question that must be answered is: what is the nature of the relationship between 'motor vehicle' and 'saloon car', and, more generally, what is the relationship between such general and particular terms of our language? It is submitted that there is no *logical* link between 'motor vehicle' and 'saloon car', or between the general and the particular, but rather the tie is of a contingent, semantic, and empirical nature. For instance, we cannot, it is suggested, deduce (in the strict sense) a rule about saloon cars from a rule about motor vehicles. Nor can we infer, as a matter of logic, that any particular word is an instantiation of a more general verbal category, or vice versa, for the relationship is one established through our linguistic usage and is not one dictated by logic.[68] Logic is concerned with form and not with semantic content. The operation of subsuming the particular under the general in legal reasoning is not therefore a logical operation, and that is the heart of most renditions of the Argument from Particularity of Facts.

In relation to expert systems, it would seem to follow, then, that the process of classifying and subsuming the facts of any case within the terms of the knowledge base cannot be executed by the system, because an initial human subsumptive judgment based on know-

[68] Cf. Harris, *LLS*, pp. 87–8; Kelsen, *GTLS*, p. 112, *ELMP*, pp. 246–7; Alchourron and Bulygin, *NS*, p. 33.

ledge of linguistic usage must be made. Yet surely an extensive array of law-predictions, law-derivations, and legal meta-rules might assist in the classification and subsumption by giving instances of accepted or predicted subsumptive relations? Given that instructions on how to engage in the procedure of determining if fact situations fall within that scope of a particular rule can be expressed, in Kant's words, 'by means of another rule', then classification and subsumption may also be carried out, in part, by deductive methods[69] and by expert systems. By this it is meant that we are assisted in the task of labelling, creasing, and folding the facts by a collection of productions that are, in a sense, about classifying and subsuming. In that way, a *strong* thesis of deductive legal reasoning is espoused. (On the logic of this subsumptive process, see Section 6.5.)

A legal knowledge base can be envisaged, therefore, within which are represented law-statements, phrased often in legalistic terms and usually pitched at a high level of generality. Further legal heuristics, at a higher level of specificity, will also be included, and will be represented as descendant nodes in a decision tree, tending, downwards in the tree, from 'institutional' to 'brute' fact (see Section 4.5). In an interaction with a system with such a knowledge base, the user could effectively request for progressively more simplified questions until such a stage at which he no longer requires assistance, or when the questions based on the primitive productions have been posed. Then he must, as Kant argued, exercise his judgment (for there could be no infinite regress of productions). It is that part of the reasoning process, of course, that cannot be regarded as deductive, and with which the expert system can be of no help. The user must answer 'yes', 'no', or 'don't know' to all the questions asked of him (other than to those that demand the input of basic data). To a great extent it does seem that his 'mother-wit' is brought to bear simply by a process of what might be called *linguistic pattern matching*—his conception of the facts are compared with what Dworkin, in *Law's Empire*, terms the 'acontextual meaning' of the questions posed.[70] But this itself raises two difficulties: first, what if the language of a question is unclear? and, second, do we not neglect important aspects of legal

---

[69] Cf. Sinclair, 'Legal Reasoning: In Search of an Adequate Theory of Argument' (1971), pp. 840–1 and n. 97.

[70] Dworkin defines acontextual meaning as 'the meaning we would assign them [words] if we had no special information about the context of their use or the intentions of their author' (*Law's Empire* (1986), p. 17). I shall refer to this useful term again in this book.

reasoning if our inferences are guided solely by linguistic convention? These two questions are addressed in Sections 5.6 and 5.7 respectively.

Note lastly, for jurisprudential purposes, that it is possible, in principle, to have a system with such extensive knowledge that any judgments made in relation to questions actually answered by the user would be so far removed from judgments of law that it would be obtuse to withhold the term 'deductive' in relation to the process of legal reasoning executed by the computer. In which event, it might be argued that legal reasoning is entirely deductive. Strictly speaking, even on that account, however, there are non-deductive parts of the process: first, the Kantian 'mother-wit' element (the Argument from Particularity of Facts, in this respect, collapses into the Argument from Act of Will), and secondly, any operation of identifying empirical data—such as the reading of rules. But these two non-deductive components, it might be contended, are also present in mathematical reasoning, the paradigm of deductive reasoning. That is true, but the thoroughgoing deductivist must still then offer a retort to the first strand of the Argument from Legal Rule Choice regarding knowledge representation as a human and non-deductive activity. Such a reply has not been formulated. In any event, I can now offer a semi-formal summary of the weak, strongish, and strong deductivist theses.

1. Weak Thesis

(1) if we take it to be axiomatic that the facts of a case are an instance of 'p' and,
(2) if we accept the validity of the legal rule, '$p \Rightarrow q$' then
(3) we may conclude 'q'.

This is really an affirmation, in a legal context, of the logician's rule of inference, *modus ponens*. Note that even this thesis is challenged: by the Arguments from Unimportance, Implied Exception, and Truth-Value.

2. Strongish Thesis

This thesis accepts the weak thesis, but adds that:

(1) if we take it to be axiomatic that the facts of a case are an instance of 'p' and,

(2) if we accept the validity of the rule of inference,
'$p \Rightarrow$ a legal rule that has p as its antecedent is applicable', and
(3) if we accept the validity of the legal rule, '$p \Rightarrow q$' and,
(4) if we accept, in virtue of some acceptable rule of conflict resolution, that rule's precedence over any other rules having p as their antecedents, then we may conclude
(5) '$p \Rightarrow q$' is the applicable valid legal rule.

3. *Strong Thesis*

This thesis accepts the weak and strongish theses, but adds that it is theoretically possible for the legal heuristics, '$n \Rightarrow p$', '$m \Rightarrow n$', '$l \Rightarrow m$', '$k \Rightarrow l$', etc., to be represented, where variables tending towards the start of the alphabet tend towards propositions of brute fact, and the heuristics, therefore, assist in classification and subsumption. In Section 6.7, I show the strong thesis to be the foundation of my argument that expert systems in law may, in the future, solve not only *clear* cases, but also those that I introduce and term as *deductive* cases.

5.6 THE ARGUMENT FROM OPEN TEXTURE AND VAGUENESS

The Argument from Open Texture and Vagueness was introduced to legal theory by Hart. He explains and develops his doctrine of open texture, in particular, in many of his writings,[71] and most fully in *The Concept of Law*.[72] His expression of the argument in 1958, however is perhaps the most convincing:

If we are to communicate with each other at all, and if, as in the most elementary form of law, we are to express our intentions that a certain type of behaviour be regulated by rules, then the general words we use ... must have some standard instance in which no doubts are felt about its application. There must be a core of settled meaning, but there will be, as well, a penumbra of debatable cases in which words are neither obviously applicable nor obviously ruled out ... We may call the problems which arise outside the hard core of standard instances or settled meaning 'problems of the penumbra'; they are always with us whether in relation to such trival things as the regulation of the use of the public park or in relation to the multidimensional

---

[71] See the Introduction, and Essays 2, 3, and 12 of *EJP*.
[72] (1961), pp. 121–32.

generalities of a constitution. If a penumbra of uncertainty must surround all legal rules, then their application to specific cases in the penumbral area cannot be a matter of logical deduction, and so deductive reasoning, which for generations has been cherished as the very perfection of human reasoning, cannot serve as a model for what judges, or indeed anyone, should do in bringing particular cases under general rules. In this area men cannot live by deduction alone.[73]

The related problem of the vagueness of terms of natural language must also be mentioned here. Although Hart sometimes seems to ascribe similar characterizations to the notions both of open texture and vagueness,[74] Waismann—the ordinary language philosopher from whom Hart explicitly borrows the doctrine of open texture— distinguished the two:

Vagueness should be distinguished from *open texture*. A word which is actually used in a fluctuating way (such as 'heap' or 'pink') is said to be vague; a term like 'gold', though its actual use may not be vague, is non-exhaustive or of an open texture in that we can never fill up all the possible gaps through which a doubt may seep in. Open texture, then, is something like *possibility of vagueness*.[75]

It is apparent that the notions of vagueness and open texture are very closely connected. Waismann's analysis might be clarified by suggesting that words are vague when they clearly have no definite set of necessary and sufficient conditions governing their use and application. Terms such as 'fair' and 'reasonable', in this sense, can be seen as being vague. Our use and definitions of many other words, however, indicates that not all terms are vague in this way. For instance, chemists' definitions of the substance (not the colour) 'gold' seem to lay out precise conditions governing our use of that empirical concept, and, prima facie, render it far from vague. Waismann's point, however, is that, in respect of borderline cases, we can never rule out the possibility of having to modify those definitions that are sufficient for standard cases: we can never reject the possibility of vagueness. MacCormick seems to confirm this analysis: he discusses vagueness as a feature of rules 'over and above' the question of open texture, and suggests an example of vagueness in law to be where 'a

---

[73] 'PSLM', pp. 63–4. Note Hart's argument is relevant for all classes of reasoning agents.

[74] See e.g. 'Dias and Hughes on Jurisprudence' (1957–8), p. 144.

[75] See 'Verifiability' (1951), p. 120. Original emphasis.

common law rule or statute imports some general standard such as that of "reasonableness"'.[76] Other rules might contain no such obviously vague terms: but the doctrine of open texture reminds us that there may arise cases to which such rules are neither clearly applicable nor inapplicable. While it is important to be aware of the above distinction, it is often sufficient to consider their combined implications for expert systems under the same heading. The two problems of open texture and vagueness, then, may be referred to collectively as the problem of *semantic indeterminacy*.[77]

The three important consequences of semantic indeterminacy for jurisprudence are: first, that 'we have no way of framing rules of language which are ready for all imaginable possibilities'[78] (see Section 5.8); secondly, legal rules can offer the reasoning agent only a limited degree of guidance; and thirdly, as Hart argues in the quoted extract, doubt is cast on the possibility of deducton in legal reasoning. These matters, as this chapter establishes, are also of import to legal knowledge engineers. The particular concern of this section is with the question of deduction, because, as I said in Section 5.1, the utility of an expert system will depend on the extent to which legal reasoning can be executed deductively.

From the extract above, and from later works,[79] it is apparent that Hart accepts deductive legal reasoning is possible. But he does remind us that surrounding every rule there is a penumbra of doubt—a fringe of uncertainty of scope—and in those cases that relate to this penumbra, in bringing particular facts within the ambit of the more general categories of legal rules, the reasoning agent, and, it may be inferred, the expert system, cannot rely solely on deductive inference mechanisms.[80] But when, more precisely, according to the Hartian appraisal, is deduction possible? At this stage I shall follow Hart's earlier views on the matter, but shall subject them

---

[76] *HLAH*, p. 125.

[77] I shall not be discussing 'semantic ambiguity' which relates to the use of words that bear more than one meaning. Ambiguous words, of course, need not be vague. Following Allen, in 'Language, Law and Logic: Plain Legal Drafting for the Electronic Age' (1980), p. 75, it can be taken that ambiguity in legal language is usually inadvertent rather than deliberate; it may be eliminated at the knowledge representation or tuning stages, and so should not affect the user of an expert system.

[78] Hart, *EJP*, p. 274.

[79] See e.g. 'PPL', p. 106. There he talks of '[t]he decisions of cases which cannot be exhibited as deductions', implying thereby that some decisions can indeed be deductively exhibited.

[80] I am very grateful to Professor Hart for clarification of this matter.

to further scrutiny in the following section in my discussion of *purpose.* In his early work,[81] as the previous quotation indicates, Hart seems to argue that deductive legal reasoning is possible in those cases in which the *meaning* of the words of a rule render it applicable to a factual situation. As he said much later, he treated it then as if it was 'purely a linguistic matter' at stake.[82] The applicability of rules could be settled, he thought then, in accordance with 'the settled conventions of language'.[83]

Accepting Hart's early analysis, then, it follows that all expert systems whose inference procedures are solely deductive will be of little aid in solving 'problems of the penumbra' (but may well function effectively where part of the knowledge base's core of settled meaning is involved). This substantially jurisprudential conclusion, however, must now be placed in the context of legal knowledge engineering. Semantic indeterminacy is relevant for expert systems in law at the point of the user interface. I submitted in Section 2.7 that research and development should focus on systems which ask users questions phrased in natural language to which only affirmative, negative, or 'don't know' responses would be appropriate. The replies of the user are based both on the facts of the instant case as he has conceptualized and categorized them prior to any consultations, and also on the classifications and categories offered to him by the system during any interactions. As I said in Section 5.5, the responses result in the subsumption (or not) of the instant facts within the antecedent(s) of some legal production(s). According to Hart, if the system asked a question to which there was an incontrovertible reply, given its 'acontextual meaning' (see the previous section) and our accepted ordinary, and legal, linguistic usage, then, in that event, a conclusion would follow logically from the response of the user (although whether we might call this whole process a deductive one is called into question by the Argument from Act of Will). A problem of the penumbra would result if the antecedent(s) of the legal productions, that is, the questions, 'are neither obviously applicable nor obviously ruled out', and so 'linguistic pattern matching' (as I called it in the previous section) is not possible. In that situation, there is no clear reply and logic dictates no decision (although once a

---

[81] 'PSLM' was written in 1958.
[82] Introduction to *EJP*, p. 7.
[83] Ibid., pp. 7–8.

choice between the responses is made, the system will indicate the logical consequences of that selection).[84]

The doubt over the applicability of the questions may be due, on the one hand, to the vagueness of the language in which they are couched. For instance, the Oxford prototype system might ask a vague question regarding behaviour of one spouse being such that it would be *unreasonable* for the other to cohabit with the first. On the other hand, the doubt may stem from the open texture of the general classifying terms used. Thus, a user concerned with a skateboard and its use in a public park, while using an expert system that asked whether a 'vehicle' was driven, would be faced with a problem of classification of an entity that fell on the fringes of a class. The Argument from Open Texture and Vagueness, as extended for present purposes, simply states that expert systems cannot assist in solving those aspects of problems that arise because of vagueness or open texture, for these cannot be resolved through the application of any logical system.

Yet that argument does require some refinement for surely, as I have hinted periodically throughout this chapter, the use of more particular law-statements and of legal heuristics, such as law-derivations, in the formulation of more specific questions, would go some way to reducing the open texture and vagueness of many questions. Where a user on the basis of a question finds his case to be penumbral, he should be able to command the display of a query framed at a higher level of specificity and in that way perhaps render his case clearer. Thus, in the last example, the vague question with the word 'unreasonable' might be rendered less penumbral by the appearance of questions based on case law-statements that indicate just what activities have satisfied the statutory subsection regarding behaviour and grounds of divorce. Or again, questions based on law-derivations may be of help. In either event, it might be that the more detailed questions relate very closely to the facts of the instant case, whereas the original, more general query offered little guidance. The problem of open texture arising from the skateboard case and the question regarding the use of vehicles might also be similarly solved if within the knowledge base there were law-statements or law-derivations pertaining precisely to skateboards. For further

---

[84] The Argument from Open Texture and Vagueness would also apply, *mutatis mutandis*, to those systems whose interface involved the input of restricted natural language in reply to questions phrased in natural language.

queries based on such statements or derivations would allow of straightforward 'yes' or 'no' responses in accordance with ordinary language. The utility of more detailed law-statements and law-derivations that I have suggested accords with Alchourron and Bulygin's account of possible reductions in the 'semantic indeterminacy' or 'vagueness' of 'general concepts', but heed must be paid to their qualification:

Vagueness may be considerably reduced through explicit definitions which expressly stipulate the rules of application of the concepts, but never disappears entirely. It is always possible that an atypical or unusual object may appear which slips through the net of the rules of application of the concept, no matter how numerous and detailed these may be.[85]

Legal theorists also agree that canons of interpretation (domain-independent meta-rules) may also reduce the number of penumbral cases, although they differ over the extent to which such reduction is possible.[86] Their disagreement is one of degree rather than kind, however, and it does seem undeniable that meta-rules cannot offer unlimited guidance for they themselves are phrased in natural language and must then also therefore be open textured and very possibly vague.

The Argument from Open Texture and Vagueness, then, indicates one set of boundaries beyond which deductive inference, and, therefore, expert systems, are of little aid to the lawyer. Deductive inference seems inapplicable because classical logical systems are appropriate for reasoning where the premises or conclusions have truth-value (are either true or false—see also The Argument from Truth-Value), and *not* where there is doubt as to their truth or falsity, such as when there is semantic indeterminacy. With regard to AI, although extensive knowledge representation may reduce the number of problems of semantic indeterminacy, expert systems can by no means cope with all penumbral difficulties, because they

---

[85] See *NS*, pp. 31–4, esp. p. 32. This quotation implicitly confirms the vagueness/open texture distinction. Although Waismann himself said that whereas '[v]agueness can be remedied by giving more accurate rules, open texture cannot', his remarks were directed at empirical concepts and not at legal rules: his argument does seem valid in relation to the former, but not to the latter whose 'possibility of vagueness' I have argued to be, in principle, in part reducible by 'more accurate' law-statements and law-derivations. See 'Verifiability' (1951), p. 120.

[86] See: Dworkin, 'No Right Answer?' (1977), p. 68; Raz, *AL*, pp. 72–4; Tur, 'Positivism, Principles and Rules' (1977), p. 58; Hart, *CL*, p. 123.

merely implement logical systems. There are two ways of trying to deal with this problem. First, the user is left to settle any semantic indeterminacy, once the expert system has effectively run out of useful supportive knowledge. This settling by the user seems to be akin to the process of 'precisification', whereby prior to the application of formal methods indeterminacies are rendered precise.[87] Thereafter, what I have called (in Section 2.7) *contingent conclusions* can be drawn by the computer on the basis of some classical, two-valued logic embodied in the inference engine. The knowledge base can be seen in this strategy to suffer from gaps (see Section 5.8). Secondly, an alternative logical system or inference mechanism might be developed. Haack mentions that, in logic, three-valued logics have been proposed for coping with vagueness, involving the values 'true', 'false', and 'borderline'. But, as she points out, this presupposes the unsatisfactory contention that we can draw firm distinctions between 'borderline' and 'true' or 'false';[88] and Raz has argued that this cannot be done in law.[89] A different alternative logical system is that of *fuzzy logic*—the logic underlying approximate or inexact reasoning—which is considered to bridge the 'excessively wide gap between the precision of classical logic and the imprecision of the real world'.[90] I shall not get involved here with the technicalities of fuzzy logic: suffice it to say that it is conceived as a means of coping with the vagueness of natural language, and its implications for legal reasoning by analogy have been considered.[91]

It is submitted, however, that problems of semantic indeterminacy, at this stage in research and development of expert systems in law, be tackled in accordance with the first of the two proposed options. The major problems arise only in cases that are harder than those that I call *deductive* cases (see Section 6.7), and in all modesty it would seem appropriate that workers in this field concentrate on designing systems to solve *clear* and *deductive* cases which can be done with a classical two-valued inference engine (subject to the

---

[87] See Haack, *PL*, pp. 163–4. Haack attributes the idea of precisification to the logician Carnap.

[88] *PL*, pp. 164–5.

[89] *AL*, pp. 73–4.

[90] 'Coping with the Imprecision of the Real World: An Interview with Lofti. A. Zadeh' (1984), p. 308.

[91] See Zadeh, 'Fuzzy Sets as a Basis for a Theory of Possibility' (1978), pp. 3–28, especially p. 4, and Haack, *PL*, pp. 165–9. And, in relation to legal reasoning, see Reisinger, 'Legal Reasoning by Analogy: A Model Applying Fuzzy Set Theory' (1982), pp. 151–63.

modifications noted in Section 6.5). In the future, when we seek to write more intelligent programs that themselves can cope with open texture and vagueness, we may then avail ourselves of some system of 'deviant logic'. But that will be in many years' time.

5.7 THE ARGUMENT FROM IMPLIED EXCEPTION

Examination of the Argument from Implied Exception can be begun by considering a remarkable claim made by Gottlieb after setting out the following propositions:

'X did A' (fact),

'All who do X [*sic*] are guilty of B' (rule),

'Verdict: X is guilty of B' (decision).

He boldly asserts thereafter that the conclusion of that set of statements 'does not necessarily follow from the two premises':[92] and in respect of this, MacCormick retorts that it is 'either total nonsense, or at best a very dim and obscure approach to the truth'.[93] Yet, as I show in this section, there is a sense in which Gottlieb's contention can be seen to be both true and important: ironically, it is not in the sense that Gottlieb maintains, but it is in a sense that MacCormick acknowledges elsewhere.

Gottlieb's supporting arguments suffer from two defects. Not only does he rather confusingly conflate the Arguments from Act of Will, Particularity of Facts, and Truth-Value (Section 6.4), but he does so while seemingly placing considerable reliance, yet with insufficient explanation and justification, on Toulmin's *The Uses of Argument*.[94] There is no need to dwell on Gottlieb's analysis, therefore, but it should be noted that Toulmin himself, in his discussion of the ambiguities inherent in universal quantifiers such as 'all',[95] offers a firm base from which, in turn, the Argument from Implied Exception may be developed.

In logic, the *universal quantifier* is used: it is often symbolized as '∀' and translated (approximately) into English as 'For all...'. The question arises as to whether the use of terms such as 'all' in relation

[92] *LC*, p. 70. And see ch. 5 generally.
[93] *LRLT*, p. 34.
[94] *LC*, p. 71 and ch. 5 generally. Cf. *The Uses of Argument* (1958), ch. 3.
[95] *The Uses of Argument* (1958), ch. 3.

to entities in fields of discourse beyond logic, carries with it those same implications within these fields for variables within given domains of quantification, as it does in logic. In other words, if we substitute, for the variables in the following syllogism, propositions and rules of the natural sciences or of law, would the form of the argument remain unaltered and the truth of any conclusion be as irrefutable as our abstract formulation suggests?

(1) X is an A

(2) All As are B

(3) X is a B.

'Laws' of the natural sciences, as Karl Popper has shown,[96] are tentative in nature. They are empirical generalizations and as such are not verifiable but only falsifiable (and, of course, open to corroboration). Thus, universally quantified, empirical statements of the natural sciences, of the sort 'All As are B', cannot be proven to be true. Given that X is an A, therefore, we cannot, as a matter of logic, conclude that X is a B because of the tentative universal proposition involved. In other words, in the natural sciences, we do not use 'all' in the same way that we employ this term as a universal quantifier in logic. And Harris has offered us a legal analogue. He says that 'words like 'no', 'any', or 'all', when appearing in legislative materials, do not have the function of categorical symbols in a deontic logic, because one can never rule out the possibility that reasons could be found for interpreting them as being subject to exceptions'.[97] And many other writers' ideas have similar implications: Honoré argues that rules of law are 'prima facie' in nature, because 'it is always possible to argue in favour of an exception, even if none at the time of argument has been recognised';[98] Hart writes of the 'defeasibility' of the legal concepts which make up legal rules and therefore preclude the rules' complete formulation;[99] Tapper suggests we regard rules 'as always susceptible to expansion, contrac-

---

[96] *Conjectures and Refutations: The Growth of Scientific Knowledge* (1972). Cf. MacCormick, 'The Nature of Legal Reasoning: A Brief Reply to Dr Wilson' (1982), p. 290.

[97] *LLS*, p. 5. Cf. Wilson, 'The Nature of Legal Reasoning: A Commentary with Special Reference to Professor MacCormick's Theory' (1982), p. 277.

[98] 'Real Laws' (1977), p. 109.

[99] See Hart, 'The Ascription of Responsibility and Rights' (1948–9). Cf. Baker, 'Defeasibility and Meaning' (1977), and Horovitz, *LL*, pp. 148–56.

tion and modification in the light of borderline instances, whether the boundary is linguistic or functional';[100] MacCormick claims that a 'formulation of a rule has to be read as subject to possible further exceptions... in the light of relevant legal principles already established and of possible new ones';[101] and Twining and Miers talk about 'implied exceptions' where 'even legal rules in fixed verbal form may be subject to exceptions based on rules or principles that may not themselves be in fixed verbal form, or that did not exist at the time of the creation of the rule in question'.[102]

All conclusions deduced from legal rules, therefore, are subject to all those implied exceptions to which the rules themselves are subject. If the syllogism suggested above was a legal syllogism (where (1) denotes the facts of a case; (2) a rule of law, and (3) a legal conclusion), we could not unconditionally assert B from (1) and (2); for (2), and so B, *ex hypothesi*, are subject to implied exceptions. In that light, it is possible to make sense of Gottlieb's remarkable claim in a way that Gottlieb himself does not, but that MacCormick, given the quotation just cited, most probably would: the verdict does not necessarily follow because it may be subject to implied exceptions.

The argument from Implied Exception, of course, has implications for expert systems in law. Every legal production, according to the conventional jurisprudential wisdom, may be subject to implied exceptions, and in turn, any legal conclusion presented to the user may also be subject to such exceptions. Indeed it might be wise to write the program in such a way that when any conclusions are inferred and displayed, this is accompanied by a message that indicates the conclusion may be subject to implied exceptions (of a nature I shall identify shortly). It should not be assumed, however, that the rulehood of legal productions is prejudiced by their potentiality to be subject to implied exceptions: for as Hart has said, 'A rule that ends with the word "unless..." is still a rule.'[103] It does seem, however, that even law-statements, in a sense, are perhaps not purely deterministic rules, although this is not to say they are probabilistic in the same way as legal heuristics.

Note that a legal conclusion subject to an implied exception is *not*

---

[100] 'A Note on Principles' (1971), pp. 633–4.
[101] 'Law as Institutional Fact' (1974), p. 126, where MacCormick, is speaking of institutive rules.
[102] *How to do Things with Rules* (1982), p. 216, and see pp. 216–17 generally.
[103] *CL*, p. 136.

the same as the category of 'contingent conclusion' as introduced in Section 2.7. *All* conclusions are what I shall now call *conditional* conclusions (that is, subject to implied exceptions), whereas only those conclusions that have been deduced during an interaction that was fettered in some way by *gaps* (see next section) can be called 'contingent'. Note also that an implied exception is not the same as an *exceptive qualification*: the latter, can always, in principle, be articulated in any statement of the contents of a momentary legal system and is an integral part of the production itself, whereas the former, by definition, cannot be so expressed, but emerges in the process of solving legal problems.

I must of course now explain why exceptions to legal productions might be implied by legal reasoning agents. Two reasons in particular seem to present themselves for discussion. First, exceptions to a rule may be implied on grounds of principle. Principles, most theorists seem to acknowledge, not only supplement rules in the process of deciding those cases where there are no clearly applicable rules (when there is semantic indeterminacy or there are conflicts or *normative gaps*—see next section), but can also be deployed by reasoning agents as reasons for finding exceptions to what might otherwise indeed seem to be clearly applicable rules. In Dworkin's famous example of the case of *Riggs* v. *Palmer*, the heir who murdered his grandfather so that he would inherit under the latter's will was held not to be entitled to the inheritance, *not* because of semantic indeterminacy or normative gaps or conflicts between rules, but because the court, on the grounds of some general principle of common law, found an exception to the apparently applicable rule of inheritance (literally construed).[104] 'In general', as Raz has said, 'all rules are subject to all principles and may be overridden by any of them in particular circumstances.'[105] This aspect of the Argument from Implied Exception, then, is of course a version of the Argument from Principles which I set out and dealt with in Section 5.2.

The second reason an exception to a rule may be implied is on account of the rule's *purpose*. Harris has put this aspect of the Argument from Implied Exception thus: 'Even the clearest rule may be held not to apply to a case where that would frustrate the purpose of the law or produce absurd consequences, and the decision whether

[104] *TRS*, p. 23. Also see *Law's Empire* (1986), pp. 15–20.
[105] 'Legal Principles and the Limits of Law' (1972), p. 834.

this is so or not cannot be dictated by logic.'[106] It was this question of the purpose of rules that urged Hart to refine his original and somewhat tentative formulation of his doctrine of 'clear cases' in accordance with which, as I said in the last section, the applicability (or otherwise) of rules was dictated by linguistic convention.[107] Fuller had questioned Hart's early belief that difficulties in the interpretation of law usually resulted from the meaning of words; he argued, in contrast, that it is to sentences, paragraphs, and pages of legal texts that we need to look to ascertain the *purpose* of any legal rule. Hart now seems to accept this and suggests that clear cases in law 'are those in which there is general agreement that they fall within the scope of a rule' and this agreement, he says, is both rooted in the 'shared conventions' of the legal and ordinary use of words and connected to the 'purpose' of statutory provisions.[108] If expert systems in law are to solve even clear cases (in the apparent sense of Hart's later account as depicted above), this implies that they must reason with meta-rules (legal heuristics) that identify the purpose of other productions in the knowledge base.[109]

Alternatively, as I argue in Sections 6.6 and 6.7, it might be that Hart's original account of clear cases is more satisfactory: that a case is clear where our common linguistic usage of legal and ordinary terms renders the verbal formulation and acontextual meaning of a rule unequivocally applicable to some set of facts. In that event, in any case where the terms of a rule are not so applicable, the case is not clear, and the purpose of a rule may well be relevant. Hart himself, in his most recent remarks on the subject, does say that 'the obvious or agreed purpose of a rule may be used to render determinate a rule whose application may be left open by the conventions of language'.[110] With this we may agree, but surely a case is hard where there is (and in virtue of) such semantic indeterminacy, for we are

[106] *LP*, p. 136. Cf. the case of *Baker* v. *Turner* [1950] AC 401: 'The inevitability of the conclusion is, as I think, falsified because . . . in my opinion, the rules of formal logic must not be applied to the Acts with too great strictness. As Scrutton, L. J., has more than once pointed out, they must be viewed in the light of their aim and object.' Also see Honoré, 'The Nature of Legal Argument' (1958), pp. 296–7.

[107] This refinement was occasioned by an onslaught by Fuller in 'Positivism and Fidelity to Law: A Reply to Professor Hart' (1958). See also Hart, in his Introduction to *EJP*, p. 8.

[108] 'PPL', p. 106.

[109] Cf. Thorne and Ugarte, 'Using Purposes of the Law in Legal Expert Systems' (1985), pp. 673–80.

[110] *EJP*, p. 8.

surely then unambiguously in the penumbra. If, therefore, Hart's earliest conception of clear cases is adopted (see Section 6.6), then an expert system with no heuristics relating to the purpose of legal productions may surely still be able to reason in such cases. It might be said, in other words, that any conclusion drawn by such a system would, in effect, be the result of the *literal* interpretation of that part of its knowledge base which bears on the facts of the instant case, and, moreover, the conclusion would be subject to any exceptions implied through later human *purposive* interpretations.[111]

In conclusion, Harris is correct in asserting that terms such as 'all' in legal sources do not function as universal quantifiers do in logic, but I must take issue with his assessment of the implications of that fact for knowledge-based systems in law: 'Computerisation of legislative source materials is unlikely ever to be of assistance in the application, as opposed to the storage, of the law.'[112] The existence of today's knowledge-based systems in law falsifies Harris's claim: he neglected the possibility of systems drawing conditional legal conclusions that are explicitly said to be subject to implied exceptions on grounds either of principle or of purpose.

5.8 THE ARGUMENT FROM GAPLESS SYSTEMS: GAPS IN A RULE-BASED LEGAL KNOWLEDGE BASE

Wasserstrom, one of the most articulate commentators on deductive legal reasoning, comments that the deductive theory (of which my strong thesis is certainly an instance) is regarded by many critics as 'in some sense postulating "a gapless system of pre-existing law, from which a solution for every new case could be obtained by deduction"'.[113] If it were indeed the case that the deductive theory, and, therefore, expert systems in law, presuppose the existence of a gapless system of law, then this would present insurmountable difficulties for legal knowledge engineers. For, as Hayek has suggested, there does seem to be jurisprudential consensus over this question: 'It is now probably universally admitted that no code of law can be

---

[111] On interpretation, see Walker, *SLS*, pp. 349–50, and Dias, *Jurisprudence* (1985), ch. 8. Later purposive interpretations of the type envisaged could equally be rational or 'absurd', in terms of Harris's analysis of purpose and interpretation: *LLS*, pp. 4–7, 141–2.
[112] *LLS*, p. 5.
[113] *JD*, p. 15.

without gaps.'[114] But the Argument from Gapless Systems can be disposed of with little difficulty. None of the three versions of the deductive thesis I have identified presupposes the existence of some gapless system of rules: all that is in fact postulated even by the most extreme rendition is that law-statements and legal heuristics can be represented in a way that allows them *sometimes*, in accordance with some logical system, to be related to factual data and to generate legal conclusions. It is true that in this book I have often assumed the possibility of *extensive* legal knowledge representation, but there is no suggestion, implicit or explicit, that we can (logically, or as a matter of fact) develop a legal knowledge base that will always be capable of providing legal conclusions in respect of all factual data. The formulation and generation of valid deductive legal arguments presupposes some formal logical system, but not some *system* of legal rules. For a valid deduction can be made from one individuated legal premiss, and its validity as a piece of necessary reasoning would of course in no way be prejudiced by the premiss's origin in some system riddled with gaps. All legal knowledge bases, I shall show, will have gaps, but this in no way precludes the drawing of legal conclusions from such knowledge as there is.

Any legal knowledge base designed on the basis of the discussion of this book so far, will clearly suffer from gaps, and to that extent will not contain an exhaustive legal scientific exposition of the legal sub-system that it strives to embody. Hart too would argue that all legal knowledge bases must have such gaps, for throughout his work he makes it abundantly clear that there cannot be a gapless system, complete in the sense that answers to *all* questions of law are contained within it. This is so, he maintains, because 'it is impossible in framing general rules to anticipate and provide for every possible combination of circumstances which the future may bring'.[115] Human beings' limited foresight and knowledge together with the inherent limitations of natural and legal language necessarily result in gaps when laws are formulated. In light of this chapter's findings, four species of gaps in legal knowledge bases can be distinguished. The first three are apparent where certain factual situations arise or are hypothesized that at once belong to a system's legal domain of

---

[114] *Law, Legislation and Liberty*, vol. 1 (1982), pp. 117–18. See also Finnis, *NLNR*, pp. 269 and 292.
[115] 'PPL', p. 103. Cf. *CL*, p. 125, where Hart talks in this connection of 'our relative ignorance of fact . . . [and] our relative indeterminacy of aim'.

application but yet cannot be unambiguously subsumed under the terms of any of the nodes within its decision tree. The fourth, however, will not be highlighted through any dialogue with our expert system. I shall look at each in turn.

First, there are *gaps due to the semantic indeterminacy of nodes*. The Argument from Open Texture and Vagueness confirmed that because all questions asked by our projected systems will be phrased in natural language—no matter how thorough a body of legal heuristics we represent—there may always be questions concerning the facts of a case which allow of neither 'yes' nor 'no' answers. This would be so because of the uncertainty of the language in which they are couched, and the knowledge base in that sense can be said to have gaps.[116]

Secondly, there are *gaps due to the absence of nodes*. The result of these gaps, which are equivalent to what have been termed 'normative gaps',[117] is that in some (hypothesized or real) situations, there may be no legal provisions represented within the system that cover a given set of facts. That is to say, the facts would be the instantiation of the antecedents of *none* of the rules within the system. In a dialogue with the system, the user's responses would not therefore constitute sufficient data for the system to infer any conclusions—even contingent conclusions—and the consequences of the facts at hand could not be divined. Thorough coverage of a domain of application, of course, would reduce the incidence of gaps due to absence of nodes.

Thirdly, there are *gaps due to conflicts of productions*. If a set of facts fires two or more conflicting productions within a knowledge base (being a conflict of the first sort identified in Section 5.4), and neither the certainty factors of the productions nor any embodied conflict resolution rules dictate the application of one production over the other(s), then the uncertainty with which the knowledge base speaks in that event can be conceived as a manifestation of a species of gap. For no definitive consequences of these facts can be indicated by the system.[118] However, again it must be stressed that gaps due to such conflicts of productions should not trouble legal knowledge engineers in the near future if, as suggested in Section 2.4,

---

[116] Cf. Raz, *AL*, pp. 73–4.
[117] See e.g. Alchourron and Bulygin, *NS*, pp. 17, 155–65, Hartney, 'Hans Kelsen's Theory of Norms' (1985), pp. 196–204. Cf. Gottlieb, *LC*, p. 18.
[118] Cf. *AL*, pp. 74–5.

fields of law containing many conflicts are considered to be unsuitable legal domains of application for the development of current systems.

Fourthly, there are *gaps due to the possibility of implied exceptions*. The Argument from Implied Exception established that the knowledge represented in any system must be conceived as subject to mutation in light of principles or purpose. Yet knowledge pertaining to principles and purpose will not be represented in systems of the sort this book describes. In that respect, the knowledge base suffers from a type of gap: an interaction will reveal neither the likelihood of exceptions being implied, nor will it generate conclusions based on principle or purpose even if that were wanted.[119]

I should, in passing, distinguish the above categories of gaps in legal knowledge bases from those *gaps in the user's knowledge* that arise from an incomplete familiarity with the facts of a case.[120] This may result in an unhelpful consultation, but, in a sophisticated system, may be ameliorated through the use of law-statements of evidence, and legal heuristics, relating to proof (see Section 3.7).

Another way of understanding the phenomenon of gaps in legal knowledge bases is by equating it with the absence of one or more rules of inference within a system, the result of which is that no legal conclusions can be drawn. It is in this light that we can see how one case for the reduction of gaps might be made. For it is conceivable that the designers of a system, to cope with the eventuality of gaps, might include within their knowledge base a sort of all-purpose, back-up rule of inference, perhaps a heuristic, which would prompt a further series of questions, permit a legal conclusion to be drawn, and thereby eliminate what would otherwise have been a gap. This would be a *closure rule*, the most obvious instance of which in respect of gaps due to absence of nodes is the injunction 'everything that is not prohibited is permitted'. The question of closure rules has been addressed in great detail both by logicians and philosophers,

---

[119] Gaps due to the possibility of implied exception may sometimes be what Alchourron and Bulygin term 'axiological gaps'. These involve the presence of a node under which the facts could be subsumed but unsatisfactorily and inadequately so, because of some prescriptive criteria of relevance within the system. See *NS*, pp. 106–16. However, the category of axiological gaps is, of course, not exhaustive of that of gaps due to the possibility of implied exceptions. The latter may also include what Raz refers to as gaps that 'arise because of indeterminate intentions independently of the language employed.' See Raz *AL*, p. 72, 17.

[120] See Alchourron and Bulygin's discussion of 'gaps of knowledge': *NS*, pp. 31–4.

and their inclusion in legal systems is often considered to result in the transition from 'open' to 'closed' systems.[121] Examination of the literature on this topic shows many of the technical and highly complex implications to be irrelevant for present purposes, for my concern is not as theirs is with judicial legal reasoning in the context of entire legal systems, but with deductive reasoning with the rules of some legal sub-system.

The question arises for legal knowledge engineers as to whether closure rules (of some sort) should be represented *explicitly* within legal knowledge bases. It is submitted that to do so would be to side unnecessarily with those who defend a purely rule-based conception of legal systems. In this book, I have argued that rules are central to all tenable theories of law, but I have not committed myself to any account of legal reasoning that relies only on rules. I have said that expert systems will be useful aids in that part of the problem-solving process that is devoted to the manipulation of rules. To stipulate that closure rules provide the correct solution in all those cases where there are no applicable (non-closure) rules is to preclude the possibility in such penumbral cases of reasoning with non-rule standards, and this would be far from espousing any consensus theory of law. Moreover, while it may well be satisfactory in a conceptual analysis of legal systems to posit the existence of closure rules, in the context of building expert systems, when we cannot sensibly be confident that we have full coverage even of a legal sub-system, the very idea of including such rules is presumptuous. It presupposes a profundity of representation that, as a matter of fact (if not of logical necessity) we will not manage to achieve: for closure rules are relevant only when *all* non-closure rules of a system are inapplicable,

---

[121] See e.g. von Wright, *NA*, ch. 5, especially pp. 87–90; Alchourron and Bulygin, *NS*, pp. 116–44; Raz, *AL*, pp. 75–7; Tammelo, 'On the Logical Structure of the Law Field' (1959) and 'On the Logical Openness of Legal Orders' (1959); Stone, *LSLR*, pp. 188–92; Smith, *Legal Obligation* (1976), p. 2; Golding, 'Kelsen and the Concept of "Legal System"' (1961), pp. 379 and 382; Singh, *Law from Anarchy to Utopia* (1986), pp. 47–54. Kelsen's discussion of gaps is clearly relevant here: he denies there to be any gaps in the law, that is, he seems to argue for the legal system as a type of closed system. He claims this on the ground that it is always logically possible for judges—who are always authorized to do so—to apply the existing legal order in resolving a dispute: e.g. *GTLS*, pp. 146–9. On Kelsen in this respect, see Hartney, 'Hans Kelsen's Theory of Norms' (1985), pp. 199–204, and Alchourron and Bulygin, *NS*, pp. 130–3. The suggestion that a legal system is 'a closed logical system' has been held to be a version of legal positivism: see Hart, 'PSLM', pp. 57–8 (n. 25) and *CL*, p. 253. Hart said in 1958 that he knew of no analyst who had held such a view of the legal system ('PSLM', p. 58).

that is, when an entire legal system is held within a legal knowledge base, and the facts of some case cannot be subsumed under the terms of any of its productions.

5.9 CONCLUSION

In this chapter, I have considered some limitations to the power of deductive legal inference engines. I conducted the examination in the light of some jurisprudential objections to deductive legal reasoning which I showed to be relevant to legal knowledge engineering. I said that expert systems in law, as described in this book, will not reason with non-rule standards, but suggested this deficiency to be of little significance. In order to counter several arguments that deny the applicability of deductive logic to legal reasoning, I developed a *strong* thesis of deductive legal reasoning, in accordance with which factual and legal premises can be selected, and legal inferences made, using the canons of formal logic. Yet I acknowledged that for every conclusion drawn, and, consequently, during every consultation with an expert system, there must ultimately be some human judgment. Expert systems, I also said, may not be of any help on those occasions when the questions they pose give rise to problems of semantic indeterminacy: but legal heuristics will minimize the occurrence of such problems. I further accepted that all conclusions of expert systems are conditional in the sense that they may be subject to implied exceptions on grounds of principle or purpose. Finally, I argued that legal knowledge bases need not be gapless systems and I identified the nature of those gaps that they may (and sometimes must) have.

Rule-based expert systems in law, on the analysis so far, have emerged as devices for the generation of literal interpretations of the legal implications of given sets of facts. I said tentatively that cases are *clear* when, in light of the instant facts, the literal interpretation of some body of pre-existing rules generates incontrovertible conclusions. Yet the notion of clear cases is itself far from clear, and is certainly not as simple as I have so far stated. In the next chapter, then, I need to examine this matter further, for it is on the basis of consensus amongst legal theorists over clear cases that expert systems should be designed. I shall also look in greater detail at the actual operation of deductive legal inference engines.

6

A Jurisprudential Specification of a Deductive Legal Inference Engine

IN this chapter, I am concerned more closely with the actual workings of a deductive legal inference engine, and in that way I introduce greater precision to the account of legal knowledge utilization developed so far. In Section 6.1, by way of jurisprudential preamble, I consider the implications for AI and the law of the suggestion that human legal reasoning agents do not in fact reason deductively. The truth of that claim is further scrutinized, *inter alia*, in Section 6.2, where I examine the notions of forward- and backward-chaining, and consider their suitability as strategies for embodiment in expert systems in law. In Section 6.3, I propose in some detail an efficient way of searching legal decision trees. A further objection to deductive legal reasoning, based on the inapplicability of logic to normative concepts, is introduced in Section 6.4, and I reply to that charge in Section 6.5, by articulating a very limited theory of deontic logic. In Section 6.6, I show how expert systems may reasonably be expected to assist in solving *clear* cases and I assess a challenge to the utility of such systems. Section 6.7 is devoted both to expert systems designed to solve *deductive* cases on the basis of their heuristic knowledge, and to the notion of the computer judge, the unlikelihood of its realization and some objections to it. Finally, in Section 6.8, I conclude by summarizing my computational approach to legal reasoning.

6.1 THE ARGUMENT FROM EMPIRICAL INADEQUACY

This argument against deductive legal reasoning, when intelligibly formulated, is different in nature from those discussed in the previous chapter. For it relates not to the possibility, the desirability, nor the extent of the applicability of deduction in legal reasoning, but rather seems to be a challenge to one aspect of the deductive theory: to the claim that reasoning agents, while engaging in the processes of selecting premisses and drawing legal conclusions, *do as a matter of fact* reach their decisions through the application of deductive inference procedures. Notice that this statement of the argument is silent as to the desirability of its implications. Nor does the argument so articulated *necessarily* deny the possibility of deduction. What is being asserted, by way of empirical counter-generalization, is that one version of the deductive theory persistently fails to accord with empirical evidence of the social phenomenon of legal reasoning. In short, it is maintained, legal reasoning agents do not tend to reason applying the techniques of deductive logic.[1]

Clearly this challenge is a broad one extending to all classes of legal reasoning agents. It affects the enterprise of building expert systems in law to the extent that legal knowledge engineers seek to embody *descriptive*, and not *prescriptive*, accounts of legal reasoning in their systems (see Section 2.2). It is, of course, not easy to assess the validity of the Argument from Empirical Inadequacy because legal reasoning involves complex mental processes that are not susceptible to direct observation. All we can do is reflect on our own experiences and also draw inferences based on all external manifestations of legal reasoning processes. However, perhaps the most convincing reply in this connection can be found in important discussions of legal knowledge acquisition, such as those of Waterman and Peterson, who implicitly falsify the empirical claim embodied in the Argument from Empirical Inadequacy, by demonstrating, on the basis of their consultations with legal experts, that reasoning agents do in fact sometimes reach their conclusions by use of deduction.[2]

The Argument from Empirical Inadequacy ought to be distinguished from the superficially similar assertion that reasoning agents, because of the nature of the psychological processes involved in human decision-making, *cannot* reach legal decisions in a deductive manner. This averment does deny the possibility of deductive legal reasoning but constitutes no more than verbal stipulation under the deceptive guise of a plausible tenet of deterministic psychology. Or, to phrase it differently, reasoning agents are said, by definition, to be psychologically incapable of deductive legal reason-

---

[1] For discussion of this argument and related issues, see Wasserstrom, *JD*, pp. 17, 19–21. See also Guest, 'Logic in the Law' (1961), p. 187.
[2] See e.g. *Models of Legal Decisionmaking* (1981), and 'Evaluating Civil Claims: An Expert Systems Approach' (1984). Also see Waterman, *AGES*, ch. 15.

ing. Little of intellectual significance can follow from such a stipulation as it eliminates the possibility of dialogue between deductivists and their adversaries. Moreover, if this proposition is intended to be one of deterministic psychology then it renders irrelevant all the anti-deduction arguments that focus on *desirability*, as there is little point in criticizing a process that cannot be engaged in.

Frank is a prominent exponent of the position just outlined. For in *Courts on Trial* he suggests that we reject the formula 'R × F = D' which he asks us to accept as a shorthand representation of the notion that legal rules can be applied by the judge to the facts of a case resulting in the mechanical production of a decision. In its stead he offers a replacement formula 'S × P = D' ('S' being the stimuli that affect the judge, 'P' his personality). But Frank argues that because the personality of the judge is 'an exquisitely complicated mass of phenomena', and the stimuli are 'a horde of conflicting stimuli', then this latter formula is also of minimal value as a predictive and critical tool, and, moreover, is an inaccurate account of what the courts do in fact.[3] Frank provides us with no empirical backing for his replacement formula but simply forwards it to the reader in quasi-psychological jargon, suggesting that it is not psychologically possible for any judge to reason deductively because of the nature of the human personality. While this may seem like a principle of deterministic psychology, in light of the absence of evidence adduced by Frank to corroborate his hypothesis it might more realistically be regarded as no more than a verbal stipulation. Clearly his intention is to convince his audience that deduction is to be wholly rejected in the context of judicial reasoning and he has chosen a powerful way of delivering that message. Yet such an outright eschewal precludes further discussion on the matter for there can be no common ground between followers of Frank and those who defend the deductive theory. Furthermore, his challenge seems to preclude the development of an expert system based on any descriptive theory of judicial legal reasoning. Although I am not directly concerned with *judicial* legal reasoning in this book, Frank's argument does merit attention, for it is possible that it might be generalized to cover all human legal reasoning agents, and to deny thereby the worth of modelling legal experts' reasoning processes.

Consider the following argument which also seems to concern the

---

[3] See *Courts on Trial* (1949), p. 182.

psychological make-up of the judge. In many cases that reach the courtroom, the applicable law is not in dispute but there is disagreement over the facts. In such cases, the stimuli 'S' are not, as Frank would have us believe, 'social forces' and undiscoverables. What affects the judge are the facts as presented and the knowledge that there exist applicable rules and meta-rules (including rules of evidence), that is, 'R × F = S'. With regard to the personality 'P', is it not true (certainly in this country), that judges are appointed to the Bench in virtue of their integrity, stability, and lack of radical tendencies? Thus, where there are clearly applicable rules (say, in 'clear cases'), the personality 'P' aspect varies little, that is, 'P' is a constant where the applicability of 'R' is clear. This is not to suggest the absurdity that all judges have identical personalities. What is being contended is that, in Hartian terminology, these judges not only obey the rules, but they take a 'critical reflective attitude' towards them.[4] In 'clear cases', they share both a conscious knowledge and acceptance of the rules together with a conscious desire to comply with them. The unconscious aspect may still be in play, but because of their stability and non-corruptibility and so forth, by dint of which they attained their positions, this also encourages the applicability of 'R × F'. In short, in such cases 'R × F = S × P'.

How are we to assess the relative merits of the suggestion set out in the previous paragraph as against Frank's formulation, both of which allegedly rely on assertions about the psychological processes of the judge? There would seem to be no readily available technique for this purpose. It would certainly be unsatisfactory to accept the more intuitively plausible account; intuitive plausibility is no sound criterion for the acceptance or rejection of claims in psychology. The second argument, however, remains open to the suggestion that in *some* cases deduction is psychologically possible and therefore avoids the restrictions of the stipulation inherent in the first. In an area of jurisprudence as controversial as this, it might be concluded, there is little room for verbal tricks that exclude further debate. As long as reasonable doubt exists as to the validity of an argument, stipulative assertions are to be regarded with suspicion. Therefore, although Frank's book does cast doubt on the utility of modelling legal experts' reasoning processes, it is submitted that we do not accept it uncritically. Rather, we should conduct extensive experi-

[4] See e.g. *CL*, p. 56.

ments both in 'tuning' and, in the future, in legal knowledge acquisition, and in that way test all such relevant empirical hypotheses.[5]

Frank's observations, of course, do not prejudice the development of deductive legal inference engines, because these mechanisms need not presuppose any theories of *human* psychology. All that they assume is that computers can reason deductively; and no one can sensibly deny that fact. The Argument from Empirical Inadequacy does, however, remind us that *some* theory of legal reasoning must be presupposed in the development of all expert systems in law. For present purposes, it is insufficient to say that that theory is deductive. I must offer further details of how the legal productions are manipulated, and whether this is done in accordance with a descriptive or prescriptive account of legal reasoning. In the following two sections, I shall provide these supplementary details.

6.2 FORWARD-CHAINING AND BACKWARD-CHAINING

Let us suppose that we have settled on the method of legal knowledge representation outlined in the previous chapter: legal subsystems as decision trees whose nodes together constitute legal productions of the structure specified. Let us further suppose that we have represented some legal knowledge within this formalism. We can regard that representation as constituting a set of possibilities— a 'search space', as AI scientists refer to it[6]—within our selected part of the universe of legal discourse. Within that search space, if our coverage of the domain has been sufficiently profound, for any set of facts relevant to that domain there will always be a production whose consequent holds the 'appropriate' legal conclusion (at least in 'clear cases', as I shall argue). Legal reasoning, on this account, involves searching through a set of possibilities established by the law, until the facts of the case can be subsumed under, or are satisfied by, the conditions, qualifications, limitations, and exceptions embodied in one legal production or in a sequence of legal productions. The consequent of the final production in the sequence holds the legal conclusion that can be drawn within the universe of legal discourse

---

[5] Note that rejection of Frank's theory does not entail acceptance of the alternative account of judicial legal reasoning that I have offered. That account is included largely as an indication that plausible alternatives can be formulated.

[6] See e.g. *BES*, p. 66, *AINM*, p. 346.

embodied in the system's knowledge base. In order that we may utilize a legal knowledge base to its best advantage, it is necessary to select one or more appropriate 'search' or 'control' strategies (methods of legal knowledge utilization), that allow us, first, to traverse the search space in a manner appropriate to our requirements and, secondly, to do so efficiently.[7] I shall discuss this first matter in this section and the latter in the following section.

Computer systems of the type I am suggesting expert systems in law to be, which characteristically make deductions through the use of rules, are often referred to as 'rule-based deduction systems'.[8] Two of the most fundamental ways of searching in rule-based deduction systems are by means of 'forward-chaining' and 'backward-chaining', both of which inference methods have been used in the AI/legal reasoning field (see Appendix I). In order to understand these search strategies, it is helpful to return to the model of legal sub-systems as decision trees at the top of which is the consequent of the most basic production—the foundation rule—of the sub-system. Below this, held within the tree, is an interconnected network of other more specific productions. Next, imagine turning this image ninety degrees clockwise so that the consequent of the foundation rule—the root node—is now rightmost in the picture. In short, forward-chaining involves finding the antecedent of a rule on the left-hand side that is satisfied and then moving through the tree from left to right until a conclusion is reached, whereas backward-chaining entails starting at the conclusion on the right-hand side, as it were, and progressing leftwards in a search for antecedents that apply to the facts.

More specifically, forward-chaining, or 'data-directed inference', is a control structure that demands movement forward through a system of rules, from antecedent to consequent, by means of the recursive application of rules whose antecedents are satisfied. When the system recognizes that the antecedent of a particular rule is satisfied by the problem data, AI scientists speak of that rule being *triggered*. If the rule is actually used by the system in the reasoning process, then it is said to have been *fired*. In some expert systems (with user interfaces unlike the one advocated in Section 2.7), not all the rules that are triggered during an interaction are necessarily

---

[7] On searching generally, see: *AI*, chs. 4, 5, and 6; *AINM*, ch. 12; *BES*, pp. 59–82 and 89–119; *PAI*, chs. 2, 3, and 6.

[8] See *PAI*, p. 196.

fired: because the antecedents of more than one rule might be satisfied simultaneously by a set of problem data, and, in absence of any concurrent reasoning facility, some conflict resolution strategy (see Section 5.4) might dictate the firing of one rule to the exclusion of, or before, the others.[9] The triggering/firing distinction need not be dwelt upon here, because, as shall be seen in the next section, lawyers tend to want to fire all rules that are triggered in their reasoning processes so as to prepare as strong a case as possible. It is important simply to remember, then, that forward-chaining involves recursive progression through a sequence of rules that are fired.

The contrasting control structure, backward-chaining or 'goal-directed inference' (equivalent to TAXMAN's 'top down' reasoning mechanism), requires a reverse reasoning process whereby it is sought to confirm or deny the truth of an assumed, desired, or hypothesized conclusion by recursively seeking to identify and then establish the truth of all those antecedents that would permit the drawing of the conclusion in question. The reasoning process can be said to be successful if the required antecedent facts are known to be true, and unsuccessful if the antecedent facts are known to be false or incapable of being established. In that latter event, then, either the assumption is ill-grounded, or the desire incapable of fulfilment, or the hypothesis is falsified.

From a computational point of view, it has been argued that both forward- and backward-chaining have their limitations, and systems that combine the two search strategies have been shown to be advantageous in many respects.[10] For our purposes, however, from the point of view of the jurisprudential question of which control structure is best suited for expert systems in law, it is useful to consider the two reasoning procedures in isolation rather than in combination. Do we want expert systems that reason forwards or backwards through the law? The answer to this question depends very much on the role of the person for whom the system is designed, that is, on the function of the legal reasoning agent whose faculties are being augmented. I shall consider here two possible reasoning agents—the lawyer and the judge—and this will be sufficient for me to arrive at a conclusion. (It must be stressed at this stage, and this point is discussed more fully in Section 6.7, that there is absolutely no question

---

[9] See *AI*, pp. 172 and 174.
[10] See *PAI*, ch. 6.

of replacing human judges by expert systems in law but merely of providing them with a new form of research aid.)

Dewey, in 1924, in an influential article entitled 'Logical Method and Law', argued quite clearly for a model of the lawyer as an essentially backward-chaining reasoning agent (while acknowledging the potentiality of mechanizing the forward-chaining process):

As a matter of fact, men do not begin thinking with premises. They begin with some complicated and confused case, apparently admitting of alternative modes of treatment and solution. Premises only gradually emerge from analysis of the total situation. The problem is not to draw a conclusion from given premises; that can best be done by a piece of inanimate machinery by fingering a keyboard. The problem is to *find* statements, of general principle and of particular fact, which are worthy to serve as premises. As matter [*sic*] of actual fact, we generally begin with some vague anticipation of a conclusion (or at least of alternative conclusions), and then we look around for principles and data which will substantiate it or which will enable us to choose intelligently between rival conclusions. No lawyer ever thought out the case of a client in terms of the syllogism. He begins with a conclusion which he intends to reach, favorable to his client of course, and then analyses the facts of the situation to find material out of which to construct a favorable statement of facts, to *form* a minor premise. At the same time he goes over recorded cases to find rules of law employed in cases which can be presented as similar, rules which will substantiate a certain way of looking at and interpreting the facts. And as his acquaintance with rules of law judged applicable widens, he probably alters perspective and emphasis in selection of the facts which are to form his evidential data. And as he learns more of the facts of the case he may modify his selection of rules of law upon which he bases his case.[11]

Such an empirical generalization concerning the psychological processes of many a lawyer is probably fairly accurate: the Scots lawyer, no doubt, will often acknowledge the goal of the research stage of his consultation, namely (because his important client wants a divorce) to find for inclusion in the condescendence of an initial writ, *inter alia*, both factual and legal premises that will justify his crave and plea-in-law: that the pursuer is entitled to decree of divorce. Yet it would be an over-simplification to suggest that a lawyer always operates in this fashion and never forward-chains. A client may want to be apprised of the legal consequences of a proposed course of action, in which event it may very well be the case that there is no

[11] (1924), p. 23. Original emphasis.

assumption to be confirmed, desire to be fulfilled, or hypothesis to be verified: the lawyer may not always, then, have any goal to which his reasoning activities are directed and he may then find himself either forward-chaining or bringing to bear a more subtle interplay of the two search strategies. If this is so, then it must be concluded that backward-chaining is a necessary but not sufficient method of legal knowledge utilization for an expert system in law whose users will be lawyers.

With regard to the judge, what control strategy should be adopted to amplify the reasoning powers of this reasoning agent who is the impartial arbiter of forensic disputes? It would be pointless to detail all those attempts that have been made to describe how judges actually go about coming to their decisions, as the literature is both extensive and often confused. However, it is generally agreed by theorists that in so far as any set of facts before a judge fall clearly within the scope of a set of rules, the judge *ought* to apply these rules and draw the conclusion(s) that the combination of the factual and legal premises entails. This is the essence of the value that Harris calls 'legality'.[12] This normative theory of judicial legal reasoning seems to present a forward-chaining model of inference, as it recommends that a judge (in light usually of the litigants' pleadings), both must identify the rules that are applicable in the circumstances, and, in the words of Socrates, 'must follow the argument wherever it leads'.[13] If taken not as a recommendation but as a piece of descriptive psychology, this notion of judicial forward-chaining is, of course, patently inconsistent with the theory of the 'judicial hunch' as expounded most famously by Hutcheson who consequently espoused a descriptive thesis of judicial backward-chaining: 'And having travailed and reached his judgement, he struggles to bring up and pass in review before his eager mind all of the categories and concepts which he may find useful directly or by analogy, so as to select from them that which in his opinion will support his desired result.'[14] If a judge does indeed hunch and then rationalizes *ex post facto* and does not forward-chain, this is surely no reason to seek to incorporate the hunching and rationalizing in the control structure

---

[12] *LLS*, p. 2.
[13] Quoted at the start of Flew, *Thinking about Thinking* (1975).
[14] See 'The Judgement Intuitive: The Function of the "Hunch" in Judicial Decision' (1929), p. 286. Also see Prott, 'Updating the Judicial "Hunch": Esser's Concept of Judicial Predisposition' (1978).

of any expert system in law provided that we are indeed agreed that he ought not so to backward-chain. If a new research tool might minimize hunching then this is probably to be welcomed, and it might be concluded that an expert system designed for judicial users ought to use forward-chaining search strategies.

To conclude this discussion of whether forward- or backward-chaining strategies are required for a useful expert system in law, it seems that the lawyer will require both forward- and backward-chaining facilities (and probably a combination of the two) while the judge ought to require no more than a forward-chaining function (although in the next section, it is shown why purely forward-chaining is never appropriate for our type of system). The lawyers' system, then, could also be used by the judge. More than this, however, there is no obvious reason why that same system could not be used to *assist* those other reasoning agents that were identified in Section 2.2 in their tasks of justifying legal conclusions, persuading given audiences, and predicting rulings of courts, in so far as these activities entail forward- and backward-chaining inference procedures. An expert system could serve several classes of reasoning agents (for their own very different and respective purposes) with only *one* knowledge base if it had an inference engine that provided a range of search strategies. Remarkably, in 1949, Frank anticipated the possibility and utility of such a forward- and backward-chaining 'logic machine':

> It is conceivable that an 'ultra-rapid' legal-logic machine could promptly answer questions like these: (1) Given a specific state of facts, F, what possible alternative legal rules, R's, will logically lead to a desired decision, D? (2) Given a legal rule, R, and a desired decision, D, what possible alternative states of fact, F's, will logically yield that decision? (3) Given a specific legal rule, R, and a specific state of facts, F, what is the logically correct decision, D?[15]

It is all the more remarkable, in light of Frank's renowned antipathy towards mechanical jurisprudence, that he suggested that 'there is much merit in the idea of such a machine'.[16] Today too, the development of such a flexible inference engine for expert systems in law I recommend as a goal for workers in the field of legal knowledge utilization.

---

[15] *Courts on Trial* (1949), p. 206. (1) and (2) correspond to backward-chaining, and (3) to forward-chaining.
[16] Ibid., p. 207.

6.3 EFFICIENT SEARCHING IN A LEGAL DECISION TREE

Let us imagine once more the legal decision tree, growing from right to left, as I suggested in the previous section. In this section, I shall consider how the computer might search through this repository of knowledge efficiently, and in so doing I shall clarify what it is expert systems in law are able to do.

The desirability, and often the necessity, of efficient searching can be appreciated after examination of what Boden would call the 'prime example of brute force thinking',[17] namely, exhaustive search of the legal decision tree without any regard to the likelihood of the relevance of the questions/nodes. In that event, during every consultation, the computer would explore the legal possibilities in a way we would expect no legal expert to do: it would simply pose a series of questions based on its indiscriminate, sequential progression through the nodes of the tree, starting from some arbitrary or predetermined slot of a node. Thus in the Oxford project domain of application, the first question confronting the user might be as specific and (more than likely) senseless as, for example, 'did the defender hit the pursuer with a heavy object?' (being perhaps a law-derivation of the law-statement pertaining to behaviour). We would be reluctant to call a system 'intelligent', and would deem it *undesirable*, if it simply demanded of the user answers to highly specific questions with no regard to the nature of his particular problem. More than this, however, it would almost certainly be *necessary* to implement non-brute force search strategies in expert systems with very large legal knowledge bases, for consultations would take unacceptably long periods of time if the computer had to ask questions based on slots held within the vast majority of nodes in the entire tree.

It is necessary therefore to devise an efficient strategy for traversing legal decision trees. In doing this I shall confine my attention to the user who at once wishes to find the legal consequences of some set of facts, but yet is not desirous of any particular conclusion.[18] Such would be forward-chaining according to the previous section,

---

[17] *AINM*, p. 346.
[18] The design of other legal inference engines—that operate on the same legal knowledge base but are for other users—is a job for legal knowledge engineers of the future.

but as shall emerge later, this bald characterization is in need of refinement. The strategy I shall propose aspires to efficiency, simplicity, and generalizability: it is intended to be a suitable set of procedures for all legal domains. Together these procedures constitute general legal problem-solving knowledge and they should be held in the legal inference engine. (The discussion also bears on the user interface—see Section 2.7.) It should be noted that the jurisprudential literature can offer little help in this context, for those legal theorists who have schematically represented the law in tree structures have not addressed, in detail, the question of how that search space might be traversed. Note also that, in a sense, my account is a prescriptive theory of legal reasoning of limited scope, as it recommends a way of manipulating legal productions so as to yield legal conclusions.

The best way of understanding the proposed inference mechanism is in terms of the facilities it offers: (1) storage of basic data and of the facts of the instant case at any given time; (2) interaction with the user through both menus and questions; (3) sensible searching in accordance with its heuristic problem-solving knowledge (and the user's knowledge of the problem being investigated); and (4) intimation during consultation of its ability to draw inferences. I shall deal with each of these features in turn.

At the start of all consultations, and sometimes during the dialogue, the system asks the user some general questions or some domain-specific queries, such as the names of the defender and the pursuer, and some dates and locations of relevant events. Responses to such questions are not restricted to 'yes', 'no', or 'don't know'. Such *basic data* will, of course, vary between domains, but are generally those pieces of information that the domain expert has indicated to be pertinent to most cases within the chosen domain of application. The basic data are stored in the part of the computer memory that holds the facts of the instant case: I shall call that store the *store of known facts* (or, simply, the *store*).[19] The store of known facts is an important component, because it is consulted by the system before any question is asked of the user. If the store provides an answer, then the system will not present the query to the user, but

---

[19] AI scientists sometimes refer to the set of facts that have been established as true (during the consultation) as the *data base*. See e.g. Waterman, *AGES*, p. 67. I shall refrain from this practice, as confusion could result from that and my usage of the term 'legal database systems': see Section 1.3.

will utilize the store as the source of the response and proceed to the next question. The store of known facts holds not only the basic data, but also the facts of the case (or interim legal conclusions) as established through positive or negative answers during the dialogue. The store, therefore, eliminates the possibility of repetition of questions. (Facts of the case can be of the form 'it is false that . . .' as well as 'it is true that . . .'.)

There are two principal ways in which the user controls the direction of the search. First, he is required to answer 'yes', 'no', or 'don't know' to questions asked of him. The questions may be of the form 'is it true that [proposition held in slot of node]?' If an affirmative or negative answer results in a store of known facts from which a conclusion can be drawn, then the system will indeed indicate (as shall be seen) that there is such a sufficiency of data. On the other hand, the replies of 'yes' and 'no' may simply augment the store, but not allow any inference to be made. If the user replies 'don't know' to a question, then no new data is added to the store of new facts. Unless the question—to which the user does not know an answer—is based on a slot of a terminal node, 'don't know' will simply prompt a further, more detailed search in the knowledge base, thereby perhaps eventually assisting the user to answer 'yes' or 'no' to a more specific question (to the generalization of which he did not feel he could reply). Of course, it might well be that the question to which the user does not have a response is indeed based on a terminal node, or again, that the successive 'don't know's' and searching result in arrival at such a node. On these occasions, unless the user retorts 'yes' or 'no', no conclusion can be inferred from that part of the knowledge base.[20]

The idea of *contingent conclusions* is introduced to cope with this (see Section 2.7). The system informs the user that it can indicate what inferences can be drawn given 'yes' *or* 'no' replies. The user may then hypothesize a positive or negative response—he tentatively opts for a 'yes' or 'no' retort—and may examine the resultant contingent conclusion(s). Thereafter, he can alter his original choice, and find out the contingent conclusion(s) that may be inferred from that later hypothesis. A conclusion is said to be contingent because it

---

[20] There is then what I called in Section 5.8 a gap in the user's knowledge. See Alchourron and Bulygin, *NS*, pp. 31–4.

is not based entirely on the store of known facts but partly on the assumed truth-values assigned by the user. These truth-values are explicitly appended to the conclusions when displayed to the user. For example, the system may conclude that 'the court may grant decree of divorce, if it is true that . . .'. This is a useful device when, as is not uncommon, all the relevant facts of the case are not known to the lawyer. However, it can be computationally complex when there are many questions within the one line of reasoning to which the user does not have answers. (Note that this is not an example of using a three-valued logic. The user is not denying that the proposition upon which the question is based has truth-value, but is indicating that he does not know what that value is.) The second principal way that the user may interact with the system is through selection from a menu. The contents of the menus, I suggest, are the condition of application slots of nodes, or summaries of them. The user selects one or more items from the menu, that is, he identifies the possibilities he would like to explore. (If there are no relevant items, then it is likely that the part of the system on offer does not have an answer to his problem.) Response to the menu will prompt further menus or questions.

I must now explain precisely when it is that the system offers these alternative modes of interaction (for it is not under the user's control). The basic search strategy can be summarized in terms of the inverted tree described in Section 4.5, and can be encapsulated in the form of rules. These rules are central to the legal inference engine; they are the principal legal domain-independent rules of heuristic search. (As I said in Section 3.7, some domain-independent legal meta-rules/heuristics are held in the inference engine.) The four most important rules are as follows:

1. If the search is at a node that has only one child that holds a (principal) condition of application slot, then the system asks a question based on that slot.

2. If the search is at a node that has more than one child that holds a (principal or alternative) condition of application slot, then a menu is presented, being a list of all the condition slots (or summaries of them) of the generation in question.

3. If more than one item on a menu is selected by the user, then the system searches down, as far as is necessary, through the descendant nodes of the first selected item, after which the descend-

ant nodes of the other items are similarly and consecutively explored.

4. If the search is at a node that has no children, then the system states it is at a terminal node and that only contingent conclusions may be inferred if the user can answer neither affirmatively nor negatively.

If these rules are applied to a hypothetical legal decision tree, starting at the root node, and assuming an interaction and search during which the reply 'don't know' is given to all questions, then the possibilities at the beginning would be thus. If the root node has only one child that has a condition of application slot, then the system asks a question. If, in turn, there is only one node in the next generation of search space that has a condition slot, then the system once again asks a question. That process is repeated through successive search spaces until the search arrives at a generation where there is more than one node that has a condition slot. At that point, as well as when the root node has more than one child that has a condition slot, a menu is presented. If only one slot is selected and *qua* conclusion slot it has just one child that has a condition slot, then a question based on that slot will be offered. But if only one slot is selected from the menu, and that slot *qua* conclusion slot itself has more than one child that has a condition, then a further menu will appear. If, on the other hand, more than one slot is selected from the menu, then the system examines, in turn, the branches emanating from each chosen item. This application of Rules 1, 2, and 3 would continue until Rule 4 was applied (subject to the intervention of the other rules introduced later in this section).

This recommended search strategy can be clarified in light of a simplification of the Oxford project domain. The foundation rule states, in summary, 'if the marriage has broken down irretrievably, the court may grant decree of divorce'. The root node of the knowledge base is the consequent of that rule, and it only has one child: the principal condition (that is, the rule's antecedent). According to the search strategy, the system then asks some such question as 'Has the marriage broken down irretrievably?' Both 'yes' and 'no' would result in obvious conclusions but only a foolish user would give either of these answers to questions at this level of generality and at this point in the decision tree.[21] Given the likely response, 'don't

---

[21] Of course, a knowledgeable user who had no need of such a system might be in a sound position so to answer.

know', the system then finds that the node 'the marriage has broken down irretrievably' has five children that have condition of application slots—those pertaining to adultery, behaviour, desertion, two years' separation, and five years' separation. A menu indicating these grounds of divorce appears, therefore, and the user selects those that might be relevant. (A sensible rule of thumb for any user is that he should select every item from a menu unless he is sure it has no bearing on his problem.) Let us imagine that the spouse of a lawyer's client has been having sexual affairs with another. The lawyer would clearly select the 'adultery' item, and, if he was thorough, the 'behaviour' choice. In that way, the search space would be radically reduced in one step, because the remaining three grounds would no longer be searchable. This then avoids the generation of all those irrelevant questions regarding desertion and separation that would ensue in a brute force search. In our hypothetical example, the system would go on to search through the part of the tree pertaining to adultery and would thereafter explore the possibility of satisfaction of the behaviour ground. Our rules of search together with the user's responses would continue heuristically to prune the legal decision tree, as the consultation progressed.

It will be observed that the above account pertained only to the nodes that have condition slots, and are functioning *qua* conditions. (It is unnecessary to distinguish—as I did in my theory of the structure of productions—between principal and alternative conditions, because there is no logical distinction between these disjuncts as regards their function and status in a decision tree. The distinction I drew in my theory of structure (see Section 4.4) was, as I said in my discussion of individuation (see Section 4.3), for ease of exposition: when the legal knowledge engineer is reducing the formal sources of the law to a system of legal productions, the principal and alternative condition slots contribute towards rules that are *manageable* units for his task.) The inference engine must also allow for the temporal and spatial limitations and the conjunctive and exceptive qualifications that may govern conditions. These sub-slots and slots never appear in menus, for it would be inefficient to allow the presentation of a barrage of questions regarding limitations and qualifications of conditions of application whose status is not yet recorded in the store of facts. Limitations and qualifications are of relevance only when the user has responded to queries about the conditions of application in a way that could possibly yield a conclusion. A further three rules of heuristic search can now be formulated:

5. If the user responds to a query about a condition of application slot in a way that could possibly yield a legal conclusion, and if that conclusion has one or more filled temporal or spatial limitation sub-slots attached to it, then the system asks one or more questions based on the sub-slot(s).

6. If the user responds to a query about one or more limitation sub-slots in a way that could possibly yield a legal conclusion, and if that node is subject to nodes with conjunctive or exceptive qualification slots, then the system asks one or more questions based on the slots.

7. If the user responds to a query about one or more qualification slots in a way that could possibly yield a legal conclusion, and if these slots themselves have one or more filled temporal or spatial limitation sub-slots attached to them then the system asks one or more questions based on these sub-slot(s).

In other words, once a condition of application is satisfied, the system asks about its limitations, and if they in turn are satisfied, the system asks about the condition's qualifications, and if these qualifications themselves are subject to limitations then the system must ask about these. Of course, questions regarding qualifications can themselves lead to further questions or menus, for then the qualification slots function as conclusion slots of more specific productions that themselves must have one or more conditions.

Further rules of heuristic search may also be needed to cope both with accessing the legal addenda sub-slot and with searching through descendants of the limitations and legal addenda sub-slots. Moreover, heuristics are required to handle the following scenario. If a question about the occurrence of an act, action, event, and so forth is capable of being answered positively or negatively in respect of more than one occasion, then the system should be capable of asking questions about each occasion which may result in the relevant proposition (with all its qualifications, limitations, and so forth), being established as true or false. For instance, if the user is asked if it is true that 'the defender has committed adultery', then a positive response may be appropriate in connection not just with one adulterous act but with many. And each of these acts may itself have been performed under distinct circumstances (with different parties, for example). The system must be capable of inquiring about each act separately; and for that type of situation, further domain-independent heuristics must be embodied in the system.

The seven rules alone indicate that the search process may indeed be a complex one; and one which many users may find difficult to follow without help. A facility that told the user that he was, say, 'on level 4 of what may be a 10-node branch' would be most helpful. For the user would thereby have some sense of his stage in the search. This proposed facility may also be useful in another respect. It may often be unclear to a user whether or not a question posed is one composed of terms of relative brute or institutional fact and he may wonder if a 'yes' or 'no' response is premature. If the system could indicate the search position, then it may frequently be apparent to the user that it holds a great deal more knowledge relating to the question at hand, in consequence of which a 'don't know' rejoinder may be more sensible.

So that the user does not overlook valuable knowledge held within the system, it is also sometimes appropriate to present him with what may be called a *definition facility*. This is desirable when the production contains a word or phrase that, when presented within a question, might be thought by the user to bear its ordinary, everyday meaning, whereas in fact it is defined quite precisely in the repositories of the law. The term 'continuous period' in the *Divorce (Scotland) Act 1976* is an example here: it is defined in s.2(4) in a way that does not accord with common usage. The user should be alerted to this, perhaps by the highlighting of such words on the screen. By marking these words in some fashion when building the knowledge base—this is done in Appendix II by underlining them—the system can be programmed to detect them during the search and simultaneously to offer the definition facility. And during a consultation, the user may use this facility in order to clarify any particular word or phrase brought to his attention.

I turn finally, in my discussion of the features of the proposed system's inference engine, to its ability to intimate when its store of known facts is sufficient for it to draw a conclusion. This can be indicated permanently through some small message continually held on the screen. A more sophisticated system gives two messages: one that confirms it can draw a *final* conclusion, by which is meant it could assert the truth-value of the conclusion slot of the root node, and another that confirms it can infer an *interim* conclusion, by which is meant it could assert the truth-value of the conclusion slot of some descendant node, the truth or falsity of which had not been indicated by the user.

It is also possible to have the facility whereby at any time during a consultation the user can request, first, the display of all the conclusions that can be drawn given the current state of the store, and, secondly, simply the display of all the known facts in the store. (The size of such displays may be constrained by users' selections from menus.) With regard to the latter, just as we might want to recapitulate what we have told a human expert, we might similarly like to know what we have told our system at any given stage in the dialogue. While it is true in respect of the former facility that a human expert is unlikely to proffer his conclusions when not yet apprised of all the facts, he may nevertheless be inclined to respond to an anxious instructing solicitor who demands some interim analysis prior to relaying all his knowledge of the facts of a case. The former facility proposed would satisfy that very demand if the solicitor were a user of an expert system.

It is important to note that even when the system can draw a final conclusion, unless instructed to do otherwise it will nevertheless continue to consider all further possibilities. This reflects the research habits of any competent lawyer who will seek to present as powerful a case as possible. Thus in pursuance of the maxim 'belt and braces', the thorough divorce lawyer will prefer to establish as many grounds for divorce as possible and cite as many instances of, say, adultery and behaviour, as the facts of the case will allow. There is no need therefore for the inclusion of heuristics that determine the order of search, from the items of a menu, in accordance with the likelihood of the applicability of nodes. For the system must explore all the possibilities that remain after the application of the seven legal heuristics; and the order of exploration is of little moment. In other words, the competent lawyer will want to know the implications of *all* the productions that may be *triggered* (see Section 6.2): he will require that all rules that may be triggered will be fired.

I said tentatively at the start of this section that, because the inference mechanism I recommend is designed for a user who has no particular goal in mind, our system forward-chains. In light of this section, however, the limitations of such a characterization of legal reasoning—in so far as our legal inference engine is concerned—can be recognized. Forward-chaining, in the first instance, involves searching for the most specific antecedent that can be fired; but it is difficult to see, if the search traverses in a purely forward direction and is governed by the type of user interface I recommend, how this could be done in any way other than a brute force, and therefore invariably unsatisfactory, fashion. For that reason, it is desirable, as I have shown in this section, to use what might be termed a 'user-controlled backward-chaining strategy' to prune the legal decision tree; although it is crucial to note that this does not mean the system favours any particular conclusion. But it is undeniably inaccurate to say that our system forward-chains, if that description is presented as an informal specification of its inference mechanism.[22]

6.4 THE ARGUMENT FROM TRUTH-VALUE

The Argument from Truth-Value claims to be yet another denial of the possibility of deductive legal reasoning and, therefore, of some types of deductive legal inference engines. It has been expressed most lucidly by Hart:

It has been contended that the application of legal rules to particular cases cannot be regarded as a syllogism or any other kind of deductive inference, on the grounds that neither general legal rules nor particular statements of law (such as those ascribing rights or duties to individuals) can be character-ised as either true or false and thus cannot be logically related either among themselves or to statements of fact; hence, they cannot figure as premises or conclusions of a deductive argument.[23]

In relation to expert systems, this argument casts doubt on the pos-sibility of designing inference engines that can apply the legal pro-ductions of a knowledge base to the facts of any case. Moreover, the argument challenges my claim that legal productions can be related to one another, and chained together in the reasoning process, in the way my theory of legal sub-systems (Section 4.5) suggests.

The Argument from Truth-Value can best be appreciated in the light of certain fundamental aspects of the discipline of logic.

---

[22] The image of forward-chaining may nevertheless be retained by legal theorists as a tool for: (1) the comparative analysis of the activities of different legal reasoning agents; (2) the evaluation of current practice in, and of descriptive theories of, legal reasoning; and (3) the development of prescriptive theories of legal reasoning.

[23] 'PPL', p. 100. Note that the Argument from Truth-Value can be employed in opposition to the weak, strongish, and strong deductive theses.

Central to the operation of techniques of classical logic, it is generally held, are the notions of truth and falsehood. Thus, in theoretical reasoning, that is, reasoning about what *is* the case, if the premisses are true and the argument is valid, then the conclusion is necessarily true. The rules of theoretical reasoning, as Kenny puts it, are 'truth-preserving'.[24] The method of determining the truth or falsity of any statement is based on the concept of *truth-value*. A statement has truth-value, in ordinary logic, if and only if it is *either* true *or* false. A problem of theoretical logic arises, therefore, in relation to those classes of statement that do not have truth-value, that is, that are neither true nor false. For it seems, at least on the face of it, that it makes no sense to talk of logical relations, such as contradiction and entailment, in respect of statements that have no truth-value. It is fashionable to regard *norms* or *normative statements* as examples of such statements,[25] and it is equally commonplace to conceive of the law as a system of norms or normative statements. Thus, it is argued, the application of the laws of logic to the laws of the state is precluded because of the normative nature of legal rules, and therefore, their lack of truth-value.

This is clearly an important and sophisticated objection to deductive legal reasoning, and, in turn, any adequate jurisprudential theory of legal knowledge utilization must offer some kind of reply. Hart's own retort indicates a direction that might be taken: 'Although considerable technical complexities are involved, several more general definitions of the idea of valid deductive inference that render the notion applicable to inferences the constituents of which are not characterized as either true or false have now been worked out by logicians.'[26] The more general definitions of valid deductive inference to which Hart is no doubt alluding are the 'extended' deontic, modal, and imperative logics that were referred to in Section 5.1. These, as I said, are themselves formal logical systems. Whereas traditional and classical logics provide us with formal canons for reasoning with empirical statements that have truth-value, extended

---

[24] 'Practical Reasoning and Rational Appetite' (1975), p. 71.

[25] See Kelsen, 'Law and Logic' (1973), especially p. 229, and Hilpinen (ed.), *DLISR*, pp. 7–8. Note, however, not all theorists agree that norms lack truth-value. Alchourron and Bulygin suggest that some writers (and they mention Kalinowski and Rodig) 'readily ascribe truth-values to norms'. See 'The Expressive Conception of Norms' (1981), pp. 95 and 121, n. 3. Also see Morscher, 'Antinomies and Incompatibilities within Normative Languages' (1982), pp. 97–8.

[26] 'PPL', p. 100.

logics furnish us with standards for reasoning with statements that lack truth-value, such as, say, imperative and normative statements.[27] In designing legal inference engines, therefore, legal knowledge engineers must identify the nature of the entities represented within their knowledge bases and decide whether these can be subjected to the application of classical or of extended logics in the process of legal reasoning. Of course, it is difficult to imagine an expert system in law whose knowledge base is entirely devoid of normative elements, as it is generally thought that the law is normative in nature; we invariably say of the law that it lays down obligations, permissions, prohibitions, rights, duties, and so forth. Moreover, characteristically we find in our law-formulations the use of typically normative vocabulary such as *must, ought, may, should, shall,* and variants thereof. How indeed might knowledge of law-formulations be manipulated while reasoning other than by the application of some deontic logic (logic of normative concepts)? The necessity for the inclusion of some deontic logic within a legal inference engine would seem beyond dispute in respect of those rule-based systems whose rules have deontic content.

Yet the extent of the practical relevance of deontic logic for expert systems in law has been denied.[28] It should be stressed, however, that any computer system that manipulates entities with deontic content necessarily makes assumptions about, and presupposes a theory of, deontic logic. For instance, if an inference engine simply implements some first-order classical logic in order to reason with norms or normative propositions, then that in itself constitutes an approach to the logic of deontic propositions or predicates. All the current systems analysed in Appendix I presuppose some theory of deontic logic, but only McCarty, the field's pioneer, has offered a thorough exposition of the underlying deontic logical system.[29]

There are extremely complex philosophical and technical issues involved in the development of deontic logics, however, and it must be noted that there is not any system of deontic logic that commands the degree of general support that many systems of classical logic currently do. Disagreement in this context is largely explicable in

---

[27] Problems of deontic, modal, and imperative logic concern not only legal theorists but scholars of ethical and practical reasoning too.

[28] See e.g. Sergot, 'Representing Legislation as Logic Programs' (1985), p. 13.

[29] 'Permissions and Obligations' (1983).

terms of current philosophical insolubility, and consensus, as shall be seen, can be achieved only at a fairly mundane level. There is, of course, no lack of philosophical source material in this area. It is generally recognized that the intellectual forerunners of modern deontic logicians were Leibniz and Bentham,[30] although it has been argued that even fourteenth-century philosophers developed fairly sophisticated normative logics.[31] However, Bentham's logic of 'the will' or of 'imperation' was not fully developed, and the first sustained treatment of deontic logic was by Mally in 1926.[32] The foundations of today's systems of deontic logic were laid by von Wright in 1951 in 'Deontic Logic',[33] in which he developed his logical system on the basis of *modal* logic, that is, a logic of possibility and necessity (another extended logical system). Since then, von Wright himself has written much of relevance for legal theory and other important jurisprudents like Ross, Castberg, Tammelo, and Alchourron and Bulygin have contributed to the field.[34] Moreover, Kelsen devoted much of the final decade of his life to the question of the logic of norms.[35]

For the purposes of this book, it is necessary to articulate a logic of legal productions, and to do so with the many problems of deontic logic in mind. Note that our concern with legal productions shall now be confined to consideration of law-statements. These are linguistic expressions articulated in the form of compound conditional statements, and—broadly speaking—they describe statutes and judicial precedents as found in law-formulations. A possible source of confusion here is the fact that such linguistic expressions are susceptible to interpretation at several different levels. In absence of a context within which these conditional statements may be fully understood, the sentential form in which they are found may often

---

[30] See von Wright, 'On the Logic of Norms and Actions' (1981), pp. 3–35, and Hart, *EOB*, pp. 112–18.

[31] Knuuttila, 'The Emergence of Deontic Logic in the Fourteenth Century' (1981), pp. 225–48. Hart mentions there to be 'scattered hints of the possibility of a logic of imperatives' in the work of Anselm (1033–1109): *EOB*, p. 112.

[32] See von Wright, 'On the Logic of Norms and Actions' (1981), p. 3.

[33] Since that article, von Wright has been one of the leading commentators on deontic logic. See e.g. *NA*, 'Deontic Logic Revisited' (1973), and 'Norms, Truth and Logic' (1982).

[34] See *DN*, *PLP*, *Modern Logic in the Service of Law* (1978), and *NS*, respectively.

[35] See Hartney, 'Hans Kelsen's Theory of Norms' (1985), p. 116. Hartney also tells us that almost half of Kelsen's *Allgemeine Theorie der Normen* (1979) concerns the applicability of logical principles to norms. Also see Weinberger, 'Logic and the Pure Theory of Law' (1986).

reasonably be taken to be law-formulations, law-statements, or indeed law-predictions.[36] Moreover, law-statements might seem to be a rather heterogeneous collection of entities: some are directed at definite subjects indicating what they are obligated or permitted to do, or prohibited from doing, while others seem simply to regulate the meaning of other legal terms. Yet, as I said in Sections 4.3 and 4.4, all law-statements individuated as legal productions can be conceived as rules of inference, stipulating what may, must, or may not be inferred from given premisses and states of affairs. They are, as I have argued, existential statements about the law, declaring what is true within the universe of legal discourse, and stipulating what legal consequences legal reasoning agents may attach to facts of cases.

Given my characterization of law-statements, it is useful now to consider a distinction introduced by Alchourron in 1969: between a 'logic of norms' and a 'logic of normative propositions'.[37] According to Alchourron, and all deontic logicians seem to agree with him in this respect, the logical systems identifying the properties and relations of norms and those of (descriptively understood) normative propositions are not identical. A normative proposition, on Alchourron's analysis, is a proposition 'to the effect that a norm has been issued'.[38] In *Norm and Action*, von Wright draws a similar distinction.[39] Accordingly, if it is accepted that law-statements are descriptive in nature, then our concern here is with a logic of normative propositions (the propositions that are the meaning of law-statements) and not with a logic of norms. It might be thought, then, that all problems of deontic logic can be conveniently side-stepped, because legal reasoning and expert systems employ as their premisses statements or propositions *about* the law which do have sufficient truth-value within the universe of legal discourse to allow of logical relations and to be susceptible to the techniques of classical, and not deontic, logic.[40] Yet deontic logicians have shown this to be

---

[36] Cf. *NA*, p. 102, where von Wright points out that '[w]hether a given sentence is a norm-formulation or not can never be decided on "morphic" grounds, *i.e.* seen from the *sign* alone' (original emphasis). See also Atwool, 'Legal Precepts' (1982), in which it is argued that legal linguistic expressions can operate on different levels: directive, normative and predictive.

[37] 'Logic of Norms and Logic of Normative Propositions' (1969).

[38] Ibid., p. 242.

[39] (1963), pp. 104–6.

[40] MacCormick seems to imply this: 'The Nature of Legal Reasoning: A Brief Reply to Dr. Wilson' (1982), pp. 289–90. Cf. Hart's criticism of Lyons's interpretation of Bentham: *EOB*, pp. 114–22.

a misguided approach. Alchourron, for instance, has shown that a logic of normative propositions in fact *presupposes* a logic of norms,[41] and, in the following section, it will become apparent, for present purposes, why a logic of normative propositions must extend beyond classical logic.

6.5 DEONTIC LOGIC AND EXPERT SYSTEMS IN LAW

From the previous section, and from the findings of this book so far, three conceivable problems of deontic logic can be identified as relevant for legal knowledge engineers. These concern: (1) the application of legal productions to factual propositions; (2) the logical relationships between legal productions; and (3) the deontic implications of legal productions.[42] I shall deal with each in turn (confining my attention to non-probabilistic legal productions).

It might be thought that the most fundamental question of the logic of legal productions relates to the first concern—the possibility of relating individual productions to factual descriptions in a way that, as a matter of logic, necessitates a particular conclusion. This point is made by Hart in his statement of the Argument from Truth-Value (as can be seen from the previous section), is laboured by Castberg during his consideration of the 'norm-syllogism',[43] and is examined also by Guest.[44] The matter can be summarized by asking if the following are valid arguments (where '*d*' denotes some deontic phrase such as 'it may be established that', or 'it shall be established that'):

(a) 1 $A \Rightarrow d(B)$
      2   A
      3   Therefore $d(B)$

(b) 1 $\forall(x)(Ax \Rightarrow d(Bx))$
      2   Az
      3   Therefore $d(Bz)$

[41] 'Logic of Norms and Logic of Normative Propositions' (1969). Cf. Horovitz, *LL*, p. 99 n. 6. The issue is far from simple. Whether deontic logic was to be regarded as a logic of prescriptions or descriptions was a question to which von Wright, in *NA*, confessed he did not know 'the best answer' (p. 133).

[42] I am not suggesting that these are the only problems of deontic logic. Rather, these are the issues raised by this book and by the Argument from Truth-Value.

[43] *PLP*, pp. 52–62.

[44] 'Logic in the Law' (1961), pp. 183–6.

In light of the discussion of Section 5.7, it might be denied that '3' in either of the arguments above necessarily follows from the premisses '1' and '2', on the grounds that exceptions to the rules, '1', may be implied for reasons of principle or policy. Yet this is not due to the deontic terms within the rules. Given, as I said, that all conclusions are conditional, there is no good reason in logic to deny the propriety of drawing such conditional conclusions and the presence of deontic terms within the rules in no way precludes this operation; nor can they prejudice the normal functioning of the conditional logical operator or the universal quantifier. The arguments above are valid in virtue of the propositional and predicate calculi respectively, and the mechanism denoted is the logic of subsumption (see Section 5.5). Of course, it is also relevant that most human legal reasoning agents, including experts, seem to accept the validity of the arguments above, and have no difficulty in relating legal rules to facts. This, then, should be reflected in the architecture of legal inference engines.

The Argument from Truth-Value is misplaced with regard to relating legal productions to facts of cases. Note that I am not here reducing deontic logic to traditional or classical logic, but am showing deontic logic, in this context, to be irrelevant. When the problem, as raised by Hart, Castberg, and Guest, is subjected to careful scrutiny, it can be seen to dissolve.

The second respect in which deontic logic seems to be relevant for legal knowledge engineering concerns the logical relationships between productions; and this raises more fundamental difficulties. It can be understood easily from the following problems (where 'O' denotes 'it shall be established that', 'P' denotes 'it may be established that', and 'Ph' denotes 'it shall not be established that', and 'a', 'b', 'c', and 'd' are propositional variables):

(*a*) Fact:	a	(*b*) Fact:	a
Rules:	$a \Rightarrow O(b)$		$a \Rightarrow P(b)$
	$b \Rightarrow O(c)$		$b \Rightarrow P(c)$
	$c \Rightarrow O(d)$		$c \Rightarrow P(d)$
Problem:	What can we conclude from 'a'?	Problem:	What can we conclude from 'a'?

(c) Fact: a
    Rules: a ⇒ *Ph*(b)
               b ⇒ *Ph*(c)
               c ⇒ *Ph*(d)
    Problem: What can we
               conclude from
               'a'?

(d) Fact: a
    Rules: a ⇒ *O*(b)
               b ⇒ *P*(c)
               c ⇒ *O*(d)
    Problem: What can we
               conclude from
               'a'?

(e) Fact: a
    Rules: a ⇒ *O*(b)
               b ⇒ *Ph*(c)
               c ⇒ *O*(d)
    Problem: What can we
               conclude from
               'a'?

(f) Fact: a
    Rules: a ⇒ *P*(b)
               b ⇒ *Ph*(c)
               c ⇒ *P*(d)
    Problem: What can we
               conclude from
               'a'?

In most classical logics of empirical statements the following *transitivity* rule of inference is accepted.

$$((a \Rightarrow b) \wedge (b \Rightarrow c) \wedge (c \Rightarrow d)) \Rightarrow (a \Rightarrow d)$$

(In English, this would read (approximately) as follows. For any propositions a, b, c, d: if a implies b, and b implies c, and c implies d, then a implies d.) It is not clear, however, that such a transitivity relation holds between legal productions, and would therefore be applicable to the six problems. (What *is* clear is that the problem is with us even if we treat the rules as descriptive and not prescriptive in nature.) The problem, then, concerns the extent, if any, to which we can chain together or conjoin statements with deontic content in the process of legal reasoning. Surprisingly, most of the legal writers who have talked of chaining legal rules together seem oblivious to the attendant logical problems.[45] Yet every legal knowledge engineer must have, or assume, a solution to this difficulty. The solution I shall now propose accords with my theory of individuation, and also reflects the reasoning habits of lawyers, who, after all, seem not to be hindered by this logical conundrum.

It will be remembered that my theory of individuation commits us to non-probabilistic legal productions of the form of rules of infer-

---

[45] In notes 76–9 of ch. 4, I noted that Stone, Gottlieb, MacCormick, Horovitz, Ross, and Honoré acknowledge legal reasoning as involving the conjunction of legal rules. But although all these writers are well aware of deontic logic, none of them provides a helpful, thorough solution to the current difficulty.

TABLE 5

Obligation	Permission	Prohibition
shall	may	shall not
must	can	may not
ought	power	ought not
should	authorized	should not
duty	privilege	must not
obligatory	permitted	prohibited
necessary	liberty	forbidden

ence indicating what may, must, or may not, be inferred within the universe of legal discourse. These rules are directions to legal reasoning agents. These rules, therefore, are not norms of conduct, or prescriptions for action or behaviour, directed at citizens in general, although they are laden with implications for these persons. One of the reasons for preferring this mode of individuation can now be appreciated. If, in the six earlier problems, we substitute for 'O', 'P', and 'Ph' the phrases 'it is obligatory that', 'it is permitted that', and 'it is forbidden that' respectively, then the difficulties are magnified beyond any reasonable expectations of solution. For answers to these problems would demand a deontic logic of richness and complexity over which consensus, as is noted again later, is sadly lacking. Case reports, legal documents, and legal textbooks suggest that lawyers do not (and probably could not) reason with such deontic units, but prefer individuated rules of the sort I propose, for which, it is submitted, a relatively simple (and limited) logic can be developed.

The first step is to show how I propose that the deontic language of legislation and judicial precedents can be reduced to three basic deontic categories (the normative categories of the theory of structure of Section 4.4). This can be done as shown in Table 5 (whose headings, but *not* contents, are conceived as exhaustive). It is, of course, not to be inferred from the table that all the terms within the same categories are synonymous. Clearly they are not. Nor, in proposing such a taxonomy, am I thereby committing the 'imperative fallacy', that is, confusing imperative and normative statements.[46] For it is submitted that although many of the words in the same

[46] On the 'imperative fallacy', see MacCormick, 'Legal Obligation and the Imperative Fallacy' (1973).

grouping differ both in meaning and in philosophical status, they nevertheless perform the same logical function in the context of searching through a legal decision tree.[47] In other words, all phrases that contain terms belonging to the same grouping will have corresponding normative category sub-slots (in accordance with the proposed structure for productions), and will be treated alike by the inference engine. For example, 'it shall be established that' is, for our purposes, logically and functionally equivalent to 'the court ought to decide that'. Sometimes, the deontic phrase is not explicitly present in the law-formulations. Section 21 of the *Theft Act 1968*, for instance, states that 'A person is guilty of blackmail if X'. In the proposed structure, this would be translated as a production that has X as its antecedent, 'A person is guilty of blackmail' as its conclusion, an interpolated insertion in the deontic phrase slot to the effect that 'it shall/ought to/should/be established that', and a filled '*O*' normative category sub-slot. (It must be remembered that my normative categories are not identical to the notions of obligation, permission, and prohibition as appear in norms of conduct directed at citizens.)

Turning now to the proposed method of concatenating legal productions, it should be stressed that the following is no more than a very brief outline of a technique that requires further development and eventual formalization. (The introduction of a logical system in terms of definitions, axioms, rules of inference, and so forth is beyond the scope of this book.) The mechanism for drawing inferences with obligations, permissions, and prohibitions (of the sort tabulated above) can be summarized by stating the effect of these notions on a search through a decision tree. I shall look at each in turn, thereby providing further rules of heuristic search. It should be noted that the direction of the search I have in mind now is from antecedent to consequent. I am assuming that the system has searched backwards through the tree in response to the user's prompts (in the way outlined in Section 6.3), and that the truth-value of an antecedent has been settled. The system is now seeking to draw inferences and move towards the root node.

---

[47] Cf. Tammelo, *Modern Logic in the Service of Law* (1978), p. 129: 'The linguistic difference between "must" and "shall" is irrelevant for logical analyses, since it is mainly one of emphasis or of conative force which the corresponding sentences are intended to carry.' For the wide diversity of *modal* terms (many of which linguistic forms are shared in deontic usage), see White, *Modal Thinking* (1975).

1. If the system encounters a filled '*O*' normative category sub-slot, then the conclusion slot of the production in question is presumed true and that production is deemed applicable.

Thus the transitivity rule of classical logic noted above is held applicable to legal productions with filled '*O*' normative category sub-slots (assuming the obligation operator is inserted in the consequents of each rule in the transitivity rule itself). The effect of this heuristic is that where there is a large chain of legal productions all stipulating what 'shall be established' (or the equivalent), then, as lawyers seem to do, the deontic phrases can effectively be ignored, and draw the final conclusion as though the productions were simply empirical statements. In absence of this rule, it is difficult to understand how legal conclusions can ever be inferred. Note that this heuristic accords with the logic presupposed by those researchers of the Prolog Projects who claim most legal rules to be *definitional* in character.[48]

Note, however, that not all productions with filled '*O*' normative category sub-slots are definitional. It is true that those productions with what I called (in Section 4.4) bi-conditional logical operator slots—the 'if and only if... then...' rules—seek to lay out the necessary and sufficient conditions which must be satisfied for their consequents to hold. Yet not all productions are of that sort. For productions with conditional logical operator slots—'if... then...' rules—do not *define* in the way just mentioned. Rather, they *exemplify*: they stipulate sufficient conditions, which, if satisfied, sanction an inference. (They also, but perhaps less commonly, indicate simply what conditions are necessary for some inference to be drawn.)

In any event, on the basis of this first heuristic, the answer to problem (a) above would be: 'b, c, d', all three rules being applicable.

2. If the system encounters a filled '*P*' normative category sub-slot, then: first, the production that holds the sub-slot is deemed applicable; secondly, the user is informed it is permissible to assert the production's conclusion to be true or false; and, thirdly, the user is asked to hypothesize the truth-value of the conclusion (any inference drawn from such hypothesis being contingent).

---

[48] See e.g. Sergot, 'Representing Legislation as Logic Programs' (1985), p. 13. Cf. *NS*, p. 73, where Alchourron and Bulygin discuss 'conceptual rules' as 'definitions'.

If we consider a production that states 'if X, then the court has the power to Y', and further imagine that X is established, then our system does not simply assume that the power will be exercised, but it allows the user to hypothesize either that Y or ¬ Y is the case, and then draws contingent conclusions on the basis of any such hypothesis. For the system does not know the truth-value of Y: and the best it can offer is contingent indications of the possible consequences of any known facts together with any hypotheses (just as it presents contingent conclusions when the user does not know the answer to a question based on a slot from a terminal node). When a lawyer is aware that the court has a discretionary power, for example, if he is cautious he will note the consequences of that power being both exercised and not exercised. Our heuristic embodies that caution. (The likelihood of it being exercised, however, may usefully be embodied in a law-prediction.)

On the basis of this second heuristic, there could be several answers to problem (*b*), depending on what the truth-values of 'b', 'c', and 'd' are hypothesized to be. If 'b' and 'c' are initially hypothesized to be true, for example, then all three rules are applicable, and the further option to hypothesize 'd' as true then arises. However, if 'b' is hypothesized to be false, then (from the available information), we can say that the first rule is applicable, the second and third rules are not, and the option of hypothesizing 'c' and 'd' to be true does not arise. With regard to problem (*d*), in any event we can conclude 'b', and the first rule is applicable. If 'c' is hypothesized to be true, we can also (contingently) conclude 'd', all three rules being applicable. But if 'c' is hypothesized to be false, then (from the available information), the second rule is applicable, the third is not, and 'd' cannot be (contingently) concluded.

3. If the system encounters a filled '*Ph*' normative category sub-slot, then: first, the conclusion slot of the production in question is presumed neither true nor false; secondly, the production is deemed applicable; but, thirdly, the search goes no further towards the root node.

The case of *MacLennan* v. *MacLennan*, 1958 SC 105, clarifies the operation of this heuristic. (Also see Appendix II.) As I said in Section 3.3, that case establishes that artificial insemination by a donor does not constitute adultery: that is, 'if the defender has been artificially inseminated by a donor, then *it shall not be established for that reason that* there has been adultery'. This production does not allow us to infer adultery. Nor does it preclude the establishment of adultery on the basis of other facts. It simply—as do all productions with filled '*Ph*' normative category sub-slots—indicates a set of conditions that together are not sufficient to sanction an inference. Given there has been AID, we then know it to be neither true nor false that there has been adultery; nothing about adultery is input to the store of known facts, and no further inferences can be made premissed on either the truth or falsity of the statement 'there has been adultery'. The search along the branch towards the root node, therefore, stops at the node that is the consequent of this AID/adultery rule. Notice when the inference 'there was adultery' cannot be made in these circumstances, that in itself constitutes an interim conclusion and is useful information and can be stored to enhance the system's transparency: the user should be able to receive an illuminating repsonse to an inquiry about why adultery may not have been established by the system. This can be done through a 'why not?' question facility, which would function on the basis of a store of applicable productions with filled prohibition slots.

On the basis of this third heuristic, in respect of problem (*c*) we could say that the first rule is applicable; and the answer to problem (*e*) would be '*b*', the first two rules being applicable. With regard to problem (*f*), if '*b*' is hypothesized to be true, then the first and second rules are applicable. If '*b*' is hypothesized to be false, the first rule is applicable, but the second is not.

The third issue concerning deontic logic and expert systems is that of the deontic entailments or implications of legal productions. A great deal of work on deontic logic has been devoted to the development of systems that provide axioms and rules of inferences which allow us to express normative modalities in terms of one another. For instance, some have argued for the interdefinability of obligations and permissions, while others assert permissions and obligations to be irreducible atomic deontic categories.[49] Much of this was anticipated by Hohfeld in his seminal work on jural relations,[50]

---

[49] On the relationships between permissions and obligations, see von Wright, *NA*, pp. 85–92, where it is argued that permissions and obligations are irreducible deontic categories. But, as Alchourron and Bulygin point out, in *NS*, p. 120, von Wright changed his mind on this point. Also see Ross, *DN*, pp. 116–24, where permissions are said to be translatable into obligations.

[50] Hohfeld, *Fundamental Legal Conceptions* (1919).

and very recently Allen and Saxon have formalized Hohfeld's fundamental legal conceptions.[51]

On the face of it, the utility of such logical systems for expert systems is clear. Given facts of a case, not only could one legal conclusion be drawn, but that conclusion could be expressed in terms of all manner of deontic modalities. Moreover, the deontic consequences of legal productions could be derived and articulated as a body of deontically equivalent productions. One could imagine, then, that the power of a legal knowledge base could be enhanced greatly by the generation of the full set of legal productions implicit in a legal decision tree. However, in respect of my proposed legal inference engine that operates on rules of inference for legal reasoning agents (because of the theory of individuation), it would not be particularly helpful to have, say, all the legal productions with P operators redefined in terms of Ph operators. In fact, the facility to propagate the deontic consequences of legal productions would be far more useful if legal productions were norms of conduct or prescriptive rules of action or behaviour (and this might be thought to be an argument against my theory of individuation). In that event, the citizen could be apprised of his position in terms of obligations, permissions, prohibitions, rights, duties, liabilities, disabilities, and so forth, as he so wished.

There is no doubt that classical logics do not provide us with the tools to realize this seductive possibility (whether or not it is norms or normative propositions that are to be manipulated). Yet nor is there any widely accepted deontic logical system that can help us here: debate has raged over the relationships between deontic modalities but consensus cannot be located.[52] Moreover, there is no doubt that the kind of system that might eventually be deployed for this purpose would require the representation of closure rules within

---

[51] Allen and Saxon, 'Analysis of the Logical Structure of Legal Rules by a Modernized and Formalized Version of Hohfeld's Fundamental Legal Conceptions' (1985).

[52] The recent collection, Hilpinen, *New Studies in Deontic Logic* (1981), indicates the diversity (and the complexity) of current theories of deontic logic. For the lack of 'firm footing' for deontic logic, see von Wright, 'Deontic Logic Revisited' (1973), p. 37. The profusion of 'deontic paradoxes' is an indication of the difficulties to which many deontic systems have given rise. See *DLISR*, pp. 21–6. Cf. Castaneda, 'The Paradoxes of Deontic Logic: The Simplest Solution to All of Them in One Fell Swoop' (1981). Note that in this section, I have avoided many controversies by resisting the reductionism that often results from seeking to define the three deontic categories in terms of one another.

legal knowledge bases—a possibility I rejected as presumptuous in Section 5.8. It is submitted, then, that current systems should not implement any such systems for the propagation of all the deontic consequences of facts and productions alike. Rather, they should reason in terms of the deontic modalities as represented, in accordance with the principles I have suggested in this section (and the proposed theory of individuation). It would be no great deficiency if systems lacked the ability to generate deontic entailments of norms of conduct, for this is neither a reliable feature of human experts' reasoning, nor is it required by the characterization of expert systems in law offered in Chapter 1.

6.6 CLEAR CASES AND THE ARGUMENT FROM UNIMPORTANCE

The subject-matter of this book reflects my belief that research into expert systems in law should be conducted within the confines of realistic expectations. Thus, as I explained in Section 4.6, I have concentrated here on rule-based, as opposed to the more ambitious conceptual, approaches to legal knowledge engineering, and, as is stressed in the following section, it has never been my concern to discuss systems to replace judges. Given this relatively modest ambition, however, it might well be asked whether the systems that might flourish on the basis of my analysis will indeed be of any use to legal practitioners. In this section I answer that question, through clarification of the concept of a clear case, and an assessment of the Argument from Unimportance. The development of a theory of clear cases is desirable not only as a means by which (as shall be seen) the province of expert systems with weak/strongish deductive inference engines can be delimited, but also as a contribution to jurisprudence; for the articulation of a descriptive and prescriptive account of the resolution of clear cases will perhaps provide legal theorists with solid common ground upon which fruitful dialogue pertaining to hard cases might be carried out in the future.[53]

It is necessary at the outset to clarify that the adjective 'clear' in this context qualifies the noun 'case': 'clear' attributes a property to 'case'. A 'case' is a generic term used to denote a particular state of affairs, set of circumstances, a series of events, states, or actions and so forth, whose legal consequences fall for consideration, and whose

[53] Cf. Hart, *EJP*, p. 169.

features are referred to as 'the facts of the case'. When we talk of a clear case, it is, then, a *case* that is clear and not a *rule*: Leith's critique of Hart and rule-based expert systems in law, based on the alleged 'philosophical invalidity of the notion of a *clear legal rule*' does not seem to acknowledge this distinction, and loses force when this point is clarified and my theories of law-statements and individuation are borne in mind.[54] Of course, on grounds of open texture, Hart himself would reject the notion of 'clear rules': because all rules must have a penumbra of doubt. What can be clear, he stresses, is their applicability in certain cases. (That is not to deny, however, that some rules are *clearer*—have a larger core of certainty—than others.) The attribute 'clear', therefore, speaks of the ease, and indirectly of the mode, of resolution of a case in light of the existence of legal rules. Yet it is necessary, of course, to be more precise than this.

Jurisprudential controversy has raged over how judges do and ought to resolve hard cases. Far less has been said about clear cases and much that has been said conflates two senses in which a case can meaningfully be said to be clear. It is submitted that a case can be *retrospectively* clear or *potentially* clear. To understand our distinction, first note an observation made by Walker: 'The only real test for a legal adviser's [or indeed an expert system's] solution for any legal difficulty or problem in issue is to have the matter decided by the court.'[55] An authoritative answer to particular legal problems, then, can only emanate from some authoritative institution whose function is to resolve disputes. So, when we are confronted with a case and suggest it to be clear, we might be saying one of two things. First, we might be musing retrospectively that a court's finding confirmed our own legal conclusions on some matter, and that the solution was indeed in no way contentious. Yet few such legal cases are judicially resolved, for legal advisers will invariably settle beyond the courts. More commonly, and secondly, when we say a case is clear we are making some kind of implicit prediction: that if the case in

---

[54] Leith, 'Clear Rules and Legal Expert Systems' (1985), p. 381 (emphasis added). Also see Leith, 'Law and Computer Program: The Limits to Logic' (1985), pp. 6–7. It is submitted that those infrequent occasions on which Hart does indeed talk of 'clear rules', (see e.g. *EJP*, p. 135), can best be construed as references to syntactically unambiguous rules, or clearly applicable rules, or rules with a small penumbra of doubt, or, finally, law-statements whose accuracy is past dispute. In any event, there is no need to talk of clear rules in this book.

[55] *SLS*, p. 453.

question came before our courts, it would undoubtedly be decided in one particular way and thereby disposed of in a fashion with which none of us could reasonably quarrel. Such a case is therefore potentially clear, and it is precisely in virtue of this potential clarity that out-of-court settlement can occur.

If my analysis of legal productions and legal rules in Section 5.7 is accepted, then it transpires, strictly speaking, that the only cases we can correctly term as clear are those that are retrospectively clear. For all rules, I said, are open to implied exceptions (on grounds of principle or purpose). And the only reasoning agent who can authoritatively imply such an exception is the judicial agent: that is to say, a conditional conclusion only becomes unconditional after a judicial decision has been made. Therefore, we can only be *certain* that a case is clear *ex post facto*: when we have judicial confirmation of our own conditional conclusions (assuming the judicial decision itself is not defective in some way).

However, when most non-judicial legal reasoning agents speak of a case being clear they do not mean this in the retrospective sense, but rather they are characterizing their problem in terms of its potential clarity. Yet this potential clarity, it must be stressed, lacks the certainty of retrospective clarity, and the suggestion that a case is potentially clear can never be regarded as more than a conditional assertion (because all rules are open to implied exceptions). The question legal theorists must face, then, is how best to account for the widespread practice of characterizing, or implicitly treating, cases as potentially clear (hereafter simply 'clear cases'), given that the foundations of such practice can be called into question. My point of departure once more will be consensus in jurisprudence, for I shall now examine three elements common to many accounts of clear cases:[56]

1. A theory of clear cases is concerned with law-statements. This

---

[56] A great deal has been written that is relevant for the topic of clear cases, but usually the material is found in the context of *hard* cases (see Section 6.7). See e.g. Hart, 'PPL', pp. 105–8, and *CL*, pp. 119 & 125–6; Dworkin, *TRS*, pp. 15, 62, 81, 83, 112, and 337, and *Law's Empire* (1986), pp. 124–5, 128–9, and 350–4; Harris, *LLS*, pp. 6, 9, 132, 142, 143, 157–8, 159, 164 and 168, and *LP*, pp. 173 and 204; MacCormick, *LRLT*, pp. 197–200 and 227–8, and *HLAH*, p. 125; Raz, *AL*, ch. 10 (where the term 'regulated dispute' usually seems to correspond to clear case). A fine discussion of hard *and* clear ('easy') cases, is Hutchinson and Wakefield, 'A Hard Look at "Hard Cases"': The Nightmare of a Noble Dreamer' (1982), especially, pp. 91–5; on which see Dworkin, *Law's Empire* (1986), pp. 353–4, and 449.

is implicit in all theorists' characterizations of clear cases: discussions focus on the applicability of rules from legislation, or of *rationes*, to facts of cases. When we reason with rules with certainty factors, we are not, therefore, dealing with clear cases. (Of course, theorists disagree over the sufficiency of law-statements for solving even the clearest of cases.)

2. When we say a case is clear, we assume that the law-statements have been individuated with no difficulty, for problems of individuating relevant rules would *ipso facto* deny a case its clarity. Ease of individuation does not, of course, lead to 'clear rules' that lack penumbrae of doubt, but simply to statements whose description or interpretation of law-formulations is agreed upon, and deployed, by legal practitioners (and, in particular, by legal experts).

3. A wide diversity of theorists, including Hart, Dworkin, Harris, and MacCormick, leave us in no doubt that they deem the mode of resolution in clear cases (after individuation and subsumption) to be weak or strongish deductive inference.[57]

Beyond these three basic points, however, there is disagreement within jurisprudence, particularly, as noted in Section 5.7, in connection with the role of purpose in legal reasoning. The heart of the issue is over the sufficiency of the following semantic and empirical account of clear cases: a case is clear where our common linguistic usage of terms of law and of ordinary language allow us—beyond all sensible doubt and independent of any alleged purpose of the law-statements in question—to subsume the facts of the case within the terms of the acontextual meaning of the relevant law-statement(s), as conveyed by the verbal law-formulation. This was Hart's earlier thesis—see Section 5.6.

Fuller and the later Hart, however, as I said in Section 5.7, argue for the insufficiency of this semantic account, and their purposive account, in effect, classifies as clear all those cases where the conclusions of purposive reasoning coincide with those of the semantic approach. In other words, if a case is clear according to the semantic thesis, *and* the conclusion dictated by that model accords with the inference derived from the alleged purpose of the relevant law-statements, then, and only then, it seems according to Fuller and the later Hart, can we properly term that case clear. Therefore, a case

---

[57] See e.g. Hart, *EJP*, p. 64, Dworkin, *TRS*, p. 337, Harris, *LLS*, p. 142, and MacCormick, *LRLT*, p. 197.

that is clear on the semantic model would not be so on the purposive model if the purpose of the legal rules in question seemed to dictate a different conclusion.

It is submitted that it is preferable to propound a theory of clear cases that does not address the question of purpose but whose concern is solely with reasoning towards conditional conclusions. (I am not denying the importance of the role of purpose in hard cases in, say, implying exceptions or in individuating rules where law-formulations are ambiguous—see Section 6.7.) For it would be far from accurate to suggest that purposive reasoning can ever be straightforward. Purposive reasoning is not a matter, as reasoning under the semantic model is, of linguistic pattern matching which most of us can undertake on many occasions on the basis of our familiarity with language. Rather, it is a formidable task involving on every occasion, as Tur has noted, 'an empirical hypothesis about the actual intentions of an actual human being or a group of human beings, or about the social effects of a particular body of rules'.[58] How could it ever be clear how we should formulate such a hypothesis? Surely we cannot sensibly maintain that a case is clear only once we have undertaken a daunting exercise of sociological inquiry. On the contrary, if we are to remain faithful to the ordinary meaning of 'clear', a clear case is best understood in terms of the semantic and empirical account I have been examining. Notice we are thereby constantly alerted to the *potential* clarity of clear cases in a way that the purposive account may not remind us: for the latter may often misleadingly obscure the potentiality of clear cases if it is not emphasized that non-judicial purposive interpretation lacks the legal authority of judicial purposive interpretation.

The semantic account is, of course, not entirely faultless, for it renders clear some cases which seem, from a non-semantic vantage, patently unclear. For example, Fuller's imaginery case of a patriotic group, by way of a memorial gesture, taking a World War Two truck into a park in which vehicles are prohibited,[59] and Dworkin's leading illustration, *Riggs* v. *Palmer*,[60] would both be clear cases on the semantic model. In the former, the group would

---

[58] 'Positivism, Principles and Rules' (1977), p. 51. Also see *IJ*, p. 1139 n. 98. On the complexity of 'purpose', see Summers, 'Professor Fuller on Morality and Law' (1971), pp. 117–19. Relevant too is Dworkin, *Law's Empire* (1986), pp. 315–37.

[59] 'Positivism and Fidelity to Law: A Reply to Professor Hart' (1958), p. 663.

[60] See Section 5.7.

be guilty, and in the latter, the murderer would inherit. This high-lights the nature of the semantic theory of clear cases: it identifies as clear those cases in which a *literal* interpretation of law-statements yields an undeniable solution.[61] The resultant peculiarities as in the cases just mentioned, however, are considered to be a lesser jurisprudential evil than the unwarranted and unrealistic assumptions of the ease of identification of purpose inherent in any purposive account. Moreover, we must be mindful of the widespread correspondence between conditional conclusions of potentially clear cases and the unconditional conclusions of retrospectively clear cases, which, together with the prevalence of out-of-court settlements, suggest that the peculiarities of the semantic account belong more to esoteric legal theory than to the daily practice of law.[62] (Note, however, that the correspondence to which I have just referred can, on some occasions, be purely coincidental: when judges come to conclusions at one with the product of the semantic model, yet reached through principled or purposive reasoning. It might be considered more accurate to classify such cases as retrospectively hard—see next section.)

Expert systems in law with knowledge bases containing only law-statements, therefore, can solve what might be called semantically clear cases: conclusions can be *deductively* drawn on the basis of the user's responses to questions asked of him and these responses themselves are made simply on the basis of the user's familiarity with ordinary and legal language (and not in the light of the purpose of the underlying rules, other than the extent to which the purpose is reflected in the expression of law-statements). Yet the Argument from Unimportance—another objection to deductive legal reasoning—lays the foundations for a denial of the utility of such systems.

Examination of this argument can start usefully with MacCormick, who finds it difficult to credit that 'some people have denied that legal reasoning is ever strictly deductive'. In relation to this he says: 'If this denial is intended in the strictest sense, implying that legal reasoning is never, or cannot ever be, solely deductive in form, then the denial is manifestly and demonstrably false.'[63] And he

---

[61] On literal interpretation, see Dias, *Jurisprudence* (1985), pp. 171–3.

[62] Cf. *LLS*, pp. 4–7, where Harris convincingly minimizes the practical relevance in most cases of purposive interpretation through his idea of 'unanimity in the rejection of purposive interpretation of rules'.

[63] *LRLT*, p. 19. Note that MacCormick's work is an illustration of the *strongish* deductive thesis: see Section 5.4.

proceeds to demonstrate this falsehood via the case of *Daniels and Daniels* v. *R. White & Sons and Tarbard*, [1938] 4 All ER 258. By an approximate usage of the propositional calculus he clearly demonstrates what, as he points out in a later article, by way of reply to a critic, 'is not in doubt, viz. that deductive logic has *some* part to play in legal reasoning'.[64] The Argument from Unimportance suggests the part that deductive logic plays is unimportant (and, when extended, claims expert systems in law—that solve clear cases—perform unimportant and trivial tasks). The argument is presented unambiguously by Jensen:

[I]f there is a process of logical deduction, it only occurs in the final stage [i.e. after premiss selection] and is so obvious that it need not be, and is not, given explicit formulation... the deductive process is such a subordinate part of the total argument that the precise determination of its nature is mainly of academic interest only.[65]

Several points can be made in respect of this extract. First, it is false to suggest that the process of logical deduction has not been given explicit formulation,[66] for examples to the contrary abound.[67] Secondly, Jensen's claim can be regarded as being addressed only to the weak thesis; and if the strong thesis is true, as I shall discuss in the next section, then the suggestions that this 'only occurs in the final stage' or is 'subordinate', or is of 'subsidiary' significance, as Wasserstrom's description of the Argument from Unimportance runs,[68] could not still reasonably be made. Thirdly, a useful expert system in law with a weak/strongish deductive inference engine rebuts this argument, rendering the assertion that the deductive process is 'mainly of academic interest only' in need of urgent revision. Although some of the systems mentioned in Section 1.4 serve to refute the argument, it is appropriate now to consider

---

[64] 'The Nature of Legal Reasoning: A Brief Reply to Dr. Wilson' (1982), p. 286.

[65] *The Nature of Legal Argument* (1957), p. 16.

[66] Remember the distinction between explicitly formulating an argument in logical form to justify a decision *ex post facto*, and using logic actually to develop a legal argument: see Section 5.1.

[67] See, for instance, Guest's examples in 'Logic in the Law' (1961), p. 194. Also see the cases of *Bernard Wheatcroft Ltd.* v. *Secretary of State for the Environment and Another* [1982] JPL 37, and *Knuller (Publishing, Printing and Promotions) Ltd. and others* v. *Director of Public Prosecutions* [1973] AC 435, in which the arguments were formulated in logical (syllogistic) form.

[68] *JD*, p. 23.

how a very simple inference (weak/strongish deductive) mechanism can provide the basis of a useful system.

'The point of contention' here is the same as that which Lloyd and Freeman identify in respect of deductive legal reasoning, namely, 'whether a so-called logical conclusion can be reached in a legal argument in cases which are not legitimately to be described as "trivial"'.[69] More specifically, then: are there any semantically clear cases that are not trivial and that indeed would benefit from resolution by computer as opposed to normal human reasoning methods? It is submitted that there are such cases—*clear cases of the expert domain.*

I said in Chapter 1 that expert systems in law are designed to provide general legal practitioners with easy access to areas of law beyond their range of knowledge and experience, a means of venturing into domains of legal expertise. When a lawyer is faced with a problem of a highly specialized nature demanding a familiarity he lacks with obscure and detailed areas of law, he has no idea whether the case is one that would present difficulties for the expert. It may be that the problem is indeed a hard case (see next section) which even the legal expert is unsure about, but very often it will be one to which the expert has an immediate retort. The latter case is a clear case of the expert domain: its resolution is dependent not on intricate reasoning techniques but on extensive domain-specific knowledge applied to the problem data using deductive logic. Clear cases need not have obvious solutions, for although the logic required is deductive, profound difficulties may arise from the extreme complexity of the area of law at issue.[70] A problem of tax law, for instance, may for its resolution demand an intimacy with a vast network of interrelated rules derived from many diverse sources, but once a human being has equipped himself with a mastery of these complex and intertwining laws, solutions for that agent may be strikingly clear. (As I said in Section 2.5, such a mastery can itself be considered to constitute legal expertise.) Computers can usefully be pro-

---

[69] *IJ*, p. 1139 n. 95.

[70] Cf. Raz, *AL*, p. 182. It might be thought inappropriate to classify a case as clear when the relevant law governing the conclusion is extremely complex. (In which event, Raz's term 'regulated dispute' may be preferred (see n. 56, *supra*)). Note though that by using the term 'clear', I am referring specifically to the ease and (implicitly) the mode of resolution of a case; and I am assuming that *resolution* when there *are* clearly applicable (however complex) law-statements is easier, or at least less contentious, than when there are not.

grammed to solve clear cases of the expert domain and impose order on large bodies of rules by chaining them together in a way that no legal textbook can. For the latter has no inference engine. No matter how large a knowledge base a system has, then, it cannot function without its inference mechanism. Deductive legal reasoning is far from unimportant for clear cases of the expert domain.

6.7 DEDUCTIVE CASES, HARD CASES, AND THE COMPUTER JUDGE

Few theorists would deny that, as MacCormick has said, '[f]or all rules (except very badly drafted ones) there are some clear cases', because, as he goes on, '[i]f that were not so, the possibility of any legal system existing anywhere as any sort of guidance of anyone's conduct for any purpose would be nil'.[71] But the precise relationship between clear cases and hard cases is not agreed upon by legal theorists. MacCormick, for instance, denies that these categories are disjunctive and asserts there to be no clear dividing line between the two,[72] whereas Harris seems to find in his 'pure-norm rule' an indicator of the boundaries.[73]

For Gardner, this matter is central to legal knowledge engineering, because her system (the Stanford Project—see Section 1.4 and Appendix I) when presented with the problem data (input in computer language), then reasons with the data without seeming to ask the user further questions: and so it must be able to differentiate between those cases it can solve and those it cannot, and also, she says, between clear and hard cases, for which purposes she devises many heuristics (not based on jurisprudential consensus).[74] With my more modest (but perhaps more practical) interface, it is clear when the system lacks the knowledge to solve a given problem, for the user—remembering that he will be a general legal practitioner— will be aware that the system has not queried him about matters that seem central to his problem, or that the system has not questioned him at the level of specificity that his case seems to demand, or, finally, that the system is unable to assist him in answering a ques-

---

[71] *HLAH*, p. 125.
[72] *LRLT*, p. 197.
[73] *LLS*, p. 143.
[74] 'An Artificial Intelligence Approach to Legal Reasoning' (1984), pp. 38–65.

tion to which he does not know the answer. The legal user that I envisage himself identifies the limitations of the system (much as a lawyer does when reading a legal text), whereas Gardner's system itself has to perform that function. As a result of my user interface, it is not necessary to inquire in detail into the clear/hard case distinction (although some of the difficulties were pointed out in the previous section). It will, however, be determinable when a case is clear: if the user can answer all the questions asked of him (based on a knowledge base of law-statements only), and he feels too that there has been an exhaustive inquiry into the facts of his case, then that case can be said (with but little reservation) to be semantically and potentially clear. The question does arise, of course, over the possibility of expert systems that can solve cases that are not clear.

If a legal knowledge base contains legal heuristics as well as law-statements, expert systems in law can solve what I shall call *deductive* cases as well as clear cases. This demands the development of a system that can reason with uncertainty, because legal heuristics have certainty factors attached to them which preclude the use of the kinds of inference engines I have discussed so far. It is beyond the scope of this book to examine the notion of legal reasoning with uncertainty in detail, but it should be noted that this process need not be divorced from formal logic. For the underlying deep structure of reasoning with legal heuristics, it is submitted, is deductive. It is true that reasoning with uncertainty is often regarded as a departure from deductive logic,[75] but this need not be so in respect of legal reasoning given the proposed theories of individuation and structure.

Legal heuristics, like all legal productions, are rules of inference, but rather than indicating what ought, may, or must not be inferred, they generally allow us to draw inferences about likely court (or official) behaviour. When representing these heuristics we input a predictive phrase and certainty factor, just as for law-statements we input a deontic phrase. Yet while the nature of the deontic phrase often radically affects the progress of the search (as, for instance, the prohibition operator does), the predictive phrase and certainty factor slot only affect the force of the conclusion, or, where there is a conflict of rules, perhaps the order in which they are examined. (Certainty factors can serve as the foundations of conflict resolution

<hr />

[75] See e.g. *PRBES*, p. 24.

strategies.[76]) A legal inference engine that can reason with uncertainty can be regarded as having two components: 'some sort of certainty-computing procedure on top of the basic antecedent-consequent apparatus', as Winston says of some rule-based systems.[77] So, on the one hand there is the mechanism by which certainty factors are manipulated—on the basis perhaps of some probabilistic calculus or a fuzzy logic. And on the other hand, there is the underlying inference routine, the following being my proposal:

1. If the system encounters a filled predictive phrase and certainty factor slot, then the conclusion slot of the production in question is presumed true and that production is deemed applicable.

This is equivalent to the heuristic for filled obligation normative category sub-slots (Section 6.5), and the transitivity rule of classical logic is once more held applicable. This proposed heuristic would need to be refined by the addition of some conflict resolution heuristics, but I am not concerned with that here. What is apparent, however, is that legal heuristics, as well as law-statements, can be chained together in deductive manner. The mechanism just described is that of the strong deductive thesis. That thesis is impervious to the Argument from Unimportance, for if my riposte to the Argument from the Particularity of Facts is reflected upon (Section 5.5), in Jensen's terms (see Section 6.6) the deductive process, by definition, does *not* occur only after premiss selection, nor indeed is it a subordinate part of the reasoning process. An expert system with such a strong deductive inference engine would indeed be a useful tool.

The kind of expert system discussed in this book, however, would be incapable of solving cases harder than deductive cases (which are themselves not clear). A case might be hard for many reasons.[78] It

---

[76] See e.g. Goodall, *The Guide to Expert Systems* (1985), p. 100. We can see that where several heuristics incline towards the same conclusion, and combine to increase the certainty of the conclusion being inferred, the legal productions, as Wisdom put it, co-operate 'like the legs of a chair'. See 'Gods' (1951), p. 195. Yet surely Summers is absolutely correct, in retorting to Wisdom's later denial of the deductive nature of legal reasoning, that '[a]t least with respect to the process of establishing the "legs", it has been demonstrated [as I have done in this book] that deductive logic may be used'. See 'Logic in the Law' (1963), pp. 257–8.

[77] *AI*, p. 191.

[78] On hard cases, see references in n. 56, above. Also see Paterson, *The Law Lords* (1982), pp. 127–8, and 190–5.

should be stressed that although an expert system with a knowledge base of law-statements may confirm a case to be (potentially) clear, lack of confirmation does not render it hard: the user's inability to answer questions or suspicion that all relevant questions have not been asked may be due to incomplete coverage of the domain and not to the hardness of the case. From this book, it can be inferred that a case may be hard because of: (1) the open texture or vagueness of law-formulations or law-statements (Section 5.6); (2) normative gaps (Section 5.8); (3) apparent conflict of law-statements for which there is no determinative conflict resolution strategy (Section 5.8); (4) a difficulty of individuation (Section 4.3) such that a satisfactory law-statement cannot be expressed (when, for instance, a statutory law-formulation is syntactically ambiguous (Section 3.2), or a generally agreed upon *ratio* cannot be enunciated (Section 3.3). Moreover, a case can also be *retrospectively* hard, where the court implies an exception in a case that was potentially (semantically) clear; or a case might be *potentially* hard, where the non-judicial reasoning agent suspects the court will imply an exception in a semantically and potentially clear case (Sections 5.7 and 6.6). There is, therefore, an overlap between potentially (semantically) clear cases and potentially hard cases.

Although some clear cases may indeed reach the courtroom (perhaps in virtue of their complexity, such as those of the expert domain), it is hard cases, for the most part, that occupy the judiciary.[79] Of course, some cases contain both clear and hard *issues*, and a case may reach the courtroom because it involves just one hard issue: such a case, in virtue of that hard issue, is a hard case. Not only do hard cases fall for judicial consideration, but they are also placed before all students in their study of the positive law. Moreover, it is hard cases that legal theorists discuss at enormous length. It is perhaps not surprising, then, that many brave workers in the AI/legal reasoning field, particularly in the USA, have sought to write programs to solve hard cases.

Although the expert systems I have described cannot solve hard cases beyond those that are deductive, that is not to say that such systems will never be of use in hard cases, for cases that are hard on account of open texture or vagueness, for instance, can be answered in the form of tentative contingent conclusions (see Section 5.6).

[79] See Dworkin, *Law's Empire* (1986), p. 129, and Harris, *LP*, p. 204.

Furthermore, clear issues within hard cases can be settled by expert systems. In the main, however, hard cases cannot be solved by rule-based expert systems with deductive inference engines. Many of those who favour a conceptual approach to legal knowledge representation, however, hope that their systems will in fact be able to solve hard cases in much the same way that the systems I recommend can solve clear cases (see Section 4.6). Yet even the more modest projects whose goals are to design systems to solve limited ranges of cases that we would call hard confront profound jurisprudential obstacles and are undertaken in the realms of the jurisprudentially contentious, and the resultant systems may *ipso facto* be considered unacceptable as legal tools for today.

Talk of computers solving hard cases has inevitably led to debate on computers and their impact on judges. Such discussions of computers and judicial legal reasoning tend to be carried out on two levels. On the one hand, some have addressed the question of whether computers might ever assume the judicial function. On the other hand, writers have considered the extent to which computers might assist judges in solving cases, and expert systems present themselves in this connection as potentially useful judicial aids. It is appropriate, finally, to say a little about each of these uses of computers.

Weizenbaum tells of a discussion with AI pioneer, John McCarthy, in which the latter having himself posed the question 'What do judges know that we cannot tell a computer?', replied 'Nothing' and that the goal of building machines for making judicial decisions was perfectly in order.[80] A detailed study of this matter is sorely needed both to dispel the profusion of misconceptions and to assure the public that while computers will no doubt provide invaluable assistance to the judiciary in the future, it is neither possible *now* (or in the conceivable future) nor desirable *ever* (as long as we accept the values of Western liberal democracy) for computers to assume the judicial function. In any event, computers cannot yet (if ever)

---

[80] *Computer Power and Human Reason: From Judgement to Calculation* (1984), p. 207. See also the comments of McCarthy in Buchanan, Lederberg, and McCarthy, *Three Reviews of J. Weizenbaum's Computer Power and Human Reason* (1976), p. 19 and Gardner, 'An Artificial Intelligence Approach to Legal Reasoning' (1984), pp. 79–83. For a legal theorist's point of view, see D'Amato, 'Can/Should Computers Replace Judges?' (1977). Also see Tyree, 'Can a "Deterministic" Computer Judge Overrule Himself?' (1980). On computer use by judges generally, see Susskind, 'Computers and the Judicial Process' (1982).

satisfactorily recognize speech, understand natural language, nor perceive images. Judges can. Computers have not yet been programmed to exhibit moral, religious, social, sexual, and political preferences akin to those actually held by human beings. Nor have they been programmed to display the creativity, craftsmanship, individuality, innovation, inspiration, intuition, common sense, and general interest in our world that we, as human beings, expect not only of one another as citizens but also of judges acting in their official role.

Moreover, any legal theorist will recognize that the construction of an expert system in law that could solve all hard cases would require, for implementation in computer programs, the development (explicitly or implicitly) of theories of legal knowledge, legal science, individuation, structure, legal systems, logic and the law, and of (judicial) legal reasoning, all of a far greater richness, detail, sophistication, and complexity than those that have been generated by the most adept jurisprudents in the past.

In this book, I have never suggested it to be my goal to write programs to replace judges. As has just been noted, the computational and jurisprudential barriers to such an enterprise are so formidable as to render such a project misconceived in the extreme (not to mention the plethora of social, ethical, and political objections that could be levelled in this connection). Debates on computer judges are only useful today, it is submitted, as provocative, jurisprudential thought-experiments that promote profound reflection on the nature of the judiciary (although clearly some writers would claim more for their ideas). Even in that context, however, the notion of the computer judge should be deployed with caution, as I have shown elsewhere that such discussions can lose all impact if conducted in the absence of some computational knowledge.[81]

At most, then, I have hinted, as others have too, that expert systems might prove in the future to be useful judicial aids. This use of computers itself, however, could attract two further objections, based on arguments against deductive legal reasoning.[82] First, there is the Argument from Judicial Creativity and Flexibility which

---

[81] See Susskind, 'Detmold's Refutation of Positivism and the Computer Judge' (1986).

[82] No doubt there are other objections to deductive judicial legal reasoning, amongst which might be the Kelsenian Argument from Normative Alternatives. See e.g. *GTLS*, pp. 153–6. Also see Harris, 'Kelsen's Concept of Authority' (1977), and Paulson, 'Material and Formal Authorisation in Kelsen's Pure Theory' (1980).

asserts that deductive legal reasoning and expert systems in law can impose undesirable constraints on judges by committing them to deciding cases in particular and deductively stipulated ways which often will not, and need not, be compatible with political and social aims, individual and collective interests, and standards of morality.[83] The second and not unrelated objection is the Argument from Justice, which states that decisions reached by deductive legal reasoning or expert systems may logically and as a matter of fact, although not necessarily, result in *concrete* injustices.[84]

Neither of these arguments, however, is fatal for expert systems designed to assist judges. Notice that they both rely for their cogency on the truth of the proposition that a conclusion generated by deduction or an expert system (which may be called a (conditional) *legal conclusion*) is necessarily identical to the final judicial deternation (the (non-conditional) *judicial decision*) of any case. Yet this need not be true, as the following analysis shows. The legal conclusion is drawn, solely on the basis of a body of legal rules and the facts of a case, through the impartial and value-free application of deductive logic. The legal decision, in contrast, is the result of practical reasoning by the judge, reasoning about what he ought to do in the circumstances. The legal conclusion does not necessitate a particular legal decision but can be conceived as one premiss, and one not necessarily of overriding significance, in a subsequent and distinct process of practical deliberation. It is during this subsequent and flexible activity of practical reasoning that the judge may exercise creativity, and pay heed to the demands of justice, morality, and so forth (although whether he ought to in semantically and potentially clear cases is a matter of some dispute).

Expert systems need not preclude judicial flexibility or creativity, nor need they be conducive to injustices when deployed by judges, for they are not designed to supplant judicial decision-making, but rather are conceived as intelligent assistants well suited to identifying the specifically legal consequences of facts of given cases.

---

[83] See e.g. *JD*, p. 15. Also see Susskind, 'Objections to Deductive Legal Reasoning' (1984). But see Tyree, 'Can a "Deterministic" Computer Judge Overrule Himself?' (1980).

[84] Gottlieb summarizes this argument in *LC*, p. 18. Also see: Susskind, 'Objections to Deductive Legal Reasoning' (1984); Holmes, 'Agency' (1891), p. 50; and Spengler, 'Machine-Made Justice: Some Implications' (1963). On 'concrete justice', see Perelman, 'Concerning Justice' (1980).

6.8 CONCLUSION

In this chapter, I have been concerned mainly with providing an informal, jurisprudential specification for a deductive legal inference engine. As in Chapter 5, much of the discussion was inspired by those objections to deductive legal reasoning that can be drawn from the jurisprudential literature. The findings indicate how searches within a legal knowledge base should best proceed: jurisprudentially, so that expert systems can reason and perform as human legal experts do; and computationally, so that the program runs efficiently. I have stressed throughout the chapter that the focus of attention has not been computer programs designed to solve hard cases of the sort that regularly confront judges, but clear cases of the expert domain and deductive cases, both of which classes of case I introduced, explained, and argued to be amenable to computational treatment.

From Chapters 5 and 6, in particular, but from the book generally, emerges a theory of legal reasoning that is both descriptive and prescriptive. There would be little point in expounding it again in detail, as it is to be found throughout the foregoing, but it can be summarized in terms of four stages central to any search (computerized or manual) for a legal conclusion. First, there is the assembly and marshalling of the facts of the case in as orderly a fashion as the agent's knowledge of the legal implications of the facts will allow. This process can be computer-assisted on the basis of legal heuristics. Secondly, there is the individuation of law-formulations into law-statements that serve as manageable units with which the agent can reason. This today remains a human activity and computers can be of little aid. Thirdly, there is the subsumption of the facts of the case within the terms of the law-statements. Again, this process can be computer-assisted on the basis of legal heuristics. Finally, there is the application of deductive logic in the selection of legal rules and their application to the facts as subsumed, and at this stage the computer can be relied upon to execute the task faultlessly. Note that the four stages may not occur in linear progression. Moreover, at each stage problems can occur, and human judgment—of a sort we cannot presently account for computationally—may be required.

Yet, in each and every case that a legal reasoning agent tackles, he will arrive at these four stages. And in every case, therefore, deductive logic has a significant role to play, constituting the methodological deep structure of the process of legal reasoning. If this is so, expert systems in law are legal tools of potential to the legal profession beyond that of any others so far developed.

Conclusion

IN this book, I have made recommendations both about research methodology and about legal knowledge engineering. From the methodological point of view, my chief recommendation, most strictly construed, is that inspiration and guidance for workers in the field of expert systems in law should always be sought, in part, from jurisprudential sources. It is both possible and desirable to follow this advice since all expert systems in law necessarily make assumptions about the nature of law and of legal reasoning. As well as being a contribution to analytical jurisprudence, this book is conceived as an addition to the collection of materials that offer jurisprudential insight for those designing expert systems in law. Of course, within its limited confines, it is intended to eliminate much of the future need for extensive scrutiny of non-computationally orientated contemporary legal theory: because I have undertaken that examination, and drawn the relevant strands of agreement from that legal material for the perusal by others in the coming years. Such perusal will allow those building expert systems in law to conduct their work, at the very least, with an awareness of the related jurisprudential presuppositions and implications of any project under consideration. In turn, it is hoped, resultant systems will offer sound advice in a fashion acceptable to their legal users.

Quite aside from the range of relevant computational issues that require attention, many inquiries in this field remain to be undertaken in a sustained and sophisticated fashion by jurisprudents and lawyers. It is submitted, in particular, that the following topics require attention: (1) legal knowledge acquisition as a socio-legal matter; (2) a socio-legal investigation of communications between human legal experts and their consultees, with a view to developing an advanced user inferface; (3) computational linguistics and expert systems in law; (4) the design of inference engines to engage in legal reasoning with uncertainty; (5) techniques of legal knowledge representation and legal knowledge utilization for legal reasoning by ana-

254

logy; (6) the implementation of parts of the law of evidence in expert systems in law; (7) liability for bad advice given by expert systems in law; (8) the general ethical and sociological implications of expert systems in law; (9) testing expert systems in law and evaluating their performance; and, finally, (10) the impact of expert systems in law on the legal profession.

I am not suggesting, however, that research into expert systems in law is purely the province of legal theorists and lawyers. Rather, I would call for serious and sustained interdisciplinary collaboration. Only the polymath will succeed on his own in this field. If the jurisprudent propounds a theory in this context, it must be subjected to rigorous testing through implementation in a working system: and unless the legal theorist can himself program, he must rely on the assistance of his computational colleagues.

Consonant with the research methodology that I have advocated, my own recommendations here of vocabulary, techniques, and principles for legal knowledge engineers were formulated on the basis of extensive examination and synthesis of jurisprudential writings. Moreover, the ideas and models—the informal specifications— have been tested through implementation in the Oxford prototype system in Scottish divorce law.[1] It must be stressed again, however, that my proposals regarding the representation of legal knowledge and the design of legal inference engines are not confined to any one chosen legal domain of application, but are generalizable. Indeed they constitute the foundations of the design of a shell for expert systems in law.

This study contributes towards the development of expert systems in law both for the near future and for decades to come. In the short term, it will be possible to build systems that will solve clear cases: their knowledge bases will contain no legal heuristics and their inference engines will not reason with uncertainty. These systems—of current commercial viability—will reason only with law-statements, and will draw legal conclusions on the basis of literal interpretations of the formal legal sources. They can correctly be termed expert systems in so far as thorough familiarity with the complex interrelationships of the law-statements of a legal domain can be said to be constitutive of legal expertise. Of course, whether or not any system merits the appellation expert system is, for practical purposes, of

---

[1] For a detailed account of the system, see Gold, 'Specification and Implementation of an Expert System in Law' (1987).

little moment: if it is a useful tool, lawyers will not be worried about what they should call it.

In the long term, assuming that human legal experts are willing to make their expertise available to knowledge engineers, expert systems will be built to solve deductive cases: they will have heuristic knowledge in their knowledge bases, will reason with uncertainty, and will draw probabilistically phrased conclusions. In this book, I have identified the nature of legal heuristics and their relationships to law-statements, and I hope that my observations may serve as a jurisprudential basis for further, more ambitious, long-term research in the field.

Appendix I

No detailed comparative assessment of the leading projects in the field of AI/legal reasoning has ever been undertaken. Although such an analysis would be beyond the scope of this book, the following tables offer a summary of the salient features of the research efforts mentioned in Section 1.4. It was not feasible to tabulate all of the projects of which I am aware; there are, therefore several important projects and programs not included in this appendix, such as ExperTAX, the xi employment law system, and the LEX project of Germany (references to all of which can be found in Section 1 of the Bibliography). Nevertheless, I hope that the tables offer a general indication of the current state of the field.

The tables provide answers to a series of questions, although the insertion of '—' indicates that no answer is obvious or available, and 'NA' suggests that the question is not applicable. These questions are as follows and are to be associated with the column headings as they appear: Who are the principal researchers? What are the dates of the project (one date indicating the date of a major research report)? In what legal domain of application does the system operate? Does the system have substantial or highly specialized portions of statutory material (or its equivalent) represented within its knowledge base? Does the system have a substantial number of judicial precedents represented within its knowledge base? Did the designers attempt to include any heuristic legal knowledge within their system? Did the researchers use jurisprudence as a source of guidance in their work (the answer 'mention' indicating that jurisprudence is mentioned in the research reports but was not deployed directly)? Is the system transparent? Is the system flexible? What is the nature of the user interface; does the user communicate with the system in computer/formal language, restricted natural language, or by means of user responses to options offered by the system? In what computer language was the system written? What is a notable feature of the inference mechanism used (given the concerns of this book)? Does the system interface with any type of legal database system in law? What method of knowledge representation was employed? Is the system available on a commercial basis? Were generally acknowledged techniques of AI used in the system's design and implementation? Could the system function even as a rudimentary expert system shell for other legal domains? Can the system sensibly be described as an expert system in substantive law, given my indication of the requirements of such systems? (In respect of this last question, a negative answer does *not* imply, of course, that the system(s) in question are not of any use.) Note, finally, that where more than one system may

257

be subsumed under the project title, the tables reflect the systems' collective features.

These questions do not always allow of any one straightforward response: the entries in the tables are intended to reflect the general nature of the systems under consideration and the tables together should be regarded as offering an overview, and not a definitive and profound account, of the current achievements.

Project	Researchers	Date	Domain	Statute	Precedent	Heuristics
TAXMAN I	McCarty	1972–7	Corporate Tax Law	Yes	No	No
TAXMAN II	McCarty, Sridharan	1978–	Corporate Tax Law	Yes	Yes	No
MIT	Meldman	1975	Tort: assault and battery	Yes	Yes	No
KRL	King	1976	Tort: assault and battery	Yes	Yes	No
RAND (LDS & SAL)	Waterman, Peterson	1980–	Tort: personal injury claims	Yes	Yes	Yes
JUDITH	Popp, Schlink	1975	German Civil Code	Yes	No	No
ABF	Sprowl, Suski, Sangster	1979	NA	NA	NA	NA
LIRS	Hafner	1981	Negotiable Instruments	Yes	Yes	Yes
PROLOG	Sergot, Sharpe, Hammond, *et al.*	1980–	British Nationality, DHSS	Yes	No	Yes
LEGOL/ NORMA	Stamper, Cook, *et al.*	1973–	Family Allowance Small Domains	Yes	No	No
SARA	NRCCL	1980	Administrative Law	No	Yes	No
CORPTAX	Hellawell	1980	Corporate Tax Law	Yes	No	No
ATAXIS	Bellord	1981–	Tax Law	Yes	No	Yes
POLYTEXT/ ARBIT	Lof	1979–	Arbitration Rules	Yes	No	No
ELI	Leith	1982–	Welfare Law	Yes	No	No
CCLIPS	deBessonet	1980–	Louisiana Civil Code	Yes	No	No
STANFORD	Gardner	1984	Offer and Acceptance	Yes	Yes	Yes
DPA	Intelligent Environments	1985	Data Protection	No	No	No
TAXADVISOR	Michaelsen	1982	Tax Planning	No	No	Yes

Project	Jurisprudence	Transparency	Flexibility	Interface
TAXMAN I	Mention	Yes	Yes	Computer/Formal Language
TAXMAN II	Mention	Yes	Yes	Computer/Formal Language
MIT	Mention	Yes	Yes	Computer/Formal Language
KRL	No	Yes	Yes	Computer/Formal Language
RAND (LDS & SAL)	No	Yes	Yes	User Responses
JUDITH	Mention	No	Yes	User Responses
ABF	No	NA	Yes	User Responses
LIRS	No	NA	Yes	User Responses Restricted Natural
PROLOG	Mention	Yes	Yes	User Responses Restricted Natural
LEGOL/NORMA	Mention	NA	Yes	NA
SARA	Yes	No	NA	User Responses
CORPTAX	No	No	No	User Responses
ATAXIS	No	Yes	Yes	User Responses
POLYTEXT/ ARBIT	No	NA	Yes	Restricted Natural
ELI	Yes	No	Yes	User Responses
CCLIPS	Mention	Yes	Yes	Restricted Natural
STANFORD	Yes	Yes	Yes	Computer/Formal Language
DPA	No	Yes	Yes	User Responses
TAXADVISOR	No	Yes	Yes	User Responses

Project	Language	Inference	Database	Representation
TAXMAN I	Micro-PLANNER (LISP)	Analysis	No	Semantic Network
TAXMAN II	AIMDS	Top-down Pattern Match.	No	Frame
MIT	PSL	Legal Analysis Logical Derivation	No	Semantic Network
KRL	KRL	Analogical	No	Frame
RAND (LDS & SAL)	ROSIE	Forward Chaining	No	Rule-based
JUDITH	FORTRAN	Backward Chaining	No	Rule-based
ABF	ABF	Backward Chaining	No	Rule-based
LIRS	LISP	NA	Yes	Semantic Network
PROLOG	PROLOG	Resolution Deduction	No	Horn Clause Logic
LEGOL/NORMA	LEGOL/NORMA	Deductive	No	Rule-based & Semantic
SARA	—	Normative Analysis	No	Discretionary Rule-based
CORPTAX	BASIC	Deduction	No	NA
ATAXIS	—	—	No	Legislative Map
POLYTEXT/ARBIT	INTERLISP	Pattern Matching	No	Frame
ELI	INTERLISP	Backward Chaining	No	Rule-based
CCLIPS	LISP	Plausible/ Deductive Inference	No	Rule-based
STANFORD	MACLISP MRS	Backward Chaining	No	Rule-based Transition Net
DPA	C (CRYSTAL)	Backward Chaining	No	Rule-based
TAXADVISOR	LISP (EMYCIN)	Backward Chaining	No	Rule-based

Project	Commercial	AI	Shell	Expert System
TAXMAN I	No	Yes	No	No
TAXMAN II	No	Yes	No	No
MIT	No	Yes	No	No
KRL	No	Yes	No	No
RAND (LDS & SAL)	No	Yes	No	No
JUDITH	No	No	No	No
ABF	No	No	No	No
LIRS	No	Yes	No	No
PROLOG	No	Yes	Yes (APES)	No
LEGOL/NORMA	No	No	No	No
SARA	No	—	No	No
CORPTAX	No	No	No	No
ATAXIS	No	—	No	No
POLYTEXT/ARBIT	No	Yes	No	No
ELI	No	Yes	No	No
CCLIPS	No	Yes	No	No
STANFORD	No	Yes	No	No
DPA	Yes	Yes	Yes	No
TAXADVISOR	No	Yes	No	No

Appendix II

THIS appendix is a formalization of some of the law-statements that describe a small part of Scottish law of divorce. It demonstrates the principles of legal science, individuation, and structure recommended in this book, and conforms with generally accepted criteria for knowledge representation. The process of formalizing, as I have stressed in the book, is largely a human activity. I do not propose to detail how this process is undertaken, as this matter has been addressed extensively by others; most notably, by L. E. Allen, in his treatment of 'normalization' (see references in Sections 1 and 2 of the bibliography). This is by no means a complete representation: not all the appropriate slots and sub-slots have been filled, and only one aspect of the domain—adultery—is covered in any detail. The formalization is simply an indication of some of the ideas I have introduced. The complete legal production format is not reproduced: only the filled slots and sub-slots. For ease of understanding, conjunction, disjunction, negation, and the biconditional and conditional operators are given their (approximate) English renderings. For the sake of completeness, the relationship slots (8) have been included in square brackets. These slots indicate expressly how productions relate to one another and are of use mainly to the legal knowledge engineer of computational training who is assembling a legal knowledge base. If a production is being examined as an individual rule, however, the relationship slot may be disregarded.

ABBREVIATIONS

PCA	Principal condition of application
ACA	Alternative condition of application
CQ	Conjunctive qualification
EQ	Exceptive qualification
DP	Deontic phrase
C	Conclusion
R	Relationship
TL	Temporal limitations
A	Authority
LA	Legal addenda

No. 1

IF AND ONLY IF

1. PCA the marriage has broken down irretrievably
   A. s. 1(1) of The Divorce (Scotland) Act 1976

AND NOT

4. EQ. decree is to be withheld in respect of action under s. 1(2)(e)
   A. s. 1(5) of The Divorce (Scotland) Act 1976

THEN

5. DP. the court may decide that*
   [Permission]*

7. C. decree of divorce is to be granted

No. 2

IF

1. PCA. the defender has committed adultery
   TL. since the date of the marriage
   A. s. 1(2)(a) of The Divorce (Scotland) Act 1976

AND NOT

4. EQ. (A) the adultery has been connived at in such a way as to raise
   the defence of lenocinium
   A. s. 1(3) of The Divorce (Scotland) Act 1976

AND NOT

   (B) the adultery has been condoned
   A. s. 1(3) of The Divorce (Scotland) Act 1976

THEN

---

*The word 'may' appears here, together with the filled permission normative category sub-slot, in accordance with the principle of deontic equivalence (see Section 3.2). It is not for the legal knowledge engineer when describing the statutory material as statute law-statements to alter the deontic or normative status of the terms used in the formal source, no matter how peculiar their use may seem to be. Secondary sources in this context indicate that it was not the intention of Parliament (given the thrust of its debate on this matter) to confer an unfettered discretion on the courts to refuse decree other than as provided for in the Act. However, there seems to have been reluctance to draft the relevant portion of statute in terms of any obligation operator, because the words of the previous legislation were not used again in the Act of 1976. For the 1938 Act was worded 'it shall be competent for the court to grant decree' and this was regarded as imposing an obligation on the court to grant decree in absence of some recognized defence or bar (*Bell* v. *Bell* 1940 SC 229, at p. 260; but see also *Wilkinson* v. *Wilkinson* 1943, SC (HL) 61, at p. 68). (On this subject, see Clive, *The Divorce (Scotland) Act 1976* (1976), p. 10, and *The Law of Husband and Wife in Scotland* (1982), p. 442.) In this situation, it would be appropriate to add a heuristic—a statute law-prediction—indicating the likelihood of the court granting decree if a marriage has broken down irretrievably. The certainty factor would be extremely high. (I am grateful to Dr E. M. Clive for confirmation of this last claim.)

5. DP.   it shall be established that
         [Obligation]
7. C.   the marriage has broken down irretrievably
[8. R.   Production No. 1:1]

No. 3

IF

1. PCA. the defender has behaved in such a way that the pursuer cannot
         reasonably be expected to cohabit with the defender
         TL. at any time since the date of the marriage
         A. s. 1(2)(b) of The Divorce (Scotland) Act 1976
         LA. whether or not as a result of mental abnormality and
         whether such behaviour has been active or passive
         THEN
5. DP.   it shall be established that
         [Obligation]
7. C.   the marriage has broken down irretrievably
[8. R.   Production No. 1:1]

No. 4

IF

1. PCA. the defender has wilfully deserted the pursuer
         A. s. 1(2)(c) of The Divorce (Scotland) Act 1976
         AND

3. CQ.   the said desertion was without reasonable cause
         A. s. 1(2)(c) of The Divorce (Scotland) Act 1976
         AND NOT

4. EQ.   (A) there has been cohabitation between the parties
         TL. during a continuous period of two years immediately suc-
         ceeding the said desertion
         A. s. 1(2)(c)(i) of The Divorce (Scotland) Act 1976
         AND NOT
         (B) the pursuer has refused a genuine and reasonable offer by the
         defender to adhere
         TL. during a continuous period of two years immediately suc-
         ceeding the said desertion
         A. s. 1(2)(c)(ii) of The Divorce (Scotland) Act 1976
         AND NOT
         (C) the pursuer has resumed cohabitation within the statutory
         time period
         THEN

5. DP.	it shall be established that
	[Obligation]
7. C.	the marriage has broken down irretrievably
[8. R.	Production No. 1:1]

No. 5

IF

1. PCA.	there has been no cohabitation between the parties
	TL. at any time during a <u>continuous period</u> of two years after the date of the marriage and immediately preceding the bringing of the action
	A. s. 1(2)(d) of The Divorce (Scotland) Act 1976
	AND
3. CQ.	(A) the defender understands the steps he must take to indicate his consent to the granting of decree of divorce
	A. s. 1(4)(a)(ii) of The Divorce (Scotland) Act 1976
	AND
	(B) the defender understands the consequences of his consenting to the granting of decree of divorce
	A. s. 1(4)(a)(i) of The Divorce (Scotland) Act 1976
	AND
	(C) the defender consents in the prescribed manner to the granting of decree of divorce
	A. s. 1(2)(d) and s. 1(4) of The Divorce (Scotland) Act 1976, & Ordinary Cause Rule 131 of 1st Schedule of The Sheriff Courts (Scotland) Act 1907
	AND NOT
4. EQ.	the defender has withdrawn his consent to the granting of divorce in the prescribed manner
	A. s. 1(4) of The Divorce (Scotland) Act 1976, & Ordinary Cause Rule 132 of 1st Schedule of The Sheriff Courts (Scotland) Act 1907
	THEN
5. DP.	it shall be established that
	[Obligation]
7. C.	the marriage has broken down irretrievably
[8. R.	Production No. 1:1]

No. 6

IF
1. PCA.   there has been no cohabitation between the parties
TL. at any time during a continuous period of five years after the date of the marriage and immediately preceding the bringing of the action
A. s. 1(2)(e) of The Divorce (Scotland) Act 1976
THEN
5. DP.   it shall be established that
[Obligation]
7. C.   the marriage has broken down irretrievably
[8. R.   Production No. 1:1]

No. 7

IF
1. PCA.   the marriage has broken down irretrievably
A. s. 1(1) of The Divorce (Scotland) Act 1976
AND
3. CQ.   (A) an action of divorce has been raised because there has been no cohabitation for five years
A. s. 1(2)(e) of The Divorce (Scotland) Act 1976
AND
(B) in the opinion of the court the grant of decree of divorce would result in grave financial hardship to the defender
A. s. 1(5) of The Divorce (Scotland) Act 1976
THEN
5. DP.   the court may decide that
[Permission]
7. C.   decree is to be withheld in respect of action under s. 1(2)(e)
[8. R.   Production No. 1:4]

No. 8

IF
1. PCA.   the pursuer has continued cohabiting with the defender in the knowledge or belief that the defender has committed adultery
A. s. 1(3) & s. 2(2) of The Divorce (Scotland) Act 1976
OR
2. ACA.   the pursuer has resumed cohabiting with the defender in the knowledge or belief that the defender has committed adultery
A. s. 1(3) & s. 2(2) of The Divorce (Scotland) Act 1976
AND

3. CQ. the pursuer has cohabited with the defender
        TL. at any time after the end of the period of three months from the date of the said continuation or resumption of cohabitation
        A. s. 2(2) of The Divorce (Scotland) Act 1976
        THEN
5. DP. it shall be established that
        [Obligation]
7. C.   the adultery has been condoned
[8. R. Production No. 2:4:B]

No. 9

        IF AND ONLY IF
1. PCA. the pursuer has resumed cohabitation with the defender
        TL. after the expiry of a continuous period of two years immediately succeeding the defender's desertion
        A. s. 2(3) of The Divorce (Scotland) Act 1976
        AND
3. CQ. the pursuer has cohabited with the defender
        TL. at any time after the end of the period of three months from the date of said resumption of cohabitation
        A. s. 2(3) of The Divorce (Scotland) Act 1976
        THEN
5. DP. it shall be established that
        [Obligation]
7. C.   the pursuer has resumed cohabitation within the statutory time period
[8. R. Production No. 4:4:C]

No. 10

        IF
1. PCA. the period has been uninterrupted
        A. s. 2(4) of The Divorce (Scotland) Act 1976
        THEN
5. DP. that shall be construed as
        [Obligation]
7. C.   a continuous period
[8. R. Production Nos. 4:4:A:TL, 4:4:B:TL, 5:1:TL, 6:1:TL, 9:1:TL]

No. 11

        IF
1. PCA. any spell(s) of cohabitation interrupting the period have not exceeded six months in all
        A. s. 2(4) of The Divorce (Scotland) Act 1976

AND NOT

4. EQ. said spell(s) of cohabitation are counted as parts of the said period

THEN

5. DP. that shall be construed as
[Obligation]

7. C. a continuous period

[8. R. Production Nos. 4:4:A:TL, 4:4:B:TL, 5:1:TL, 6:1:TL, 9:1:TL]

No. 12

IF AND ONLY IF

1. PCA. the pursuer and defender have in fact lived together as man and wife
A. s. 13(2) of The Divorce (Scotland) Act 1976

THEN

5. DP. it shall be established that
[Obligation]

7. C. there has been cohabitation between the parties

[8. R. Production Nos. 4:4:A, 4:4:C, 5:1, 6:1, 8:1, 8:2, 8:3, 9:1, 9:3, 9:7, 11:1, 11:4]

No. 13

IF

1. PCA. the defender has been artificially inseminated by a donor
A. MacLennan v. MacLennan, (1958) SC 105
LA. whether or not the pursuer gave his consent

THEN

5. DP. it shall not be established for that reason that
[Prohibition]

7. C. the defender has committed adultery

[8. R. Production No. 2:1]

No. 14

IF AND ONLY IF

1. PCA. the defender has had full sexual intercourse with a person other than his/her spouse
TL. since the date of the marriage
A. MacLennan v. MacLennan, (1958) SC 105.

AND

3. CQ. the said sexual intercourse was voluntary
A. Stewart v. Stewart, 1914 2 SLT 310

THEN

5. DP.   it shall be established that
             [Obligation]
7. C.   the defender has committed adultery
[8. R.   Production No. 2:1]

No. 15

IF
1. PCA. the defender has engaged in sexual acts with a person other than.
             his/her spouse
             TL. since the date of the marriage
             A. MacLennan v. MacLennan (1958) SC 105
             AND NOT
4. EQ.   said acts did involve full sexual intercourse
             THEN
5. DP.   it shall not be established for that reason that
             [Prohibition]
7. C.   the defender has committed adultery
[8. R.   Production No. 2:1]

Bibliography

FOR ease of consultation, this bibliography is divided into four sections. Section 1 is devoted to the artificial intelligence/legal reasoning field, and the names of projects discussed in Section 1.4 and Appendix I are inserted after relevant references. Section 1 also includes references to some works that concern general computer applications to law. Section 2 contains references to jurisprudence, philosophy, and logic. Section 3 focuses on general works on artificial intelligence, expert systems, and computer science. Finally, Section 4 cites materials pertaining to Scottish law of divorce, the legal domain of application discussed in this book. The headings of the sections themselves are approximate labels, and although some writings could clearly fall into more than one category, entries appear only once (in what was deemed the most helpful grouping).

The bibliography contains references of published books, articles, and some unpublished papers. Many of these are referred to, in shortened form, in footnotes throughout the book. The others were found useful in the course of the research undertaken for this book. Many of the books are collections of essays, but where an essay from such a collection has been expressly identified in the book, or is of particular interest, it appears as a distinct item in the bibliography.

1. ARTIFICIAL INTELLIGENCE AND LEGAL REASONING, AND COMPUTER APPLICATIONS TO THE LAW

ALLEN, L. E., 'Beyond Document Retrieval Toward Information Retrieval' (1963), 47, *Minnesota Law Review*, 713.

——, 'A Language-Normalization Approach to Information Retrieval in Law' (1968), 9, *Jurimetrics Journal*, 41.

——, 'Language, Law and Logic: Plain Legal Drafting for the Electronic Age' (1980), in Niblett (ed.), *Computer Science and Law* (1980).

——, 'Towards a Normalized Language to Clarify the Structure of Legal Discourse' (1982), in Martino (ed.), *Deontic Logic, Computational Linguistics and Legal Information Systems* (1982).

——, 'Two Modes of Representing Sets of Legal Norms: Normalization and an Arithmetic Model', in Proceedings of 3rd Congress on L'Informatica Giuridica E La Comunità Nazionale Ed Internazionale (Rome, 1983).

271

272   *Bibliography*

ALLEN, L. E., and ENGHOLM, C. R., 'Normalized Legal Drafting and the Query Method' (1978), 29, *Journal of Legal Education*, 380.

——, and SAXON, C. S., 'Exploring Computer-Aided Generation of Questions for Normalizing Legal Rules' (Presented at the 2nd Annual Conference on Law and Technology at the University of Houston Law Center, 1985).

ALSCHWEE, B., and GRUNDMANN, S., 'System Design for a Computer-Aided Juridical Expert System' (1985), in Martino and Natali (eds.), *Atti Preliminari Del II Convegno Internazionale di studi su Logica, Informatica, Diritto* (1985).

ARNOLD, C. (ed.), *Yearbook of Law, Computers and Technology*, ii. *1986* (Butterworths, London, 1986).

ASHLEY, K. D., and RISSLAND, E. L., 'Toward Modelling Legal Argument' (1985), in Martino and Natali (eds.), *Atti Preliminari Del II Convegno Internazionale di studi su Logica, Informatica, Diritto* (1985).

BAADE, H. W. (ed.), *Jurimetrics* (Basic Books, London, 1963).

BELLORD, N. J., 'Information and Artificial Intelligence in the Lawyer's Office' (1982), in Ciampi (ed.), *Artificial Intelligence and Legal Information Systems* (1982). ATAXIS.

——, *Computers for Lawyers* (Sinclair Browne, London, 1983). ATAXIS.

BENCH-CAPON, T., and SERGOT, M. J., 'Towards a Rule Based Representation of Open Texture in Law' (Imperial College of Science and Technology, 1985). PROLOG.

BIGELOW, R. P. (ed.), *Computers and the Law: An Introductory Handbook*, 3rd edition (Commerce Clearing House, Chicago, 1981).

BING, J., 'Deontic Systems: A Sketchy Introduction' (1980), in Bing and Selmer (eds.), *A Decade of Computers and Law* (1980). SARA.

——, 'Legal Norms, Discretionary Rules and Computer Programs' (1980), in Niblett (ed.), *Computer Science and Law* (1980). SARA.

——, (ed.), *Handbook of Legal Information Retrieval* (North-Holland, Amsterdam, 1984).

——, 'The Text Retrieval System as a Conversion Partner' (1986), in Arnold (ed.), *Yearbook of Law, Computers and Technology*, ii. *1986* (1986).

——, and HARVOLD, T., *Legal Decisions and Information Systems* (Universitetsforlaget, Oslo, 1977).

——, and SELMER, K. S. (eds.), *A Decade of Computers and Law* (Universitetsforlaget, Oslo, 1980). SARA.

BLANK, L. J., 'Computers, Discretion, and Legal Decision-Making in Public Administration', in Bing and Selmer (eds.), *A Decade of Computers and Law* (1980).

BORCHGREVINK, M., and HANSEN, J., 'SARA: A System for the Analysis of Legal Decisions' (1980), in Bing and Selmer (eds.), *A Decade of Computers and Law* (1980). SARA.

BRODY, D. A., *The Post-Macomber Cases in a TAXMAN II Framework: A Pre-*

liminary Analysis (Rutgers University Laboratory for Computer Science Research, Technical Report LRP-TR-5, 1980). TAXMAN II.

BUCHANAN, B. G., 'The Current Status of Artificial Intelligence Research As It Applies to Legal Reasoning' (Stanford Law School Workshop on Computer Applications to Legal Research and Analysis, 28–9 April 1972).

——, and HEADRICK, T. E., 'Some Speculation About Artificial Intelligence and Legal Reasoning' (1970), 23, *Stanford Law Review*, 40.

BUTTERWORTH TELEPUBLISHING, *LEXIS Handbook* (Butterworth (Telepublishing) Limited, London, 1981).

CAMPBELL, C. M. (ed.), *Data Processing and the Law* (Sweet & Maxwell, London, 1984).

CHALTON, S., 'Legal Diagnostics' (1980), 25, *Computers and Law*, 13.

——, *Computers and Word Processors in a Solicitor's Office*, 2nd edition (The College of Law, London, 1982).

CIAMPI, C. (ed.), *Artificial Intelligence and Legal Information Systems* (North-Holland, Amsterdam, 1982).

——, 'Artificial Intelligence and Legal Information Systems' (1982) in Ciampi (ed.), *Artificial Intelligence and Legal Information Systems* (1982).

CROSS, G. R., and DEBESSONET, C. G., 'The Implementation of CCLIPS' (Presented at the 2nd Annual Conference on Law and Technology at the University of Houston Law Center, 1985). CCLIPS.

COUNCIL OF EUROPE, *Artificial Intelligence and Linguistic Problems in Legal Data Processing Systems* (Council of Europe, Strasburg, 1982).

——, *The Progress in Legal Information Systems in Europe* (Council of Europe, Strasburg, 1984).

D'AMATO, A., 'Can/Should Computers Replace Judges?' (1977), 11, *Georgia Law Review*, 1277.

DEBESSONET, C. G., 'A Proposal for Developing the Structural Science of Codification' (1980), 8, *Rutgers Computer & Technology Law Journal*, 47. CCLIPS.

——, 'An Automated Approach to Scientific Codification' (1982), 9, *Rutgers Computer & Technology Law Journal*, 27. CCLIPS.

——, 'Legislative Technique and Automated Systems', in Proceedings of 3rd Congress on L'Informatica Giuridica E La Comunità Nazionale Ed Internazionale (Rome, 1983). CCLIPS.

——, 'An Automated Intelligent System Based on a Model of a Legal System' (1984), 10, *Rutgers Computer & Technology Law Journal, 31*. CCLIPS.

——, and CROSS, G. R., 'Conceptual Retrieval and Legal Decision-Making' (1985), in Martino and Natali (eds.), *Atti Preliminari Del II Convegno Internazionale di studi su Logica, Informatica, Diritto* (1985). CCLIPS.

FEINSTEIN, J. L., and SIEMS, F., 'EDAAS: An Expert System at the US Environmental Protection Agency for Avoiding Disclosure of Confidential Business Information' (1985), 2, *Expert Systems*, 72.

FIEDLER, H., 'Functional Relations between Legal Regulations and Software' (1980), in Niblett (ed.), *Computer Science and Law* (1980).

——, 'Expert Systems as a Tool for Drafting Legal Decisions' (1985), in Martino and Natali (eds.), *Atti Preliminari Del II Convegno Internazionale di studi su Logica, Informatica, Diritto* (1985).

FINAN, J. P., 'LAWGICAL: Jurisprudential and Logical Considerations' (1982), 15, *Akron Law Review*, 675.

FREEMAN, P. R. W., 'Expert Systems and the Law' (1986), 47, *Computers and Law*, 9.

GARDNER, A. V. D. L., 'The Design of a Legal Analysis Program' in *Proceedings of the National Conference on Artificial Intelligence* (AAAI-83, 1983), 114. STANFORD.

——, *An Artificial Intelligence Approach to Legal Reasoning* (Stanford University Department of Computer Science, Report No. STAN-CS-85-1045, 1984). STANFORD.

GOEBEL, J. W., 'Consequences of Applying Legal Expert Systems in the Legal Practice of Decision-Making' (1985), in Martino and Natali (eds.), *Atti Preliminari Del II Convegno Internazionale di studi su Logica, Informatica, Diritto* (1985).

GOLD, D. I., 'Specification and Implementation of an Expert System in Law' (Oxford University D.Phil. thesis, 1987).

——, and SUSSKIND, R. E., 'Expert Systems in Law: A Jurisprudential and Formal Specification Approach' (1985), in Martino and Natali (eds.), *Atti Preliminari Del II Convegno Internazionale di studi su Logica, Informatica, Diritto* (1985).

GOLDMAN, S. R., DYER, M. G., and FLOWERS, M., 'Representing Contractual Situations' (Presented at the 2nd Annual Conference on Law and Technology at the University of Houston Law Center, 1985).

GONSER, T. A., SOMA, J. T., and WILHELM, E. I., 'The Computer as a Tool for Legal Decision Making' (1981), 27, *The Practical Lawyer*, 11.

GRAY, G. B., 'Law and Technology Conference: Expert System Workshop Report' (1985), in Walter (ed.), *Computing Power and Legal Reasoning* (1985).

HAFNER, C. D., *An Information Retrieval System Based on a Computer Model of Legal Knowledge* (UMI Research Press, Michigan, 1981). LIRS.

——, 'Representation of Knowledge in a Legal Information Retrieval System' (1981), in Oddy, Robertson, van Rijsbergen, and Williams (eds.), *Information Retrieval Research* (Butterworths, London, 1981). LIRS.

HAMMOND, P., 'Representation of DHSS Regulations as a Logic Program' (1983), in *Expert Systems 1983*, the Proceedings of the Third Technical Conference of the British Computer Society Specialist Group on Expert Systems. PROLOG.

HANSEN, J., *Modelling Knowledge, Action, Logic and Norms* (Norwegian Research Center for Computers and Law, Complex No. 8/85, Oslo, 1985).

——, *Simulation and Automation of Legal Decisions*, NORIS (57) (Norwegian Research Center for Computers and Law, Complex No. 6/86, Oslo, 1986).

HEADRICK, T. E., 'Some Further Thought on Legal Reasoning and Artificial Intelligence' (Stanford Law School Workshop on Computer Applications to Legal Research and Analysis, 28–9 April 1972).

HEATHER, M. A., 'Future Generation Computer Systems in the Service of the Law' (1985), in Martino and Natali (eds.), *Atti Preliminari Del II Convegno Internazionale di studi su Logica, Informatica, Diritto* (1985).

HELLAWELL, R., 'A Computer Program for Legal Planning and Analysis: Taxation of Stock Redemptions' (1980), 80, *Columbia Law Review*, 1362. CORPTAX.

——, 'CHOOSE: A Computer Program for Legal Planning and Analysis' (1981), 19, *Columbia Journal of Transnational Law*, 339.

HUSTLER, A., *Programming Law in Logic* (University of Waterloo Department of Computer Science, Research Report CS-82-13, 1982). PROLOG.

JONES, R. P., 'The LEX Project, IBM Scientific Centre, Heidelberg and University of Tübingen' (1986), in Arnold (ed.), *Yearbook of Law, Computers and Technology*, ii. *1986* (1986).

KARLGREN, H., and WALKER, D. E., 'The Polytext System: A New Design for a Text Retrieval System' (Unpublished, May 1980). POLYTEXT/ARBIT.

KAYTON, I., 'Can Jurimetrics be of Value to Jurisprudence?' (1964), 33, *The George Washington Law Review*, 287.

KEDAR-CABELLI, S., *Analogy with Purpose in Legal Reasoning from Precedents*, Dissertation Proposal (Rutgers University Laboratory for Computer Science Research, Technical Report LRP-TR-17, 1984). TAXMAN II.

KEEN, M., and McBRIDE, S., 'Expert Systems for Clarifying Employment Law' (1986), in *Knowledge Based Systems 86* (Online, Pinner, 1986).

KING, J. J., 'Analysis and KRL Implementation of a Current Legal Reasoning Program Design' (Unpublished, 20 May 1976). KRL.

KOWALSKI, R. A., 'Software Engineering and Artificial Intelligence in New Generation Computing' (1984), 1, *Future Generations Computer Systems*, 39. PROLOG.

——, 'Logic for Knowledge Representation', in Proceedings of Conference on Foundations of Software Technology and Theoretical Computer Science (Japan, 1985). PROLOG.

——, and SERGOT, M. J., 'Computer Representation of the Law' (1985), in Proceedings of the British Computer Society Specialist Group on Expert Systems Seminar on Social Implications of Artificial Intelligence and Expert Systems (Abingdon, 10–12 May 1985). PROLOG.

LAMB, S., 'On Representing the Content of Legal Discourse in PROLOG' (Presented at the 2nd Annual Conference on Law and Technology at the University of Houston Law Center, 1985). PROLOG.

LAWLOR, R. C., 'Computer Analysis of Judicial Decisions' (1980), in Niblett (ed.), *Computer Science and Law* (1980).

LEITH, P., 'ELI: An Expert Legislative Consultant' (Conference Publication No. 212, presented at IEE Conference on Man/Machine Systems, UMIST, 6–9 July 1982). ELI.

——, 'Hierarchically Structured Production Rules' (1983), 26, *The Computer Journal*, 1. ELI.

——, 'Cautionary Notes on Legal Expert Systems' (1984), 40, *Computers and Law*, 14. ELI.

——, 'Logic, Formal Models and Legal Reasoning' (1984), 24, *Jurimetrics Journal*, 334.

——, 'Law and Computer Program: The Limits to Logic' (Presented at the 12th World Congress on Philosophy of Law and Social Philosophy, Athens, 1985). ELI.

——, 'Clear Rules and Legal Expert Systems' (1985), in Martino and Natali (eds.), *Atti Preliminari Del II Convegno Internazionale di studi su Logica, Informatica, Diritto* (1985). ELI.

LOEVINGER, L., 'Jurimetrics—The Next Step Forward' (1949), 33, *Minnesota Law Review*, 455.

LOF, S., *The POLYTEXT/ARBIT Demonstration System* (National Defense Research Institute, FOA Report C40121-M7, 1980). POLYTEXT/ARBIT.

MCCARTY, L. T., 'Interim Report on the TAXMAN Project: An Experiment in Artificial Intelligence and Legal Reasoning' (Stanford Law School Workshop on Computer Applications to Legal Research and Analysis, 28–9 April 1972). TAXMAN I.

——, 'Reflections on TAXMAN: An Experiment in Artificial Intelligence and Legal Reasoning' (1977), 90, *Harvard Law Review*, 837. TAXMAN I.

——, *Some Notes on the MAP Formalism of TAXMAN II, with Applications to Eisner v. Macomber* (Rutgers University Laboratory for Computer Science Research, Technical Report LRP-TR-6, 1980). TAXMAN II.

——, *Some Requirements for a Computer-Based Legal Consultant* (Rutgers University Laboratory for Computer Science Research, Technical Report LRP-TR-8, 1980). TAXMAN II.

——, 'The TAXMAN Project: Towards a Cognitive Theory of Legal Argument' (1980), in Niblett (ed.), *Computer Science and Law* (1980). TAXMAN II.

——, 'A Computational Theory of Eisner v. Macomber' (1982), in Ciampi (ed.), *Artificial Intelligence and Legal Information Systems* (1982). TAXMAN II.

—— (ed.), 'The Applications of Artificial Intelligence to Law: A Survey of Six Current Projects' (1982), in Council of Europe, *Artificial Intelligence and Linguistic Problems in Legal Data Processing Systems* (1982). LIRS, ABF, MIT, LEGOL/NORMA, TAXMAN, RAND (LDS).

——, 'Permissions and Obligations' (1983), in Hansen (ed.), *Modelling Knowledge, Action, Logic and Norms* (1985). TAXMAN.

——, 'Intelligent Legal Information Systems: Problems and Prospects' (1984), in Campbell (ed.), *Data Processing and the Law* (1984). TAXMAN II.

——, and SRIDHARAN, N. S., *The Representation of Conceptual Structures in* TAXMAN II. *Part One: Logical Templates* (Rutgers University Laboratory for Computer Science Research, Technical Report LRP-TR-4, 1980). TAXMAN II.

——, and ——, *The Representation of an Evolving System of Legal Concepts: I. Logical Templates* (Rutgers University Laboratory for Computer Science Research, Technical Report LRP-TR-7, 1980). TAXMAN II.

——, and ——, *The Representation of an Evolving System of Legal Concepts: II. Prototypes and Deformations* (Rutgers University Laboratory for Computer Science Research, Technical Report LRP-TR-11, 1981). TAXMAN II.

——, and ——, *A Computational Theory of Legal Argument* (Rutgers University Laboratory for Computer Science Research, Technical Report LRP-TR-13, 1982). TAXMAN II.

MACRAE, C. D., and MACRAE, E. C., 'An Expert System for Tax Research: Interacting with Knowledgeable Users' (Presented at the 2nd Annual Conference on Law and Technology at the University of Houston Law Center, 1985).

MAGGS, B., and DEBESSONET, C. G., 'Automated Logical Analysis of Systems of Legal Rules' (1972), 12, *Jurimetrics Journal*, 158.

MARTINO, A. A. (ed.), *Deontic Logic, Computational Linguistics and Legal Information Systems* (North-Holland, Amsterdam, 1982).

——, and NATALI, F. S. (eds.), *Atti Preliminari Del II Convegno Internazionale di studi su Logica, Informatica, Diritto* (Consiglio Nazionale delle Ricerche Istituto per la documentazione giuridica, IBI, Florence, 1985).

MEHL, L., 'Automation in the Legal World—From the Machine Processing of Legal Information to the "Law Machine"' in *Mechanisation of Thought Processes*, the Proceedings of a Symposium held at the National Physical Laboratory (NPL, November 1958).

MELDMAN, J. A., *A Preliminary Study in Computer-Aided Legal Analysis* (Massachusetts Institute of Technology, MAC TR-157, 1975). MIT.

——, 'A Structural Model for Computer-Aided Legal Analysis' (1977), 6, *Rutgers Journal of Computers and the Law*, 27. MIT.

MICHAELSEN, R. H., 'A Knowledge-Based System for Individual Income and Transfer Tax Planning' (University of Illinois Ph.D. thesis, 1982).

——, and MICHIE, D., 'Expert Systems in Business' (Nov. 1983), *Datamation*, 240. TAXADVISOR.

——, 'An Expert System for Federal Tax Planning' (1984), 1, *Expert Systems*, 149. TAXADVISOR.

MICHAELSEN, R. H., MICHIE, D., and BOULANGER, A., 'The Technology of Expert Systems' (April 1985), 10, *BYTE*, 303. TAXADVISOR.

MILLER, J., 'Expert Systems—The End of the Legal Profession?' (Mar. 1984), *New Zealand Law Journal*, 85.

MORRISE, M., 'Emerging Computer-Assisted Legal Analysis Systems' (1980), 1, *Brigham Young University Law Review*, 116.

NATIONAL LAW LIBRARY, *Lawyers and Technology: Report of a Study of the Use of Technology by Solicitors (The Slot Report)* (National Law Library, 1983).

NIBLETT, B. (ed.), *Computer Science and Law* (Cambridge University Press, Cambridge, 1980).

——, 'Computer Science and Law: An Introductory Discussion' (1980), in Niblett (ed.), *Computer Science and Law* (1980).

——, 'The Computer as a Consultation Machine' (1981), in Bigelow (ed.), *Computers and the Law: An Introductory Handbook* (1981).

——, 'Expert Systems for Lawyers' (1981), 29, *Computers and Law*, 2.

OSKAMP, A., and VANDENBERGHE, G. P. V., 'Legal Thinking and Automation' (1985), in Martino and Natali (eds.), *Atti Preliminari Del II Convegno Internazionale di studi su Logica, Informatica, Diritto* (1985).

PARK, R., and BURRIS, R., 'Computer-Aided Instruction in Law: Theories, Techniques and Trepidations' (1978), 1, *American Bar Foundation Research Journal*, 1.

PHILLIPS, L., 'Using an Expert System in Testing Legal Rules' (Unpublished, Ludwig Maximilians, Universität, Munich, 1985).

POPP, W. G., and SCHLINK, B., 'JUDITH, A Computer Program to Advise Lawyers in Reasoning a Case' (1975), 15, *Jurimetrics Journal*, 303. JUDITH.

REISINGER, L., 'Legal Reasoning by Analogy: A Model Applying Fuzzy Set Theory' (1982), in Ciampi (ed.), *Artificial Intelligence and Legal Information Systems* (1982).

ROYCROFT, A. E., and LOUCOPOULOS, P., 'ACCI—An Expert System for the Apportionment of Close Companies' Income' (1985), in Bramer (ed.), *Research and Development in Expert Systems* (1985).

RUOFF, T., *The Solicitor and the Automated Office* (Sweet & Maxwell, London, 1984).

SERGOT, M. J., 'Programming Law: LEGOL as a Logic Programming Language' (Imperial College of Science and Technology, 1980). PROLOG, LEGOL/NORMA.

——, 'Prospects for Representing the Law as Logic Programs', in Clark and Tarnlund (eds.), *Logic Programming* (Academic Press, London, 1982). PROLOG.

——, 'Logic Programming and its Applications in Law: A Brief Tutorial Introduction' (Imperial College of Science and Technology, 1985). PROLOG.

——, 'Representing Legislation as Logic Programs' (Imperial College of Science and Technology, 1985). PROLOG.

——, CORY, T., HAMMOND, P., KOWALSKI, R., KRIWACZEK, F., and SADRI, F., 'Formalisation of the British Nationality Act' (1986), in Arnold (ed.), *Yearbook of Law, Computers and Technology*, ii. *1986* (1986). PROLOG.

——, SADRI, F., KOWALSKI, R. A., KRIWACZEK, F., HAMMOND, P., and CORY, H. T., 'The British Nationality Act as a Logic Program' (Imperial College of Science and Technology, 1984 & 1985). PROLOG.

——————————————'The British Nationality Act as a Logic Program (1986), 29, *Communications of the ACM*, 370.

SHARPE, W. P., 'Logic Programming for the Law' (Master of Technology thesis, Brunel University, 1984). PROLOG.

——, 'Logic Programming for the Law' (1985), in Bramer (ed.), *Research and Development in Expert Systems* (1985). PROLOG.

SHORTLIFFE, E. H., 'Expert Systems Research: Adapting Technical Knowledge for Computer-Based Consultation Systems' (1982), in Council of Europe, *Artificial Intelligence and Linguistic Problems in Legal Data Processing Systems* (1982).

SOLOMON, L. D., and GROSSMAN, G. S., 'Computers and Legal Reasoning' (Oct. 1982), *Trusts and Estates*, 43.

——, and ——, 'Computers and Legal Reasoning' (1983), 36, *Computers and Law*, 11.

SPENGLER, J. J., 'Machine-Made Justice: Some Implications' (1963), in Baade (ed.), *Jurimetrics* (1963).

SPROWL, J. A., 'Automating the Legal Reasoning Process: A Computer that Uses Regulations and Statutes to Draft Legal Documents' (1979), 1, *American Bar Foundation Research Journal*, 1. ABF.

——, 'Automated Assembly of Legal Documents' (1980), in Niblett (ed.), *Computer Science and Law* (1980). ABF.

SRIDHARAN, N. S., *A Flexible Structure for Knowledge: Examples of Legal Concepts* (Rutgers University Laboratory for Computer Science Research, Technical Report LRP-TR-1, 1978). TAXMAN I.

——, *Some Relationships between BELIEVER and TAXMAN* (Rutgers University Laboratory for Computer Science Research, Technical Report LRP-TR-7, 1980). TAXMAN II.

STAMPER, R., 'The Automation of Legal Reasoning Problems and Prospects' (LSE Systems Research Group, LEGOL Project L.6, 1976). LEGOL/ NORMA.

——, 'Computer-Aided Legal Reasoning' (LSE Systems Research Group, LEGOL Project L.39, 1979). LEGOL/NORMA.

——, 'LEGOL: Modelling Legal Rules by Computer' (1980), in Niblett (ed.), *Computer Science and Law* (1980). LEGOL/NORMA.

——, 'A Logic of Social Norms and Individual Affordances: A Proposal Arising from an Investigation in the Field of Computers and Law' (1985),

280 *Bibliography*

in Hansen (ed.), *Modelling Knowledge, Action, Logic and Norms* (1985). LEGOL/NORMA.

——, 'A Non-Classical Logic for Law Based on the Structures of Behaviour' (1985), in Martino and Natali (eds.), *Atti Preliminari Del II Convegno Internazionale di studi su Logica, Informatica, Diritto* (1985). LEGOL/NORMA.

——, TAGG, C., MASON, P., COOK, S., and MARKS, J., 'Developing the LEGOL Semantic Grammar' (1982), in Ciampi (ed.), *Artificial Intelligence and Legal Information Systems* (1982). LEGOL/NORMA.

STONE, J., 'Man and Machine in the Search for Justice' (1964), 16, *Stanford Law Review*, 515.

STRATHCLYDE BUSINESS SCHOOL, *The Use of Information Technology in Solicitors' Practices* (University of Strathclyde, 1985).

SUSSKIND, R. E., 'Computers and the Judicial Process' (University of Glasgow Ll.B. thesis, 1982).

——, 'Artificial Intelligence, Expert Systems, and the Teaching of Law' (1986), 5, *Computers in Teaching*, 26.

——, 'Expert Systems in Law: A Jurisprudential Approach to Artificial Intelligence and Legal Reasoning' (1986), 49, *The Modern Law Review*, 168.

——, 'Expert Systems in Law: A Jurisprudential Inquiry' (Oxford University D.Phil. thesis, 1986).

——, 'Expert Systems in Law and Legal Database Systems', in *Law Office Management '86* (Society for Computers and Law, 1986).

——, 'Expert Systems and Law and the Data Protection Adviser' (1987), 7, *Oxford Journal of Legal Studies*, 145.

——, 'Some Preliminary Considerations Concerning Expert Systems in Law' (1987), *Northern Kentucky Law Review* (forthcoming).

TAPPER, C. F. H., 'Lawyers and Machines' (1963), 26, *The Modern Law Review*, 121.

——, *Computers and the Law* (Weidenfeld and Nicolson, London, 1973).

——, 'Citations as a Tool for Searching Law by Computer' (1980), in Niblett (ed.), *Computer Science and Law* (1980).

——, *An Experiment in the Use of Citation Vectors in the Area of Legal Data*, NORIS (36) (Norwegian Research Center for Computers and Law, Complex No. 9/82, Oslo, 1982).

THORNE, J., and UGARTE, M., 'Using Purposes of the Law in Legal Expert Systems' (1985), in Martino and Natali (eds.), *Atti Preliminari Del II Convegno Internazionale di studi su Logica, Informatica, Diritto* (1985).

TYREE, A. L., 'Can a "Deterministic" Computer Judge Overrule Himself?' (1980), 7, *Rutgers Computer & Technology Law Journal*, 381.

WALTER, C. (ed.), *Computing Power and Legal Reasoning* (West Publishing Co., St Paul, 1985).

WATERMAN, D. A., 'Rule-Based Expert Systems' (1981), in *Machine Intelli-*

gence, Infotech State of the Art Report, Series 9, No. 3 (Pergamon Infotech Limited, Maidenhead, 1981). RAND.

——, PAUL, J., and PETERSON, M., 'Expert Systems for Legal Decision Making' (1986), 3, *Expert Systems*, 212. RAND (LDS & SAL).

——, PETERSON, M. A., 'Rule-Based Models of Legal Expertise', in *Proceedings of the First Annual National Conference on Artificial Intelligence* (1980). RAND (LDS).

——, and ——, *Models of Legal Decisionmaking* (The Rand Corporation, Report R-2717-ICJ, Santa Monica, 1981). RAND (LDS).

——, and ——, 'Evaluating Civil Claims: An Expert Systems Approach' (1984), 1, *Expert Systems*, 65. RAND (LDS).

WELCH, J. T., 'LAWGICAL: An Approach to Computer-Aided Legal Analysis' (1982), 15, *Akron Law Review*, 655.

2. JURISPRUDENCE, PHILOSOPHY, AND LOGIC

ALCHOURRON, C. E., 'Logic of Norms and Logic of Normative Propositions' (1969), 12, *Logique et Analyse*, 242.

——, and BULYGIN, E., *Normative Systems* (Springer-Verlag, New York, 1971).

——, and ——, 'The Expressive Conception of Norms' (1981), in Hilpinen (ed.), *New Studies in Deontic Logic* (1981).

ALLEN, L. E., 'Symbolic Logic: A Razor-Edged Tool for Drafting and Interpreting Legal Documents' (1957), 66, *The Yale Law Journal*, 833.

——, 'Deontic Logic' (1960), *Modern Uses of Logic in Law*, 13.

——, and SAXON, C. S., 'Analysis of the Logical Structure of Legal Rules by a Modernized and Formalized Version of Hohfeld's Fundamental Legal Conceptions' (Presented at Consiglio Nazionale delle Ricerche, 2nd International Congress, 'Logica, Informatica, Diritto', Florence, 1985).

ATIYAH, P. S., 'Common Law and Statute Law' (1985), 48, *The Modern Law Review*, 1.

ATWOOL, E. (ed.) *Perspectives in Jurisprudence* (University of Glasgow Press, Glasgow, 1977).

——, 'Legal Precepts' (Unpublished, Glasgow University, 1982).

AYER, A. J., *The Central Questions of Philosophy* (Penguin, Harmondsworth, 1973).

BAKER, G. P., 'Defeasibility and Meaning' (1977), in Hacker and Raz (eds.), *Law, Morality and Society: Essays in Honour of H. L. A. Hart* (1977).

BECCARIA, C., *On Crimes and Punishment* (1746), tr. H. Paolucci (Bobbs-Merrill, New York, 1963).

BENTHAM J., *Of Laws in General*, edited by H. L. A. Hart (The Athlone Press, London, 1970).

BRUMBAUGH, J. F., *Legal Reasoning and Briefing* (Bobbs-Merrill, Indianapolis, 1917).

CARDOZO, B. N., *The Nature of the Judicial Process* (Yale University Press, New Haven and London, 1921).

——, *The Paradoxes of Legal Science* (Columbia University Press, New York, 1928).

CASTANEDA, H. N., 'The Paradoxes of Deontic Logic: The Simplest Solution to All of Them in One Fell Swoop' (1981), in Hilpinen (ed.), *New Studies in Deontic Logic* (1981).

CASTBERG, F., *Problems of Legal Philosophy*, 2nd edition (Allen & Unwin, London, 1957).

COHEN, M., (ed.), *Ronald Dworkin and Contemporary Jurisprudence* (Duckworth, London, 1984).

COHEN, M. R., 'The Place of Logic in the Law' (1916), 29, *Harvard Law Review*, 622.

CROSS, R., *Precedent in English Law*, 3rd edition (Clarendon Press, Oxford, 1977).

DENNING, LORD, *The Family Story* (Butterworths, London, 1981).

DETMOLD, M. J., *The Unity of Law and Morality: A Refutation of Legal Positivism* (Routledge & Kegan Paul, London, 1984).

DEWEY, J., 'Logical Method and Law' (1924), 10, *Cornell Law Quarterly*, 17.

DIAS, R. W. M., *A Bibliography of Jurisprudence*, 3rd edition (Butterworths, London, 1979).

——, *Jurisprudence*, 5th edition (Butterworths, London, 1985).

DOWNIE, R. S., and TELFER, E., *Caring and Curing* (Methuen, London, 1980).

DRETSKE, F. I., *Knowledge and the Flow of Information* (Basil Blackwell, Oxford, 1981).

DWORKIN, R. M., 'No Right Answer?' (1977), in Hacker and Raz (eds.), *Law, Morality and Society: Essays in Honour of H. L. A. Hart* (1977).

——, *Taking Rights Seriously* (Duckworth, London, 1977).

——, *A Matter of Principle* (Harvard University Press, London, 1985).

——, *Law's Empire* (Fontana, London, 1986).

EBENSTEIN, W., 'The Pure Theory of Law: Demythologizing Legal Thought' (1971), 59, *California Law Review*, 617.

ECKHOFF, T., 'Guiding Standards in Legal Reasoning' (1976), 29, *Current Legal Problems*, 205.

EHRLICH, E., *Fundamental Principles of the Sociology of Law*, reprint edition (Arno Press, New York, 1975).

FARRAR, J., *Introduction to Legal Method* (Sweet & Maxwell, London, 1977).

FINCH, J. D., *Introduction to Legal Theory*, 3rd edition (Sweet & Maxwell, London, 1979).

FINNIS, J. M., *Natural Law and Natural Rights* (Clarendon Press, Oxford, 1980).

FLEW, A. G. N. (ed.), *Logic and Language*, First Series (Basil Blackwell, Oxford, 1960).

——, *Thinking about Thinking* (Fontana, Glasgow, 1975).

FRANK, J., *Courts on Trial* (Princeton University Press, Princeton, 1949).

FRIEDMANN, W., *Legal Theory*, 5th edition (Stevens, London, 1967).

FULLER, L., 'Positivism and Fidelity to Law: A Reply to Professor Hart' (1958), 7, *Harvard Law Review*, 630.

GOLDING, M. P., 'Kelsen and the Concept of "Legal System"' (1961), 47, *Archiv für Rechts und Sozialphilosophie*, 355.

GOODHART, A. L., 'Determining the Ratio Decidendi of a Case' (1930), 40, *The Yale Law Journal*, 161.

GOTTLIEB, G., *The Logic of Choice: An Investigation of the Concepts of Rule and Rationality* (Allen & Unwin, London, 1968).

GUEST, A. G., 'Logic in the Law' (1961), in Guest (ed.), *Oxford Essays in Jurisprudence* (1961).

—— (ed.), *Oxford Essays in Jurisprudence* (Clarendon Press, Oxford, 1961).

HAACK, S., *Philosophy of Logics* (Cambridge University Press, Cambridge, 1978).

HACKER, P. M. S., and RAZ, J. (eds.), *Law, Morality and Society: Essays in Honour of H. L. A. Hart* (Clarendon Press, Oxford, 1977).

HARRIS, J. W., 'Kelsen's Concept of Authority' (1977), 36, *The Cambridge Law Journal*, 353.

——, *Law and Legal Science: An Inquiry into the Concepts Legal Rule and Legal System* (Clarendon Press, Oxford, 1979).

——, *Legal Philosophies* (Butterworths, London, 1980).

——, 'Kelsen and Normative Consistency' (1986), in Tur and Twining (eds.), *Essays on Kelsen* (1986).

HART, H. L. A., 'The Ascription of Responsibility and Rights' (1948–9), in Flew (ed.), *Logic and Language*, First Series (1960).

——, 'Dias and Hughes on Jurisprudence' (1957–8), 4, *Journal of the Society of Public Teachers of Law*, First Series, 143.

——, 'Positivism and the Separation of Law and Morals' (1958), in Hart, *Essays in Jurisprudence and Philosophy* (1983).

——, *The Concept of Law* (Clarendon Press, Oxford, 1961).

——, 'Problems of the Philosophy of Law' (1967), in Hart, *Essays in Jurisprudence and Philosophy* (1983).

——, 'The Demystification of the Law' (1973), in Hart, *Essay on Bentham: Studies in Jurisprudence and Political Theory* (1982).

——, 'American Jurisprudence Through English Eyes: The Nightmare and the Noble Dream' (1977), in Hart, *Essays in Jurisprudence and Philosophy* (1983).

HART, H. L. A., *Essays on Bentham: Studies in Jurisprudence and Political Theory* (Clarendon Press, Oxford, 1982).

——, *Essays in Jurisprudence and Philosophy* (Clarendon Press, Oxford, 1983).

HARTNEY, M., 'Hans Kelsen's Theory of Norms' (Oxford University D.Phil. thesis, 1985).

HARVEY, C. P., 'A Job of Jurisprudence' (1944), 7, *The Modern Law Review*, 42.

HAYEK, F. A., *Law, Legislation and Liberty*, 1 vol. edition (Routledge & Kegan Paul, London, 1982).

HILPINEN, R. (ed.), *Deontic Logic: Introductory and Systematic Readings*, reprint edition (D. Reidel, Dordrecht, 1981).

——(ed.), *New Studies in Deontic Logic* (D. Reidel, Dordrecht, 1981).

HODGES, W., *Logic* (Penguin, Harmondsworth, 1977).

HOHFELD, W. N., *Fundamental Legal Conceptions*, edited by W. W. Cook (Yale University Press, New Haven and London, 1919).

HOLMES, O. W., 'Agency' (1891), in Holmes, *Collected Legal Papers* (1920).

——, 'The Path of the Law' (1897), in Holmes, *Collected Legal Papers* (1920).

——, *Collected Legal Papers* (Constable, London, 1920).

——, *The Common Law* (MacMillan, London, 1968).

HONORÉ, A. M., 'The Nature of Legal Argument' (book review) (1958), 74, *The Law Quarterly Review*, 296.

——, 'Groups, Laws, and Obedience' (1973), in Simpson (ed.), *Oxford Essays in Jurisprudence*, Second Series (1973).

——, 'Real Laws' (1977), in Hacker and Raz (eds.), *Law, Morality and Society: Essays in Honour of H. L. A. Hart* (1977).

HOROVITZ, J., 'Ulrich Klug's Legal Logic: A Critical Account' (1966), in Perelman (ed.), *Études de Logique Juridique* (Établissements Emile Bruylant, Brussels, 1966).

——, *Law and Logic: A Critical Account of Legal Argument* (Springer-Verlag, New York, 1972).

HOSPERS, J., *An Introduction to Philosophical Analysis*, 2nd edition (Routledge & Kegan Paul, London, 1967).

HUTCHESON, J. C. JR., 'The Judgment Intuitive: The Function of the "Hunch" in Judicial Decision' (1929), 14, *Cornell Law Quarterly*, 274.

HUTCHINSON, A. C., and WAKEFIELD, J. N., 'A Hard Look at "Hard Cases": The Nightmare of a Noble Dreamer' (1982), 2, *Oxford Journal of Legal Studies*, 86.

JAMES, M. H., 'Bentham on the Individuation of Laws' (1973), 24, *Northern Ireland Legal Quarterly*, 357.

JENSEN, O. C., *The Nature of Legal Argument* (Basil Blackwell, Oxford, 1957).

KANT, I., *Critique of Pure Reason*, tr. Norman Kemp Smith (MacMillan, London, 1929).

KELSEN, H., 'The Pure Theory of Law and Analytical Jurisprudence' (1941–2), 55, *Harvard Law Review*, 44.

——, *General Theory of Law and State* (Russell & Russell, New York, 1945).

——, 'On the Pure Theory of Law' (1966), 1, *Israel Law Review*, 1.

——, *The Pure Theory of Law* (University of California Press, Berkeley and Los Angeles, 1967).

——, *Essays in Legal and Moral Philosophy*, selected and introduced by Ota Weinberger (D. Reidel, Dordrecht, 1973).

——, 'Law and Logic' (1973), in Kelsen, *Essays in Legal and Moral Philosophy* (1973).

KENNEDY, W. B., 'Another Job for Jurisprudence' (1945), 8, *The Modern Law Review*, 18.

KENNY, A. J. P., 'Practical Reasoning and Rational Appetite' (1975), in *Will, Freedom and Power* (Basil Blackwell, Oxford, 1975).

KNUUTTILA, S., 'The Emergence of Deontic Logic in the Fourteenth Century' (1981), in Hilpinen (ed.), *New Studies in Deontic Logic* (1981).

KUHN, T. S., *The Structure of Scientific Revolutions*, 2nd edition (University of Chicago Press, Chicago, 1970).

LEMMON, E. J., 'Deontic Logic and the Logic of Imperatives' (1966), 8, *Logique et Analyse*, 39.

——, *Beginning Logic* (Nelson, Sunbury-on-Thames, 1977).

LEVI, E. H., *An Introduction to Legal Reasoning* (The University of Chigago Press, Chicago, 1949).

LLEWELLYN, K. N., *Jurisprudence: Realism in Theory and Practice* (The University of Chicago Press, London, 1962).

——, *The Bramble Bush: Our Law and its Study*, 3rd printing (Oceana, New York, 1969).

LLOYD, D., 'Reason and Logic in the Common Law' (1948), 64, *The Law Quarterly Review*, 468.

LLOYD, LORD, *Introduction to Jurisprudence*, 4th edition (Stevens, London, 1979).

——, and FREEMAN, M. D. A., *Lloyd's Introduction to Jurisprudence*, 5th edition (Stevens, London, 1985).

LUCAS, N. F., 'Logic and Law' (1919), 3, *Marquette Law Review*, 203.

MACCORMICK, D. N., 'Legal Obligation and the Imperative Fallacy' (1973), in Simpson (ed.), *Oxford Essays in Jurisprudence*, Second Series (1973).

——, 'Law as Institutional Fact' (1974), 90, *The Law Quarterly Review*, 102.

——, *Legal Reasoning and Legal Theory* (Clarendon Press, Oxford, 1978).

——, *H. L. A. Hart* (Edward Arnold, London, 1981).

——, *Legal Right and Social Democracy: Essays in Legal and Political Philosophy* (Clarendon Press, Oxford, 1982).

MacCormick, D. N., 'The Nature of Legal Reasoning: A Brief Reply to Dr. Wilson' (1982), 2, *Legal Studies*, 286.

——, 'Contemporary Legal Philosophy: The Rediscovery of Practical Reason' (1983) in Lloyd and Freeman, *Lloyd's Introduction to Jurisprudence*, 5th edition (1985).

——, 'Analytical Jurisprudence and the Possibility of Legal Knowledge' (1984–5), 49, *Saskatchewan Law Review*, 1.

——, 'The Democratic Intellect and the Law' (1985), 5, *Legal Studies*, 172.

——, and Weinberger, O., *An Institutional Theory of Law* (D. Reidel, Dordrecht, 1986).

MacIntyre, A., *After Virtue* (Duckworth, London, 1981).

Morscher, E., 'Antinomies and Incompatibilities within Normative Languages' (1982), in Martino (ed.), *Deontic Logic, Computational Linguistics and Legal Information Systems* (1982).

Munzer, S., 'Validity and Legal Conflicts' (1973), 82, *The Yale Law Journal*, 1140.

Olivecrona, K., *Law as Fact*, 2nd edition (Stevens, London, 1971).

Paterson, A., *The Law Lords* (MacMillan, London, 1982).

Paulson, S. L., 'Material and Formal Authorisation in Kelsen's Pure Theory' (1980), 39, *The Cambridge Law Journal*, 172.

Perelman, Ch., 'Concerning Justice' (1980), in *Justice, Law, and Argument: Essays on Moral and Legal Reasoning* (1980).

——, *Justice, Law, and Argument: Essays on Moral and Legal Reasoning* (D. Reidel, Dordrecht, 1980).

Popper, K. R., *The Poverty of Historicism*, 2nd edition (Routledge & Kegan Paul, London, 1961).

——, *Conjectures and Refutations: The Growth of Scientific Knowledge*, fourth edition (Routledge & Kegan Paul, London, 1972).

——, *Objective Knowledge: An Evolutionary Approach* (Clarendon Press, Oxford, 1972).

Pound., R., 'Mechanical Jurisprudence' (1908), 8, *Columbia Law Review*, 605.

——, 'Law in Books and Law in Action' (1910), 44, *American Law Review*, 12.

Prott, L. V., 'Updating the Judicial "Hunch": Esser's Concept of Judicial Predisposition' (1978), 26, *The American Journal of Comparative Law*, 461.

Raz, J., 'Legal Principles and the Limits of Law' (1972), 81, *The Yale Law Journal*, 823.

——, *Practical Reason and Norms* (Hutchinson, London, 1975).

——, *The Authority of Law: Essays on Law and Morality* (Clarendon Press, Oxford, 1979).

——, *The Concept of a Legal System: An Introduction to the Theory of Legal System*, 2nd edition (Clarendon Press, Oxford, 1980).

——, 'The Problem about the Nature of Law' (1982), extracted in Lloyd and Freeman, *Lloyd's Introduction to Jurisprudence* (1985).

ROBINSON, J. A., *Logic: Form and Function* (Edinburgh University Press, Edinburgh, 1979).

ROSS, A., *Directives and Norms* (Routledge & Kegan Paul, London, 1968).

——, 'Tu-tu' (1957), 70, *Harvard Law Review*, 812.

RUSSELL, B., *The Problems of Philosophy*, 9th impression (Oxford University Press, Oxford, 1980).

RYLE, G., *The Concept of Mind* (Hutchinson, London, 1949).

SARTORIUS, R., 'Social Policy and Judicial Legislation' (1971), 8, *American Philosophical Quarterly*, 151.

——, 'Bayes' Theorem, Hard Cases, and Judicial Discretion' (1977), 11, *Georgia Law Review*, 1269.

SIMMONDS, N. E., *The Decline of Juridical Reason: Doctrine and Theory in the Legal Order* (Manchester University Press, Manchester, 1984).

SIMPSON, A. W. B., 'The *Ratio Decidendi* of a Case and the Doctrine of Binding Precedent' (1961), in Guest (ed.), *Oxford Essays in Jurisprudence* (1961).

—— (ed.), *Oxford Essays in Jurisprudence*, Second Series (Clarendon Press, Oxford, 1973).

——, 'The Common Law and Legal Theory' (1973), in Simpson (ed.), *Oxford Essays in Jurisprudence*, Second Series (1973).

SINCLAIR, K., JR., 'Legal Reasoning: In Search of an Adequate Theory of Argument' (1971), 59, *California Law Review*, 821.

SINGH, C., *Law from Anarchy to Utopia* (Clarendon Press, Oxford, 1986).

SMITH, J. C., *Legal Obligation* (The Athlone Press, London, 1976).

STONE, J., 'The *Ratio* of the *Ratio Decidendi*' (1959), 22, *The Modern Law Review*, 597.

——, *Legal System and Lawyers' Reasonings* (Stanford University Press, Stanford, 1964).

——, *Social Dimensions of Law and Justice* (Stevens, London, 1966).

——, *The Province and Function of Law*, 4th printing (Hein, Buffalo, 1968).

STONE, M., *Proof of Fact in Criminal Trials* (W. Green, Edinburgh, 1984).

STRAWSON, P. F., *Introduction to Logical Theory* (Methuen, London, 1952).

SUMMERS, R. S., *Instrumentalism and American Legal Theory* (Cornell University Press, Ithaca and London, 1982).

——, 'Logic in the Law' (1963), 72, *MIND*, 254.

—— (ed.), *More Essays in Legal Philosophy: General Assessments of Legal Philosophies* (Blackwell, Oxford, 1971).

——, 'Notes on Criticism in Legal Philosophy' (1971), in Summers (ed.), *More Essays in Legal Philosophy: General Assessments of Legal Philosophies* (1971).

——, 'Professor Fuller on Morality and Law' (1971), in Summers, (ed.)

More Essays in Legal Philosophy: General Assessments of Legal Philosophies (1971).

SUSSKIND, R. E., 'Objections to Deductive Legal Reasoning' (Oxford University M. Litt. qualifying paper, 1984).

——, 'Detmold's Refutation of Positivism and the Computer Judge' (1986), 49, *The Modern Law Review*, 125.

TAMMELO, I., 'Sketch for a Symbolic Juristic Logic' (1955), 8, *Journal of Legal Education*, 277.

——, 'On the Logical Openness of Legal Orders' (1959), 8, *The American Journal of Comparative Law*, 187.

——, 'On the Logical Structure of the Law Field' (1959), 45, *Archiv für Rechts und Sozialphilosophie*, 95.

——, *Modern Logic in the Service of Law* (Springer-Verlag, New York, 1978).

TAPPER, C. F. H., 'A Note on Principles' (1971), 34, *The Modern Law Review*, 628.

TOULMIN, S. E., *The Uses of Argument* (Cambridge University Press, Cambridge, 1958).

TUR, R. H. S., 'Jurisprudence and Practice' (1976), 14, *Journal of the Society of Public Teachers of Law* NS, 38.

——, 'Positivism, Principles and Rules' (1977), in Atwool (ed.), *Perspectives in Jurisprudence* (1977).

——, 'What is Jurisprudence?' (1978), 28, *Philosophical Quarterly*, 149.

——, 'The Kelsenian Enterprise' (1986), in Tur and Twining (eds.), *Essays on Kelsen* (1986).

——, and TWINING, W. L., *Essays on Kelsen* (Clarendon Press, Oxford, 1986).

TWINING, W. L., 'Treatises and Textbooks: A Reply to T. B. Smith' (1972–3), 12, *Journal of the Society of Public Teachers of Law*, NS, 267.

——, *Karl Llewellyn and the Realist Movement* (Weidenfeld and Nicolson, London, 1973).

——, 'Some Jobs for Jurisprudence' (1974), 1, *British Journal of Law and Society*, 149.

——, and MIERS, D., *How to Do Things with Rules*, 2nd edition (Weidenfeld and Nicolson, London, 1982).

VILLA, V., 'Legal Science between Natural and Human Sciences' (1984), 4, *Legal Studies*, 243.

WAISMANN, F., 'Verifiability' (1951), in Flew (ed.), *Logic and Language*, First Series (1960).

WALKER, D. M., 'A Note on Precedent' (1949), 61, *Juridical Review*, 283.

——, 'The Theory of Relevancy' (1951), 63, *Juridical Review*, 1.

——, *The Scottish Legal System*, 5th edition (W. Green, Edinburgh, 1981).

——, *The Oxford Companion to Law* (Clarendon Press, Oxford, 1980).

WASSERSTROM, R. W., *The Judicial Decision: Towards a Theory of Legal Justification* (Stanford University Press, Stanford, 1961).

WEINBERGER, O., 'Logic and the Pure Theory of Law' (1986), in Tur and Twining (eds.), *Essays on Kelsen* (1986).

WEYLAND, I., 'Idealism and Realism in Kelsen's Treatment of Norm Conflicts' (1986), in Tur and Twining (eds.), *Essays on Kelsen* (1986).

WHITE, A. R., *Modal Thinking* (Blackwell, Oxford, 1975).

WHITE, P. D., 'Philosophy and Law: Some Observations on MacCormick's *Legal Reasoning and Legal Theory*' (1980), 78, *Michigan Law Review*, 737.

WILSON, A., 'The Nature of Legal Reasoning: A Commentary with Special Reference to Professor MacCormick's Theory' (1982), 2, *Legal Studies*, 269.

WISDOM, J., 'Gods' (1951), in Flew (ed.), *Logic and Language*, First Series (1960).

WRIGHT, G. H., VON, 'Deontic Logic' (1951), 60, *MIND*, 1.

——, *Norm and Action: A Logical Inquiry* (Routledge & Kegan Paul, London, 1963).

——, 'Deontic Logic Revisited' (1973), 4, *Rechtstheorie*, 37.

——, 'On the Logic of Norms and Actions' (1981), in Hilpinen (ed.), *New Studies in Deontic Logic* (1981).

——, 'Norms, Truth and Logic' (1982), in Martino (ed.), *Deontic Logic, Computational Linguistics and Legal Information Systems* (1982).

3. ARTIFICIAL INTELLIGENCE, EXPERT SYSTEMS, AND COMPUTER SCIENCE

d'AGAPEYEFF, A., 'Report to the Alvey Directorate on a Short Survey of Expert Systems in UK Business', *Alvey News*, Supplement to Issue No. 4. (April 1984).

BARR, A., FEIGENBAUM, E. A., and COHEN, P. R. (eds.), *The Handbook of Artificial Intelligence*, i and ii (Kaufmann, Los Altos, 1981 & 1982).

BODEN, M. A., *Artificial Intelligence and Natural Man* (Harvester, Brighton, 1977).

BRAMER, M. A., *Research and Development in Expert Systems* (Cambridge University Press, Cambridge, 1984).

BUCHANAN, B. G., and DUDA, R. O., *Principles of Rule-Based Expert Systems* (Stanford University Computer Science Department, Report No. STAN-CS-82-926, 1982).

——, LEDERBERG, J., and MCCARTHY, J., *Three Reviews of J. Weizenbaum's Computer Power and Human Reason* (Stanford University Computer Science Department, Report No. STAN-CS-76-577, 1976).

DAVIS, R., and LENAT, D. B., *Knowledge-Based Systems in Artificial Intelligence* (McGraw-Hill, London, 1982).

DEPARTMENT OF INDUSTRY, *A Programme for Advanced Information Technology* (*The Alvey Report*) (HMSO, London, 1982).

DREYFUS, H. L., *What Computers Can't Do: A Critique of Artificial Reason* (Harper & Row, New York, 1972).

FEIGENBAUM, E. A., 'Knowledge Engineering: The Applied Side' (1983), in Hayes and Michie (eds.), *Intelligent Systems: The Unprecedented Opportunity* (1983).

——, and FELDMAN, J. (eds.), *Computers and Thought* (McGraw-Hill, New York, 1963).

——, and MCCORDUCK, P., *The Fifth Generation* (Addison-Wesley, London, 1983).

GAINES, B. R., 'From Ergonomics to the Fifth Generation: 30 Years of Human–Computer Interaction Studies', in *INTERACT '84*, the First IFIP Conference on Human–Computer Interaction (IFIP, 1984).

GOLDSCHLAGER, L., and LISTER, A., *Computer Science: A Modern Introduction* (Prentice-Hall, London, 1982).

GOODALL, A., *The Guide to Expert Systems* (Learned Information, Oxford, 1985).

HAMMOND, P., and SERGOT, M. J., 'A PROLOG Shell for Logic Based Expert Systems' (1983), in *Expert Systems 1983*, the Proceedings of the Third Technical Conference of the British Computer Society Specialist Group on Expert Systems.

HART, P. E., 'Directions for AI in the Eighties' (1982), 79, *SIGART Newsletter*, 11.

HAWKINS, D., 'An Analysis of Expert Thinking' (1983), 18, *International Journal of Man–Machine Studies*, 1.

HAYES, J. E., and MICHIE, D. (eds.), *Intelligent Systems: The Unprecedented Opportunity* (Ellis Horwood, Chichester, 1983).

HAYES-ROTH, F., WATERMAN, D. A., and LENAT, D. B., *Building Expert Systems* (Addison-Wesley, London, 1983).

HOARE, C. A. R., *Programming is an Engineering Profession* (Oxford University Computing Laboratory, Programming Research Group Technical Monograph PRG-27, 1982).

HOFSTADTER, D. R., *Godel, Escher, Bach: Eternal Golden Braid* (Vintage, New York, 1980).

——, and DENNETT, D. C., *The Mind's I* (Penguin, Harmondsworth, 1982).

MCCORDUCK, P., *Machines Who Think* (W. H. Freeman, San Francisco, 1979).

MICHIE, D. (ed.), *Expert Systems in the Micro-electronic Age* (Edinburgh University Press, Edinburgh, 1979).

——, 'Expert Systems' (1980), 23, *The Computer Journal*, 369.

——(ed.), *Introductory Readings in Expert Systems* (Gordon and Breach, London, 1982).

——, *Machine Intelligence and Related Topics* (Gordon and Breach, London, 1982).

——, and JOHNSTON, R., *The Creative Computer* (Viking, Harmondsworth, 1984).

NILSSON, N. J., *Principles of Artificial Intelligence* (Springer-Verlag, New York, 1982).

QUINLAN, J. R., 'Semi-autonomous Acquisition of Pattern-based Knowledge' (1982), in Michie (ed.), *Introductory Readings in Expert Systems* (1982).

RICH, E., *Artificial Intelligence* (McGraw-Hill, Tokyo, 1983).

ROBINSON, J. A., 'Logical Reasoning in Machines' (1983), in Hayes and Michie (eds.), *Intelligent Systems: The Unprecedented Opportunity* (1983).

SEARLE, J. R., 'Minds, Brains and Programs' (1980), in Hofstadter and Dennett (eds.), *The Mind's I* (1982).

——, *Minds, Brains and Science* (BBC, London, 1984).

SHEPHERDSON, J. C., 'The Calculus of Reasoning' (1983), in Hayes and Michie (eds.), *Intelligent Systems: The Unprecedented Opportunity* (1983).

SLOMAN, A., 'Epistemology and Artificial Intelligence' (1979), in Michie (ed.), *Expert Systems in the Micro-electronic Age* (1979).

SUWA, M., SCOTT, A. C., and SHORTLIFFE, E. H., *An Approach to Verifying Completeness and Consistency in a Rule-Based Expert System* (Stanford University Computer Science Department, Report No. STAN-CS-82-922, 1982).

TAUBE, M., *Computers and Common Sense: The Myth of Thinking Machines* (Columbia University Press, New York and London, 1961).

TURING, A. M., 'Computing Machinery and Intelligence' (1950), 59, *MIND*, 433.

TURNER, R., *Logics for Artificial Intelligence* (Ellis Horwood, Chichester, 1984).

WATERMAN, D. A., *A Guide to Expert Systems* (Addison-Wesley, London, 1986).

WEIZENBAUM, J., *Computer Power and Human Reason: From Judgement to Calculation*, with new preface (Penguin, Harmondsworth, 1984).

WIEDERHOLD, G., 'Knowledge and Database Management' (Jan. 1984), *IEEE Software*, 63.

WINSTON, P. H., *Artificial Intelligence*, 2nd edition (Addison-Wesley, London, 1984).

ZADEH, L. A., 'Fuzzy Sets as a Basis for a Theory of Possibility' (1978), 1, *Fuzzy Sets and Systems*, 3.

——, 'Coping with the Imprecision of the Real World: An Interview with Lofti A. Zadeh' (1984), 27, *Communications of the ACM*, 304.

4. SCOTTISH LAW OF DIVORCE

BENNETT, S. A., *A Short Guide to Divorce in the Sheriff Court* (W. Green, Edinburgh, 1984).

CLIVE, E. M., *The Divorce (Scotland) Act 1976* (W. Green, Edinburgh, 1976).

——, *The Law of Husband and Wife in Scotland*, 2nd edition (W. Green, Edinburgh, 1982).

GLOAG, W. M., and HENDERSON, R. C., *Introduction to the Law of Scotland*, 8th edition (W. Green, Edinburgh, 1980).

MARSHALL, E. A., *General Principles of Scots Law*, 4th edition (W. Green, Edinburgh, 1982).

MESTON, M. C., 'Divorce Reform in Scotland' (1977), *Scots Law Times*, 13.

ROSS HARPER & MURPHY (Solicitors), *Sheriff Court: DIVORCE* (Internal Booklet, April 1984).

WALKER, D. M., *Principles of Scottish Private Law*, 3rd edition (Clarendon Press, Oxford, 1982).

WILLOCK, I. D., 'The New Divorce Law' (1977), 8, *SCOLAG Bulletin*, 12.

WILSON, W. A., 'Divorce for Abracadabra' (1976), *Scots Law Times*, 27.

Index